# THE ECONOMIC INDICATOR HANDBOOK

The Bloomberg Financial Series provides both core reference knowledge and actionable information for financial professionals. The books are written by experts familiar with the workflows, challenges, and demands of investment professionals who trade the markets, manage money, and analyze investments in their capacity of growing and protecting wealth, hedging risk, and generating revenue.

Since 1996, Bloomberg Press has published books for financial professionals on investing, economics, and policy affecting investors. Titles are written by leading practitioners and authorities, and they have been translated into more than 20 languages.

For a list of available titles, please visit our website at www.wiley.com/go/bloombergpress.

# THE ECONOMIC INDICATOR HANDBOOK

How to Evaluate Economic Trends to Maximize Profits and Minimize Losses

**Richard Yamarone**

WILEY

Published by John Wiley & Sons, Inc., Hoboken, New Jersey.
Published simultaneously in Canada.

For general information on our other products and services or for technical support, please contact our Customer Care Department within the United States at (800) 762-2974, outside the United States at (317) 572-3993 or fax (317) 572-4002.

Wiley publishes in a variety of print and electronic formats and by print-on-demand. Some material included with standard print versions of this book may not be included in e-books or in print-on-demand. If this book refers to media such as a CD or DVD that is not included in the version you purchased, you may download this material at http://booksupport.wiley.com. For more information about Wiley products, visit www.wiley.com.

*Library of Congress Cataloging-in-Publication Data is available:*

ISBN 9781118204665 (Hardcover)
ISBN 9781118228470 (ePDF)
ISBN 9781118233122 (ePub)

Cover Design: Wiley
Cover Images: Blue Whispy Flow © colecom/Getty Images, Inc.;
GDP data chart, Reprinted with permission of Bloomberg LP

Printed in the United States of America

10 9 8 7 6 5 4 3 2 1

*Dedicated to the loving memory of Milton and Nash Yamarone.*

# Contents

# Acknowledgments

This project is overwhelmingly related to economics as seen from the Bloomberg terminal. So it is only natural that I express my gratitude to the countless—and I do mean countless—Bloomberg employees that have provided invaluable help over the last 20-plus years that I have been associated with Bloomberg either as a client (since 1992) or as an employee (October 26, 2009). There's a real reason why Bloomberg, LP is so successful, and it is undoubtedly due to its employees. I've never seen such dedication to a company and to the client in my more than 30 years on the Street. If you know anyone that has ever worked at Bloomberg, you know exactly what I am talking about.

I have the great fortune to work with some of the brightest and hardest-working people in all of business. At any hour of the day or evening, weekend, or holiday, I feel I could reach out with an issue and get an immediate response . . . that's an incredible team to draw upon. I call each of them my friend as well as co-worker.

My thanks are extended first to the Bloomberg Intelligence Economics team. At the top is Mike McDonough, the global director of economics who has set up this solid powerhouse and is responsible for making it the preeminent economic research group on all of Wall Street that it is today. He is a great leader. Carl Riccadonna is the sharpest economist I have ever worked with and is the best "big picture" economics writer on the Street today; I learn from him every day. Yelena Shulyatyeva has a gifted ability to find the most meaningful detail in economic indicators, draw intelligent inferences, and place them in a macro context. She does this masterfully, despite having the tremendous misfortune of having to sit next to me for over 10 hours a day. Bless you.

Many thanks go to the rest of the team, including Richard Marquit, Felipe Hernandez, Marco Maciel, Jaime Murray, Tom Orlik, David Powell, Niraj Shaw, Mark Bohlund, Dan Hanson, Maxime Sbaihi, Tamara Henderson, Fielding Chen, Yuki Masujima, and Tricia Franceschina. Special thanks to James Callan, the brilliant editor that takes my scribblings and polishes them into coherent commentary.

Bloomberg Intelligence is an incredible research group, undoubtedly the best on the Street, and as helpful as they are insightful. Imagine what a joy it is (especially as an economist) to be able to draw upon the knowledge from industry legends—yeah, legends—like Poonam Goyal, Ken Hoffman, Kevin Tynan,

Kit Konolige, Paul Sweeney, Josh Zaret, Lee Klaskow, John Butler, Karen Ulbelhart, and Jason Miner. Seriously, who couldn't form an accurate economic perspective with so many talented professionals feeding the information channel with top-tier insights and analyses? Additional thanks are extended to Richard Salditt, Dragos Aoloie, and Mike McGlone.

There are countless employees around the globe that I work with only on occasion, but have helped me beyond measure. This includes my personal friend, Janice Slusarz; I couldn't ask for a better friend. In Multimedia there is another dear friend, Julie Hyman—I am very lucky to call her a friend. In addition, my many thanks are extended to Matt Miller, David Westin, Ted Fine, Pimm Fox, Mike McKee, Tom Keene, Kathleen Hays, Vonnie Quinn, Taylor Riggs, David Sucherman, Paul Brennan, Sam Lenga, Carol Massar, John Tucker, Cory Johnson, Emily Haas-Godsil, Paris Wald, Vielka Todd, Richard Trueman, Charlie Pellet, Rachel Wehrspann, Erik Schatzker, Joe Weisenthal, Courtney Donohoe, Lisa Abramowicz, Scarlet Fu, Mark Crumpton, and Bob Moon.

I could fill an entire book with the hundreds of salespeople that I have worked with over the last seven years, who have taught me so much about the importance of the client during the close to a thousand presentations, speeches, and one-on-one meetings I have had with our clients and prospects. My hat is tipped to Matt Nolfo, the King of university sales. No one compares to you and your seemingly never-ending ability to let people know the power of the terminal. Tom Rogers, Kevin G. Murphy, Annie Sears, Stephen Smith, Ariel Pariser, Thomas Pennella, Alex Shomber, Logan McClennan, Wayne Pasternack, Mary Briatico, Caroline Bauer, Craig Kesten, and Chris Piekarski.

My gratitude is also extended to other colleagues that I indirectly work with, including Hillary Conley, Peter Coy, Dorothy Lata, Shelly Banjo, Deirdre Fretz, James Crombie, Ben Baris, Anne Riley, Joe Mysak Jr., Jackie Jozefek, Mary Ann Thomas, Steven Moy, Mike Nol, Doug Simmons, Rose Constantino, Florent Ouelle, Mike Finnegan, Clifton Simmons, David Noguerol, Tony Bolton, Derek Pryor, Monica Betran, Jacqueline Thorpe, Caitlin Noselli, Vince Golle, Vinny DelGuidice, Alex Tanzi, Vivien Lou Chen Sho Chandra, and Doug Edler. And to a true Bloomberg giant, Ted Merz, you are a wonderful source of wisdom; I consider you a very valuable friend.

I must express my most sincere thanks to a true diamond at Bloomberg, Reileen Brown. You have saved me on hundreds of occasions. Without you, I would be lost . . . literally.

To the thousands of clients with whom I interact, thanks for all of your thoughts, comments, and idea-generating conversations. You have contributed to this project in more ways than you may realize. Along these lines, I must extend thanks to the near 700 members of the Bloomberg Macro Economic Chatroom. I cannot divulge any individual members—it is an anonymous chatroom—but I must tell you there are numerous occasions where members have inspired me to read, study, and learn about specific topics and economic issues weeks ahead of them appearing in the broader business press.

Thank you all.

# About the Author

**Richard Yamarone** is a Bloomberg senior economist with more than three decades of experience on monetary and fiscal policy, economic indicators, fixed income, commodities, and general macroeconomic conditions.

As a member of Bloomberg Intelligence–Economics, he is a contributor to the Real-Time Economics product that features analysis, data, and news on the forces shaping the global economy. Mr. Yamarone and the Bloomberg Intelligence–Economics team provide in-depth analysis of macroeconomic data, policy, and trends and how they will impact financial markets.

He is also the creator of the Bloomberg Orange Book of CEO Comments, a compilation of macroeconomic anecdotes gleaned from comments C-suite executives made on quarterly earnings conference calls. He travels extensively to speak to clients and corporate executives on the economic outlook, public speaking, and career and management coaching. The author of *Trader's Guide to Key Economic Indicators* (Bloomberg Press, 2012), Mr. Yamarone is a member of the National Association for Business Economists, the American Economic Association, the New York State Economics Association, and the Money Marketeers of New York University. He has won numerous accolades for his work, including being featured as one of the top 10 economists in the United States by *USA Today* in 2007 and "Nostradamus of the Financial Industry" by Bank Advisor in 2008 for his prediction of the financial crises.

# CHAPTER 1

# The Daily Blotter

Perhaps the best way to appreciate the most important and meaningful economic indicators used by Wall Street economists is to present them in the manner that they are used by those professionals. Every bank, money manager, hedge fund, or financial institution has an interest in economic indicators, and each of those producing the analysis possesses their own individual routine in which they obtain the data, produce a product, and disseminate their respective analysis. For the most part, Wall Street economists use the Bloomberg Professional service for their data, write a daily newsletter—with oftentimes several updates a day—and send it electronically to their clients, investment professionals, and the media.

This chapter attempts to present the most important information used on Wall Street trading desks, and how the desk economist goes about prepping for the day, understanding and appreciating anything that might move the financial markets or alter the outlook for the economy.

The traditional market reaction to news, events, and economic data—particularly the top tier economic indicators—is usually with respect to what insight the news brings to the entire financial market. While some equity analysts use economic releases to determine the trends in some of their respective industries and stocks, most investment professionals look to see how information will influence the broader markets.

For example, should news break about a refinery fire at an integrated oil company, then there may be an immediate negative reaction to that specific company's stock price. Depending on how severe the damage was to its facilities and how long that refinery would be out of commission would dictate the value of the price adjustment. Similarly, if the refinery was large, producing a tremendous amount of gasoline, then the lost supply could disrupt the commodity market, and send prices higher. This wouldn't upset the entire stock, bond, or currency market, with the damage being concentrated in just the trading of some energy products.

1

When a major economic release hits the newswires, market participants look at the details with respect to how the information contained in the report will influence the prices of a security.

When economic releases are better than expectations, that is, with a positive or bullish implication, equity prices rise and bond prices fall. Yields on bonds (or fixed-income securities) rise since they are inversely related to prices). The economics behind this is that a stronger economic posting like a large number of jobs added in a month, an increase in the orders for durable goods, or an extremely upbeat reading in consumer confidence, implies companies will be conducting a greater amount of business, which is good for revenues and profits.

The reaction to strong economic data in the fixed income market would be very different. Stronger economic conditions possess potentially inflationary conditions. An increase in demand or production is usually accompanied by greater prices. So exceptionally stronger gains in activity are viewed as inflationary, which erodes the value of a fixed income security. The yields on those bonds would rise since they are inversely related.

The opposite holds true for weak economic reports. In the event that one of the manufacturing condition surveys is less than expectations, industrial production contracts, or housing starts fall, stock prices would sour on that news and bond prices would rise (yields would fall).

While each Wall Street economist has varying responsibilities and individual routines, they do share some common traits. Knowing what releases are scheduled for any given day is atop that list. The economic calendar is so important that vacations and time off is planned around economic releases by order of importance. You never call in sick or walk in late for an Employment Situation release, an FOMC meeting, or a day when three or more top-tier indicators are slated for release.

## The Economic Calendar

The Bloomberg calendar depicted in Exhibit 1.1 may be obtained by typing ECO <GO> on the Bloomberg Professional terminal. It is the most comprehensive and trusted source for releases in all of finance, detailing the name of the release, date, time, previous value, and the current Street consensus estimate. There's also a relative importance graph identifying how the Street views each index—the larger the number of subscription alerts there are for an individual indicator, the greater the number of bars highlighted in the bar graph located in the "R" column (relative importance) to the left of the Event column. In the associated exhibit, the ISM Milwaukee index clearly is not considered to be as important as the Chicago Purchasing Managers Index.

The Bloomberg ECO calendar may be customized to include economic releases like durable goods orders and economic events like speeches by policy

**EXHIBIT 1.1** The Economic Calendar

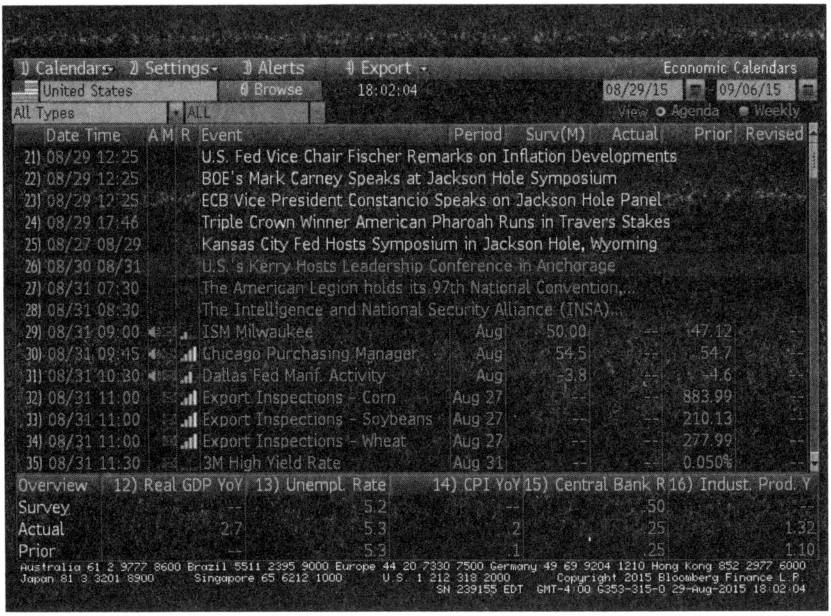

*Source:* Bloomberg

makers or Federal Reserve Open Market Committee meeting announcements. The addition of all the government conferences and speeches like those from the secretaries of the Departments of Treasury or State are also available. All Treasury financing auctions are listed as well. Even the commodity reports such as crop conditions or crude oil inventory levels are available. While we are only addressing the U.S. economic indicators, the ECO calendar is available for 189 countries and regions (e.g., Eurozone, G8, G20).

Traders, analysts, and economists always want to know what the market is thinking, so when an economic release hits the tape, they know whether the report is stronger, weaker, or in line with Street expectations.

With respect to the calendar on economic releases, right-clicking on any of the indexes will reveal the detail of all those economists polled and their respective forecast history for that specific indicator (ECOS). The most popular economic releases possess upwards of 100 individual forecasts.

## Economist Estimates and Expectations

Once in the calendar on economic releases, right-clicking on any of the indexes reveals the Street expectations, as seen in Exhibit 1.2. Here we see the graphical distribution for nonfarm payroll estimates by 74 economists, as well as the

**EXHIBIT 1.2**   Economist Estimates

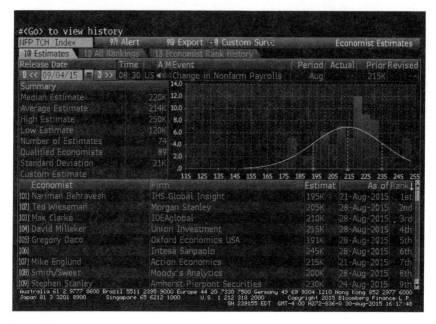

*Source:* Bloomberg

average, median, high, low, and standard deviation. There is also a ranking of the economist for that indicator in the lower-right-hand corner, which is based on two years of contributed estimates.

Then, clicking again on an individual economist or firm reveals a chart of the forecasting history of that particular forecaster for that economic release (Exhibit 1.3), as well as the median and actual number. You can also select several economists at a time. Now we are capable of seeing just how good some are at the estimating game.

And since we have the Street estimates for dozens of indicators—and history—we can plot to see how far off the experts as a consensus were with respect to the actual number. Exhibit 1.4 shows the Economic Surprise Monitor (ECSU <GO>), which contains a dashboard of the latest top-tier indicators and their associated postings (by date) and the amount that each differed from the survey median as polled by Bloomberg, divided by the survey standard deviation.

## The Bloomberg Economic Surprise Index

The Bloomberg Economic Surprise Index (ESI) shows the degree to which Street economists either under- or overestimate those top-tier indicators posted in ECO <GO>.

**EXHIBIT 1.3**   Economist/Firm Forecast History

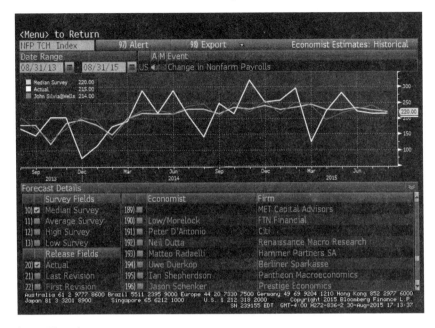

*Source:* Bloomberg

**EXHIBIT 1.4**   The Economic Surprise Monitor

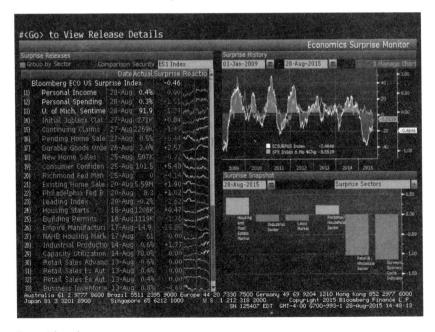

*Source:* Bloomberg

When the actual number exceeds the Street estimates, it's a sign that the measured performance of a particular economic indicator bettered Street expectations, implying the economy may be performing better than the pros believe. Conversely, lower actual values suggest weaker economic conditions compared to what the forecasters believe. The associated exhibit lists the most recent releases in the Bloomberg ECO U.S. Surprise Index and whether they missed to the up side (green) or to the down side (red).

Formal releases of economic data aren't the only incidents that move the market or may change the outlook of the economy. The daily events calendar is an extremely important tool used in the analysis of the economic environment. While there are rarely specific data or indexes revealed in the countless events that occur during any given trading session, there are nuggets of information in many of the conference calls or releases—the sharp analyst just has to know where to look.

Most analysts and economists know days in advance about what is on the docket regarding investor meetings, industry or bank-sponsored conferences, earnings calls, corporate updates, annual meetings, and special company announcements like a merger or acquisition. The Bloomberg Events Calendar in Exhibit 1.5 (EVTS <GO>) identifies one page of the thousands that exist on the terminal.

**EXHIBIT 1.5** Events Calendar

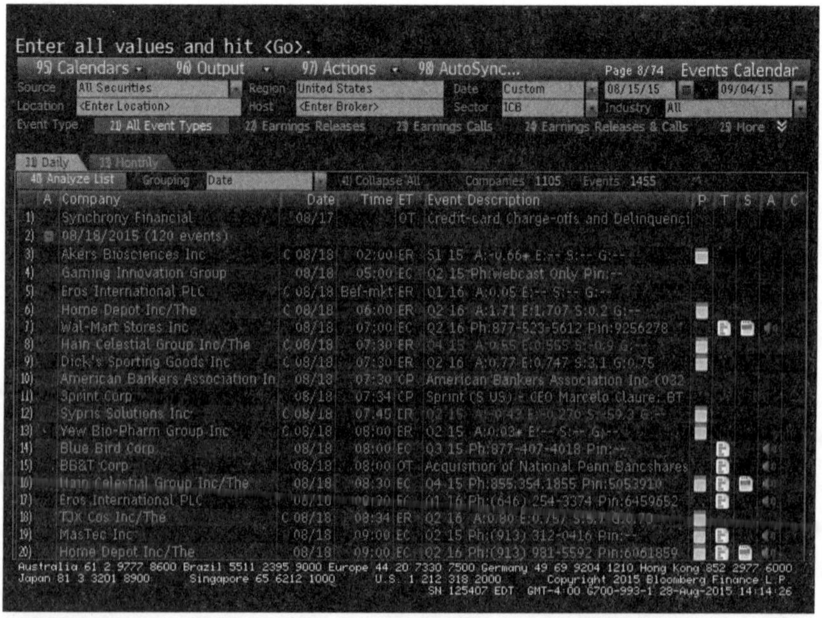

*Source:* Bloomberg

## The Events Calendar

The company is identified, as well as a description of the event type. Where applicable, the dial-in number is listed along with the necessary PIN code in the event that the listener would like to call in directly and ask questions.

The last five columns are functions that permit the user to read the associated press release (P), download a PDF file of the transcript of the entire conference call (T), read a transcript summary (S), listen to an audio file of the entire conference call (A), or sync the event to your calendar (C). These, of course, are all archived and available on an historical basis.

To be sure, not every call will generate insight to the goings on of the economy. But the wise desk economist should listen to (or read the transcripts of) the most economically sensitive companies that may be complaining of a high-interest-rate environment, stagnant spending by the consumer, or high input prices. Just about anything that can disrupt a company's performance will be mentioned in these calls. Many times, the comments made by executives on these calls forewarn changes in the economic data.

In Exhibit 1.5, it would be wise to listen to what Home Depot, Wal-Mart, and TJX Companies might have to say. The information contained in those calls might identify the underlying tone of the consumer. And since the consumer is responsible for a large portion of economic activity, the anecdotes can be invaluable to the forecasting process.

Having a treasury of economic data is essential for every economist or analyst. The Bloomberg Professional terminal provides a trove of economic and financial market data ranging from the common government reports and all the associated detail like GDP, consumption expenditures, the price indexes, and the confidence measures to the more obscure North American rail carloads of forest products. Just think of how valuable the latest data on industrial production of veneer, plywood, and engineered wood products, the retail price of carbonated drinks, or the number of persons employed in museums, historical sites, and parks can be to a housing, beverage, or not-for-profit industry analyst.

## The Economic Statistics Table (ECST)

As Exhibit 1.6 highlights, the data are available on tens of thousands of indicators and are easily searchable and downloadable with a mere click on the menu—all in one place.

Having the ability to work with data is also critical in the analysis process. All of the charts in this book were created using data from the Bloomberg terminal, and almost all have been produced in the Economic Workbench (ECWB <GO>). This function permits you to "play" with data. That is, insert different indicators or indexes and look at relationships, ideally identifying the

**EXHIBIT 1.6**   Economic Statistics Table

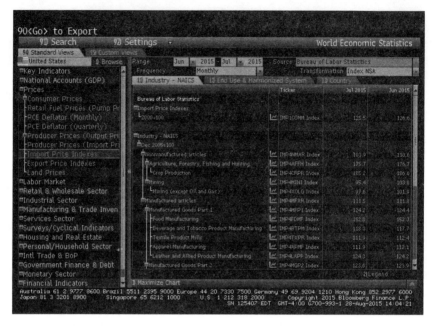

*Source:* Bloomberg

temperature of the economic climate or other key indicators to better appreciate the tone of an industry, the possible direction of a stock or bond, or changes in the business cycle.

## The Powerful Economic Workbench

Exhibit 1.7 displays the Bloomberg Economic Workbench. Basically, this is a charting tool. Any of the historical data on the terminal may be loaded into a field and then altered to identify a particular pattern or association. Sometimes economists want to compare data that are reported in different bases, like a quarterly GDP and weekly initial jobless claims, or daily commodity prices and monthly producer price indexes.

In Exhibit 1.7, we chart the U.S. Treasury cash balance of federal tax deposits withheld from employment income and tax receipts against the monthly nonfarm payrolls. The economic explanation behind this is that the more people employed, the greater will be the amount of tax withholdings by the federal government.

There are several other applications that analysts like to apply to data such as moving averages—especially for volatile economic time series or for high frequency daily or weekly data. Year-over-year analysis of indicators is often the

**EXHIBIT 1.7** Economic Workbench

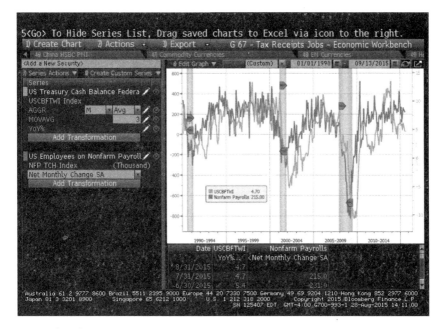

*Source:* Bloomberg

best perspective used on the Street, since this smooths so many fluctuations that may occur in data that are presented week-to-week, month-to-month, or quarter-to-quarter. In this book, the majority of data are presented on a year-over-year basis.

Other transformations frequently used in economic analysis are aggregation, whereby data points are summed or averaged. There are times when only the last data point of the month is desired. In addition, the analyst might like to perform many different applications like absolute values, logarithms, exponential, and power transformations.

Because economic indicators can adopt a leading, lagging, or coincident nature, the ability to transform the data by leading or lagging a few periods is also a common analytical tool that economists perform on data. Some indicators are lagged by sizable periods—five or six months, or even a year. You'll want to be able to make these adjustments to the many indicators.

Nearly all of the major trading floors have a morning squawk. During this internal broadcast, market participants—particularly those on the trading floor—are alerted to the top events, earnings announcements, and economic data.

Basically, this is a condensed and informative interpretation of the events and economic calendars. Discussions about potential market trends and possible market conditions are also mentioned. This is also a forum for analysts to pitch ideas, as well as investment products and securities, to the salespeople. Bloomberg has a version called the First Word Audio Squawk, and can be accessed on the terminal by typing SQUAWK <GO>.

Another type of communication on the Street is called the hoot-and-holler, whereby an economist would analyze the economic releases as they hit the tape. Admittedly, these instant analyses were much more prevalent in the 1970s through 1990s, but there are a few trading institutions that carry on this live interpretation of the data.

The task of the hoot-and-holler is not one for an amateur and is extremely difficult; a mere slip can cost traders millions. You have to be aware of the underlying market conditions, particularly the fixed-income market, and you must know what the Street expectations for the release are. It's also important to know how the markets will react to economic releases.

## The Bloomberg Orange Book of CEO Comments

The Bloomberg Orange Book of CEO Comments (Exhibit 1.8) is a creation born out of the need to improve an existing, and somewhat staid publication used by policy makers, the *Beige Book*. Every seven weeks or so—eight times a

**EXHIBIT 1.8**    The Bloomberg Orange Book of CEO Comments

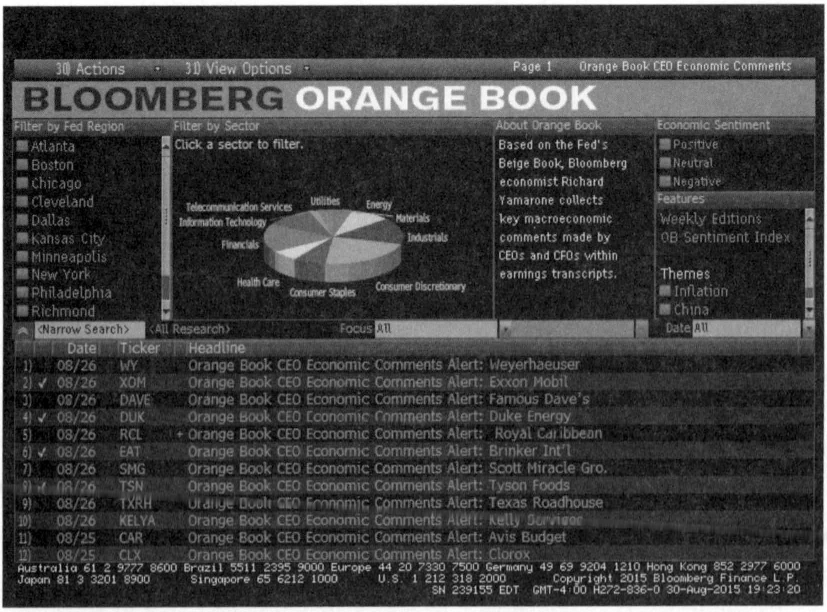

*Source:* Bloomberg

year—the Federal Reserve releases the *Beige Book Summary of Commentary on Current Economic Conditions by Federal Reserve District.* This is essentially a compilation of anecdotes gathered by economists in each of the Fed's 12 districts. Once collected, the Fed economists strip away the source information (the name of the person or company making the comment) and don't offer a date of when the comments were made.

The Bloomberg Orange Book of CEO Comments is assembled by reading some 300 quarterly earnings transcripts of the most economically sensitive companies and extracting the most economically relevant comments by C-suite executives. Anything related to hiring, inflation, capital spending, interest rates, growth, spending, consumer developments, global economic conditions, or confidence makes it to the Orange Book. They are all collated by company and posted to the terminal. These are the actual unedited comments made by executives, identified by the person making the comment and the date that it was made.

By typing ORANGE <GO> on the Bloomberg terminal, you will access the history of all entries, ordered by several different classifications. By clicking on a sector in the pie chart on the Orange Book page depicted in Exhibit 1.8, any of the companies may be found. So, for example, if you wanted to know the comments made by executives in the energy sector, a mere click would reveal the comments made by Hess, Chevron, Halliburton, or Arch Coal.

In addition, there is a search function that permits the user to filter comments by Fed District. So, if you wanted to mimic the Fed's *Beige Book* by district, you simply check the regional bank on the left, say Atlanta, and all the comments made by executives that are headquartered in the district will be revealed—for example, in the Atlanta District: Flowers Foods, UPS, Coca-Cola, Beazer Homes, Home Depot, and so on.

One of the more useful functions of the Orange Book is to identify trends in specific economic conditions. By entering a specific phrase of word like *deflation, job cuts,* or *Obamacare* in the <Narrow Search> field, any mention of those terms from a conference call would appear.

This makes the analysis of so many topics and themes considerably easy. With the Bloomberg Orange Book, you can learn what is on the minds of some of the most important business people in the United States.

In addition, the company transcripts are each scored with respect to its tone—that is, positive, negative, or neutral. Admittedly, the overwhelming majority (usually 290 of 300) are neutral since every conference call doesn't exude a definitive tone. But it is quite evident when a company is downbeat or sanguine about the economic outlook. Keep in mind, the gist of the Orange Book is not to understand how an individual company is performing, but what their perceptions are regarding the U.S. economic situation. A company can have stellar financial results, soaring earnings and escalating profits, but if they mention a near-term recession or a mass furlough of workers that might be scored a "negative." This is another reason so many companies are graded as "neutral," C-suite officials don't always mention the economic assessment.

Economists need to know where the financial markets are trading throughout the session, particularly those of Treasuries and currencies. The equity market is a very important measure as well, but its relevance is somewhat limited since it is not open as long as the fixed income and currency market. For example, when an economic release hits the tape at 8:30 a.m. ET—as so many major reports do—the U.S. stock market hasn't begun trading and will not for another hour. Not only will the fixed-income and currency markets be open and trading for the majority of economic releases, but in the event that some news or event breaks overseas (in Europe, Asia, or Africa and the Middle East) and overnight, bonds and currencies will trade with respect to the circumstances.

## The Treasury and Money Market Rates

One of the more informative sources for all of this information—and more—is the Bloomberg Treasury and Money Market page (BTMM <GO>) and is depicted in Exhibit 1.9. This is essentially a summary of the more important measures and indicators that trade throughout the day. Circled are the

**EXHIBIT 1.9**    Bloomberg Treasury and Money Market page

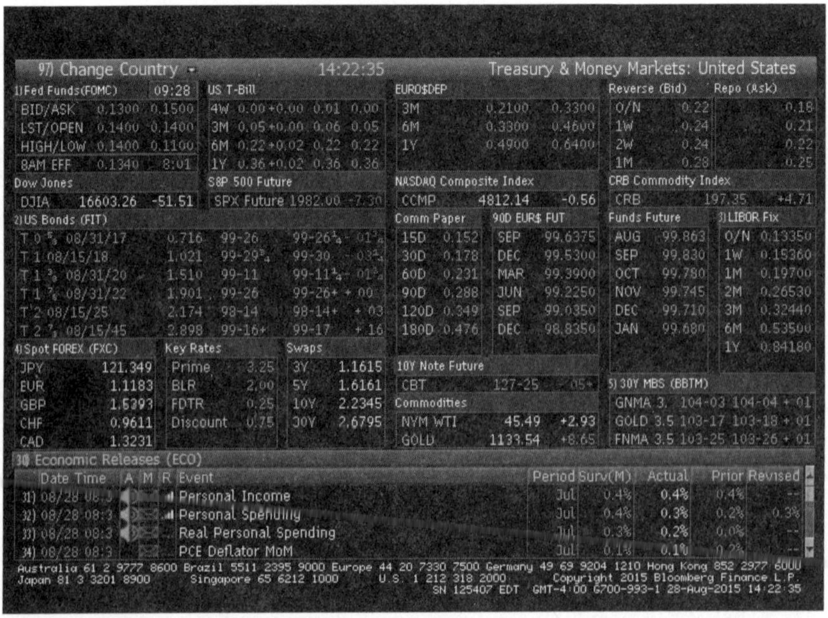

*Source:* Bloomberg

"on the run" Treasuries (the latest issues for the major maturities) and currencies of five of the most popular traded currencies with respect to the U.S. dollar, which is the world's reserve currency.

There are also many money market instruments including commercial paper, 90-day euro dollar futures, LIBOR fixings, and Fed funds futures. There are a few major stock market aggregates like the Dow Jones Industrial Average, the S&P 500, and the NASDAQ Composite.

Other important economic indicators are posted on this page as well, including the CRB Commodity Index and the latest price of gold and crude oil (West Texas Intermediate).

If something is stirring the markets, it will be identified by movements in several, if not all, of the measures on this page. Professionals can tell how severe or mild the market swings are simply by looking at a snapshot of this page.

There is a rather unique financial market metric that the Street now focuses on in order to appreciate the underlying tone of the markets.

## The Bloomberg Financial Conditions Monitor

After the 2008 financial crisis, it became increasingly important for economists to be aware of the amount of stress ruminating throughout the financial system, which lead to the creation of several financial market stress indicators.

The Bloomberg Financial Market Conditions Monitor (FCON <GO>) shown in Exhibit 1.10 contains the individual components of the U.S. Financial Conditions Index (FCON) in the three asset classes, a graphical history of the index, and the latest and 52-week range of each of the components in the FCON.

The FCON is an index of three equally weighted (33 percent each) asset classes, the Money Market, the Bond Market, and the Equity Market. The headline index comprises a total of 10 indicators. In each of the three asset classes are instruments that represent their respective category.

In the Money Market group there are three measures (the U.S. LIBOR/OIS Spread, the U.S. TED spread, and the U.S. commercial paper/T-bill spread), each carrying an 11.1 percent weight in the total index. The Bond Market section includes five measures (the BAA-10-year Treasury spread, the U.S. High-Yield-10-year Treasury spread, the 10-year swap-Treasury spread, the U.S. muni-10-year Treasury spread, and the swaption volatility index), each possessing a 6.7 percent weight in the headline index. The Equity market group contains the S&P 500 five-year moving average and the VIX Index of S&P 500 volatility, and each of these carries a 16.7 percent weight.

As Exhibit 1.11 shows, there were seven notable events/periods since late 2007, when financial conditions were flashing worry signs.

In late 2007, the liquidity issues surfaced in the interbank funding market, while the Bank of England provided a loan facility for Northern Rock, a major

**EXHIBIT 1.10**  Bloomberg Financial Market Conditions Monitor

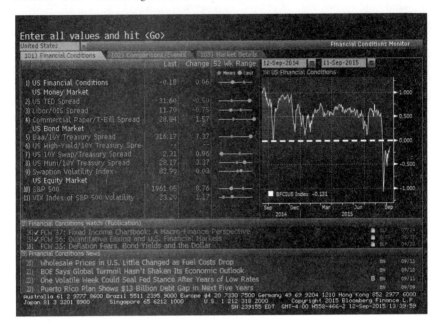

*Source:* Bloomberg

**EXHIBIT 1.11**  Bloomberg Financial Market Conditions Index—History

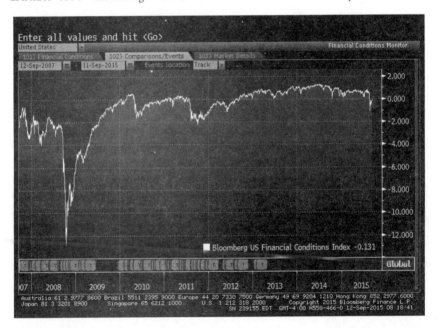

*Source:* Bloomberg

mortgage provider in the United Kingdom. This was essentially the first of several sizable declines in the Financial Conditions Index. The Federal Reserve commenced its rate-cutting campaign in September 2007 and continued to slash its target rate throughout 2008, which had a steady deceleration in financial conditions. Also in 2008, the primary cause for the momentous plunge in the Financial Conditions Index during September of that year was the collapse of Lehman Brothers. This would be the first major domino to fall in a string of global bank failures, which rattled the markets for years. Congress subsequently provided a $700 billion Troubled Asset Relief Program (TARP), purchasing the assets of failing banks and injecting liquidity into the melting financial markets. This move, in combination with monetary policy accommodation and other actions, soon resulted in an increase in the Financial Conditions Index as fears of calamity subsided through 2009.

In mid-2010, the euro area started to unravel with fears of a Greek default and possible exit from the Eurozone. The International Monetary Fund (IMF) and European nations created the Financial Stabilization Mechanism and Facility of €750 billion and agreed to loan €110 billion to Greece. This ultimately sent the Financial Conditions Index back into negative territory.

In July and August of 2011, conditions deteriorated once again on Greek fears, and the ratings agency Standard & Poor's cut America's credit rating from AAA to AA+ amid concerns that policy makers wouldn't be able to raise revenues and reduce spending enough to reduce its burgeoning budget deficit. The Bank of England made asset purchases. This stabilized the financial markets.

Then in early 2012, Europe's situation grew more dire. Spain was up against the ropes, and the Republic of Cyprus needed an emergency loan. The European Central Bank (ECB) soon announces a bond-buying program and financial market stress is arrested.

Conditions returned to a relatively safe status until a temporary hit in August of 2015, when the People's Bank of China devalued its currency and China experienced a tremendous sell-off in its stock market in 2015. This sent jitters throughout the markets, since the concerns were exacerbated by the expectations of a Federal Reserve rate increase. The Financial Conditions Index fell, but returned to less worrisome levels once the fears dissipated.

## Test Yourself

Answer the following multiple-choice questions:

1. Economists occasionally adjust data in order to:
    a. identify a relationship between economic variables.
    b. make a similar comparison of data.
    c. remove noisy timing elements from time series.

    d. none of the above.

    e. all of the above.

2. Why is the economic calendar an extremely important tool?

    a. Economists use all of the indicators in it to forecast GDP.

    b. It provides the Street consensus expectations for particular releases.

    c. It forecasts all of the economic indicators in a month.

    d. All of the above.

    e. None of the above.

3. Why are anecdotes found in company earnings transcripts and other events important?

    a. Executives have the economic releases before they are released to the Street.

    b. Executives provide an industry perspective not seen in the economic releases.

    c. Executives have the best forecasting record.

    d. All of the above.

    e. None of the above.

4. Upbeat or positive economic releases usually result in:

    a. an increase in the stock market, and a decrease in fixed-income prices.

    b. an increase in the stock market, and an increase in fixed-income prices.

    c. an increase in the stock market, and a decrease in fixed-income yields.

    d. all of the above.

    e. none of the above.

5. A financial conditions or stress index tells us:

    a. the likelihood of an economic downturn in an economy.

    b. the number of companies issuing negative assessments of the financial market.

    c. the amount of stress that exists in the financial banking system based on the levels and trends of several fixed-income assets.

    d. all of the above.

    e. none of the above.

## Answers

1. e
2. b
3. b
4. a
5. c

# CHAPTER 2

# The Business Cycle

Over time, the economy experiences periods of varying degrees of economic activity. Throughout history there have been different measures of economic activity, including the amount agricultural products produced or harvested, factory output, or the amount of commodities demanded. As recently as the Great Depression in the 1930s, policy makers were forced to implement legislature to combat the sinking economy with no formal measure of overall economic activity! In many cases, policies were initially adopted based largely upon sinking stock prices.

It wasn't until the formation of the National Income and Product Accounts in the late 1930s for an estimate of national income to be developed; and not until the early 1940s for a measure of gross national product to be calculated.

The most common way to consider the business cycle is as a graphical representation of the total economic activity of a country. Because the accepted benchmark for economic activity in the United States is currently gross domestic product (GDP), economists generally identify the business cycle with the alternating increases and declines in GDP. Rising GDP marks economic expansion; falling GDP, a contraction. We will see that there are several measures used to represent the businesses cycle—considerably more timely than the quarterly report on GDP—and that it takes several difference barometers to ultimately determine expansions and contractions.

When the economy is growing, economists refer to this phase as an expansion. Traditionally, aggregate demand advances due to several variables such as population, technological advances, and abundance of natural resources. Policies enacted by legislatures often determine the growth rate as well. In the United States, the base trend in economic growth—as measured by inflation adjusted, or real, gross domestic product (GDP)—has been positive, advancing an average of 3.2 percent since 1948. This is somewhat of a benchmark to consider when thinking of the condition of the economy.

Contractions occur less frequently—thankfully—and are often engendered by falling corporate profitability, widespread labor market weakness, escalating prices, or some other event. Rarely do economic expansions simply run out of gas. Either monetary policy makers choke off growth by aggressively increasing borrowing costs or fiscal policy makers fail to provide sufficient stimulus in the way of federal spending initiatives like infrastructure projects or by tax reductions. So-called economic shocks like an unforeseen surge in energy prices or unanticipated wars, conflicts, or skirmishes have been known to rattle underlying confidence in an economy and reduce growth.

The National Bureau of Economic Research (NBER) is the official arbiter of the business cycle in the United States. The NBER is a nonpartisan, nonprofit, private economic research institution founded in 1920 studying and analyzing a variety of economic topics. However, its work with respect to the business cycle seems to garner the most attention.

The NBER's Business Cycle Dating Committee—a group of highly esteemed economists—employs a number of economic indicators used in the determination of economic expansions and downturns.

Basically, the period from a peak in activity to the bottom, or *trough*, is called a *recession*, while the phase existing from the trough to the peak is called *expansion*. There is no single barometer used in the estimation of the particular date of recession or expansion, but rather a compendium of measures that have been known to represent the trend in total economic activity in the country. One of the most commonly used representatives of the business cycle is gross domestic product. While the NBER does in fact observe trends in this indicator, it also uses several others in the dating of business-cycle turning points. Exhibit 2.1 represents a handful of those indicators, including industrial production, real personal income less transfer payments, employment (payroll and household survey), average weekly hours worked, and real manufacturing and trade sales.

No two business cycles are the same. As illustrated in many of the exhibits in this book, the length of expansions and recessions have varied widely—although the former, especially recently, have generally been longer and steadier than the latter. The NBER has identified and dated the peaks and troughs in the U.S. economy back to 1854.

Since then, expansions have ranged from 120 months (April 1991 to March 2001) to 10 months (March 1919 to January 1920), and downturns from 43 months (August 1929 to March 1933) to 6 months (January 1980 to July 1980). The amplitude of the peaks and troughs has also differed significantly from cycle to cycle.

## Leading, Lagging, and Coincident Indicators

The Conference Board publishes a monthly report called U.S. Business Cycle Indicators, which contains three composite indexes and a detailed report

**EXHIBIT 2.1** NBER Recession Indicators (Y/Y%)

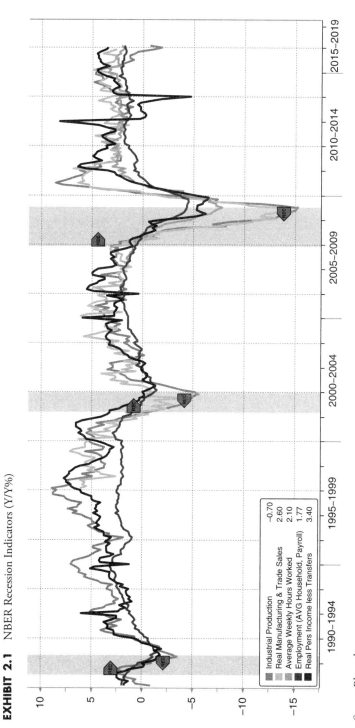

| Industrial Production | −0.70 |
| Real Manufacturing & Trade Sales | 2.60 |
| Average Weekly Hours Worked | 2.10 |
| Employment (AVG Household, Payroll) | 1.77 |
| Real Pers Income less Transfers | 3.40 |

*Source:* Bloomberg

regarding the latest trends in the business cycle. Economic indicators are classified according to how they relate to the business cycle. Those that reflect the current state of the economy are coincident; those that predict future conditions are leading; and those that confirm that a turning occurred are lagging. The Business Cycle Indicators report has the most respected measures of these three phases of the cycle.

## Coincident Indicators

The Conference Board's Coincident Economic Index (CEI) is a composite measure comprised of four components that depicts the trends of the current business cycle (Exhibit 2.2). The four components of the Conference Board's CEI are the number of employees on nonagricultural payrolls, personal income less transfer payments, the industrial production index, and manufacturing and trade sales.

The CEI is not a market mover, and it is rarely reported in the business press. Since it is not intended to estimate or project the future direction of the economy or an industry, most investors ignore it. The true value of this indicator lies in its lengthy history and accuracy as a current measure of the business cycle.

Each of the components is an excellent measure of economic conditions individually, but when used in concert as a composite, the power to identify peaks and troughs is strengthened. Since a single indicator may emit false signals due to weather fluctuations, calendar or seasonal quirks, or any host of reasons, a composite is preferred, as all of the components would have to be distorted or influenced to result in an improper or misleading reading.

The four components represent the broadest perspective of the U.S. economy—employment, incomes, production, and sales. Nonfarm payrolls are an excellent barometer since employment is essentially the lifeblood of the economy. Similarly, the associated compensation of personal income less transfer payments is an excellent gauge used in the determination of economic health. There is no indicator more important than employment. Not only are there economic consequences of not possessing a job—the loss of incomes—but there are many negative social issues associated with unemployment such as crime, divorce, depression, suicide, and even murder. Obviously, when employment is increasing, the entire economy is better off economically and socially.

The remaining two components, industrial production and sales, make economic sense because they are measures of economic output and consumption. Prior to the creation of the national income and product accounts (NIPAs)—the formal measures of economic activity including GDP—industrial production was used as the benchmark measure of overall economic activity. This was a function of two conditions: The United States was predominantly a manufacturing-based economy, so changes in industrial production were a perfect representation of overall economic activity, and production, by definition, is a measure of output.

**EXHIBIT 2.2** Conference Board Coincident Economic Index

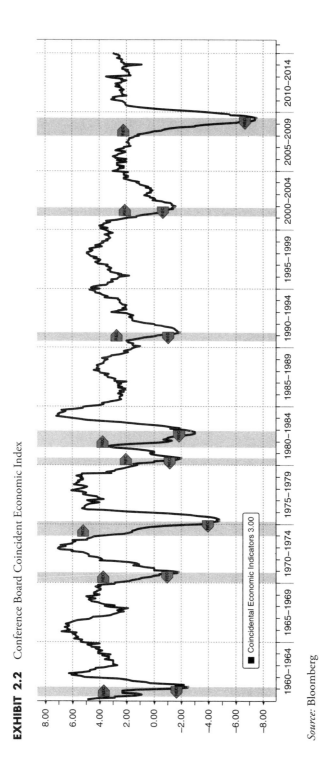

*Source:* Bloomberg

21

The CEI is released monthly, which makes it somewhat preferred to the quarterly released GDP, which is somewhat dated and prone to notable revisions. The coincident index might not measure the magnitude of economic growth that well since it is only comprised of four components, but it does highlight the vector (or direction) of the economy quite well.

## Forward-Looking Leading Indexes

Market participants don't generally pay a great deal of attention to the Conference Board's Business Cycle Indicators report because the underlying data have already been released and analyzed. As such, it doesn't possess a great deal of market-moving potential. Nevertheless, economists and businesses have traditionally looked for longer-term trends in the leading index to predict turning points in the economy (Exhibit 2.3).

The 10 components of the current index of leading economic indicators are:

1. Average weekly hours in manufacturing
2. Weekly initial claims
3. New orders for manufacturers—consumer goods
4. New orders ISM Report
5. New orders, nondefense capital goods ex-aircraft
6. Building permits
7. Stock prices
8. Leading Credit Index
9. Interest rate spread
10. Consumer sentiment—expectations

Each of these measures will be discussed, with varying degrees of attention, in coming chapters.

Over time, the components have changed as new measures and findings provide a more accurate representation of the business cycle and one that yields better predictive powers.

Some noteworthy issues regarding these components: For starters, some are what economists call hard or concrete measures. That is, they actually measure stuff—that is, the level of building permit applications or the level of new orders for consumer goods manufactures. This differs from what economists call sentiment or opinion indicators. The consumer expectations index or the Institute of Supply Management's (ISM's) new orders survey are sentiment indicators. They attempt to capture feelings or opinions about where the consumer believes the economy is headed, or what the ISM purchasing managers anticipate about the future pace of new orders will be. Economists tend to favor those gauges that actually measure products ordered, sold, or shipped, to those that are proxies for feelings or guesstimates. Nevertheless, the Conference Board Leading Economic Index (LEI) is the foremost index available that predicts the business cycle.

**EXHIBIT 2.3** Conference Board's Index of Leading Economic Indicators, Real GDP %

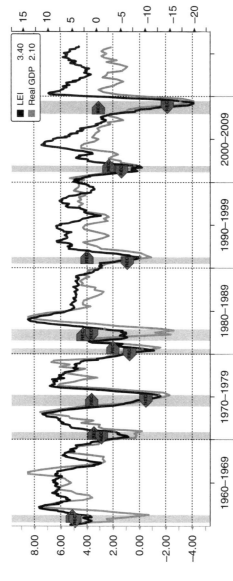

*Source:* Bloomberg

At one time, there was a rule of thumb that three consecutive monthly declines in the LEI signaled a recession within a year, whereas three consecutive increases suggested a recovery. This rule was roughly accurate but managed to predict several recessions that failed to materialize. One reason for false recession predictions could be that although the index contains components representing the manufacturing, consumer, financial, employment, and business investment sectors, it has none that reflect demand for, or investment and employment in, the services industries that now dominate the economy. Moreover, the financial sectors that are represented often move in ways that don't parallel movement in the broader economy, generating both volatility and some of those false signals.

The LEI's record of predicting, as a popular quip has it, "seven of the last five recessions" has led some cynics to term it the index of misleading indicators. That's not really a fair appraisal since it is exceptionally good at predicting changes in the cycle, and has a long history of doing so. It's just that at times there are false signals emitted, which have turned some investors off from this measure. One should never get in the habit of banking on one indicator, especially since *all* indicators possess flaws.

Economists often consider the LEI's moves in three dimensions—duration, depth, and diffusion—instead of just one, duration, as the three-month rule suggests. That is, in addition to requiring that changes extend over three months, the refined method looks at how large changes are and how many components are involved. For example, if 8 of the index's 10 components show increases, but two fall, an expansion is more certain than if only four components increase, three decrease, and three are unchanged.

The rationale behind including some of these indicators is clear from their names: *orders* and *expectations*, for example, are by definition forward-looking since they imply action in the future. The inclusion of others is less self-evident. All the components, however, are there for a reason, and work together well in the prediction of economic trends.

## The Lagging Index and the Coincident-to-Lagging Ratio

The Conference Board Lagging Economic Index (LAG) is a composite of seven indicators (average duration of unemployment, inventory-to-sales ratio, labor cost per unit of output in manufacturing, the prime rate, commercial and industrial loans, consumer credit-to-income ratio, and the CPI for services). These components tend to change months after the business cycle has turned, and when used as a composite doesn't provide too much of an explanation as to what is going on in the economy.

As much as the coincident index is ignored by the Street, the lagging indicator index may not have been noted or mentioned in an economist note in decades. So why look at a series of indicators that are going to tell you where the economy has been several months after the fact? That's a legitimate question, and we will see that there are some very desirable uses for the lagging index, which ultimately provide.

One reason to observe trends in this series is to confirm, or refute, what the LEI, or even the CEI, may have signaled. Keep in mind that all of the individual components of the Conference Board's business cycle measures (leading, coincident, and lagging)—or any indicator, for that matter—experience constant changes, and have a propensity to emit an errant reading. Sometimes a revision occurs and alters what an individual indicator might have been suggesting. So the LAG may also be used as another check to see if any false signals have been transmitted.

Interestingly, economists have found that computing the ratio of the coincident index to the lagging index yields a highly predictive measure of the business cycle. The theory behind this ratio, informally referred to as the coincident-to-lagging ratio, is this: In the early stages of a recovery, coincident indicators are rising while lagging indicators, reflecting the conditions of earlier months, remain unchanged, resulting in a rising ratio. When an expansion is peaking, both sets of indicators will be rising, but the rate of increase for the coincident indicators will be slower, so the ratio will fall. Similarly, near the nadir of a recession, all the component indicators will again be moving in the same direction—this time, down—but the coincident indicators will fall more slowly, so the ratio will rise.

As you can see from the chart in Exhibit 2.4, the coincident-to-lagging ratio has declined before every recession since 1970. Similarly, it has climbed along with, and during, all expansions. The simple logic behind this relative success is that the coincident and lagging indexes do a better job of representing current and past economic performance, respectively, than the leading index does of assessing future activity.

## The Chicago National Activity Index

One of the more recently developed measures of overall economic activity is the Chicago Fed National Activity Index (CFNAI), which is estimated and released by the Federal Reserve's Chicago District. This series is a weighted average of 85 monthly indicators of U.S. economic activity. Some of the components include detailed data from industrial production, ISM, retail sales, nonfarm payrolls, initial claims, consumer expenditures, housing starts, and inventories. In addition to a headline measure, the Chicago Fed provides four major subcomponents and associated indexes for (1) production and income; (2) personal consumption and housing; (3) sales, orders, and inventories; and (4) employment, unemployment, and hours.

This highly respected, robust representative of overall economic activity doesn't move the financial markets—many on the Street may not even know of its existence. That neglect may be due to the fact that most of the underlying data

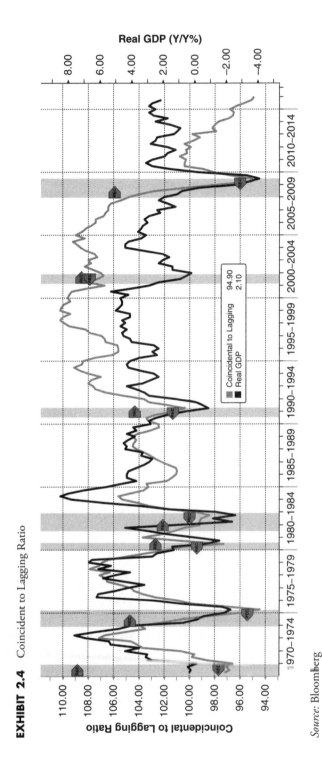

**EXHIBIT 2.4** Coincident to Lagging Ratio

*Source:* Bloomberg

26

are already known, and some observers tend to have their own individual favorite indicators. But collectively and when observed on a less volatile three-month moving average, this index is a true powerhouse with regard to estimating the economic business cycle.

Rather than representing the pace of economic activity, the CFNAI is constructed to have a reading of zero, which corresponds to an economy advancing at its historical trend. Positive values therefore imply periods when the economy is advancing at a pace above its trend, while negative values denote a slower pace.

According to the folks at the Chicago Fed, the key threshold for recession occurs when the three-month moving average (MA3) of the CFNAI falls below −0.7 as shown in each of the seven recessions depicted in Exhibit 2.5. This series has a somewhat scattered history in timing of recessions, but a definitively successful predictive history.

The CFNAI-MA3 fell below −0.7 within the second or third month of the 1969–1970, 1981–1982, 1990–1991, and 2007–2009 recessions, and the fourth month of the 1980 downturn. It wasn't until the eleventh month of the 1973–1975 recession that the index fell below −0.7. The measure's greatest day was when it foreshadowed the 2001 recession by falling below −0.7 one-month prior to the downturn that year.

There have only been two false signals, July 1989 and December 1991. The Fed had been engaged in a rate tightening campaign from 1988 through early 1989, which more than likely resulted in a curtailment of many of the index's interest rate–sensitive components.

The CFNAI is also used to identify periods of a sustained increase in inflation. When the three-month moving average of the CFNAI rises above +0.7 for more than two years into an expansion, there is an increased likelihood that the economy has entered a period of sustained elevated inflation.

An extremely informative addition to the CFNAI report came in 2012 with the estimation of the CFNAI Diffusion Index. This is truly one of the more secretive economic measures in the world of economic indicators. And boy is it accurate. When the three-month moving average of the CFNAI Diffusion Index falls below −0.35, you better prepare for some turbulent times. Only once since 1971 has this index sent a false signal.

## The Yield Curve as a Predictor of the Business Cycle

One of the most accurate forecasting measures of economic activity, and component of the Conference Board's index of leading economic indicators, is the slope of the yield curve. The yield curve is simply the graphical relationship between the yield on U.S. Treasury securities and their maturities.

When economists want to know if the economy is headed into recession, there is no better place to look than at the interest rate spread. That is, the

28

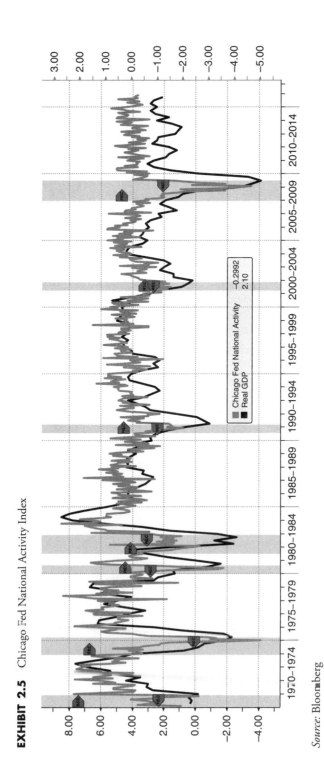

**EXHIBIT 2.5** Chicago Fed National Activity Index

*Source:* Bloomberg

difference between longer-dated maturity Treasury fixed-income instruments like the benchmark 10-year Treasury note, and one of the short-term measures like the Fed funds rate, the 3-month Treasury bill, or the 2-year Treasury note. The most common measure on the Street is the Fed-funds, 10-year Treasury note spread. How does this work?

For example, if the federal funds rate is 1.00 percent and the 10-year Treasury is yielding 3.15 percent, the spread is 2.15 percent, or 215 basis points (a basis point is one-hundredth of a percent). The interest-rate spread embodies fixed-income traders' expectations about the economy.

Longer-term rates are usually higher than shorter-term rates, because more things can affect the value of the bond in 10 years than in overnight, 3 months, or 2 years, and lenders require greater rewards for undertaking these greater risks. Thus, under "normal" economically favorable conditions, interest-rate spreads are positive, and the shape of the yield curve is gently convex—rising somewhat more steeply at the short end and leveling off a bit at the longer maturities.

Steep curves—very large spreads—may temporarily be the result of current economic weakness. The Federal Reserve seeks to counter such weakness by reducing the overnight rate, thus lowering borrowing costs and encouraging business investment and consumer spending on interest rate–sensitive goods and services like housing and automobiles. This move stimulates the economy but can spark inflationary fears among the fixed-income community. Inflation erodes the value of future interest and principal payments. In anticipation, fixed-income investors sell off longer-term (more inflation-sensitive) bonds, depressing their prices and raising their yields. This, combined with the Fed's lowering of the short-term rate, steepens the yield curve. Conversely, when the economy seems to be running too hot, the Fed may seek to forestall a rise in inflation by raising its target overnight rate, discouraging spending and so slowing growth. The result is a flatter yield curve (smaller spreads).

At times, the curve may become "inverted," with short-term rates higher than long-term rates and spreads below zero. This situation is generally associated with economic downturns, and if sustained in recessions, as illustrated in Exhibit 2.6.

Why does an inverted yield curve predict recessions? There is no definitive answer. One possible explanation may be that an inverted curve may result from the Fed's overdoing it—raising rates so high they not only cool but stifle growth (as well as any fears of inflation). What is clear is that expectations of weak economic conditions may encourage expectations of lower interest rates. This, in turn, leads to more purchases of longer-term bonds, pushing up their prices and lowering their yields. The result is an inverted curve.

While there has never been a recession without an inverted yield curve, there have been occasions where the yield curve has been inverted, with no associated economic downturn. In other words, an inverted yield has engendered a false recession signal. While it is not failsafe, the yield curve is one of the most respected measures of the economic cycle that investors have today.

**EXHIBIT 2.6** Yield Curve

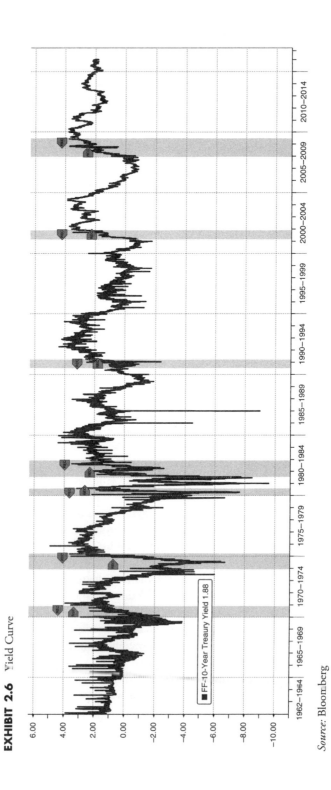

*Source:* Bloomberg

## "Nowcasting" Economic Activity

The latest, and arguably greatest, contribution to economic forecasting in the last decade comes out of the Atlanta Fed, particularly the work of economist Patrick Higgins, who created the Atlanta Fed's GDPNow—a model that employs monthly data to estimate a *nowcast* of the upcoming quarterly GDP report. While this report has only been around since 2015, the results to date are truly quite impressive.

About five or six times a month, economists at the Atlanta Fed run the model with data from the releases of several economic indicators—essentially all presented in this book—and a latest forecast is generated and posted on their website. This is not an official forecast of the Federal Reserve System, the Atlanta Fed, or any individual. It is simply a guide—a highly accurate one—that investors are encouraged to view over the course of the quarter when they would like to see how the U.S. economy is trending prior to the release of the GDP report.

The forecasts are generated and presented several times a month, with at least one estimate given following each of the six data releases: the ISM Report on Business, U.S. international trade balance, the monthly retail trade report, new housing starts report, the durable goods report, and the personal income and spending release.

Exhibit 2.7 shows just how successful the GDPNow has been at predicting the quarterly change in the BEA's real GDP release. Over the course of the economic calendar, the forecasts are generated and posted. Many times, the Atlanta Fed's GDPNow trends along a path until it comes to a quarterly point, which is not too far off from the actual quarterly change in real GDP.

Economists do not forecast this series; It is used as a convenient, accurate measure for investors that do not have the wherewithal to gather data, create and run their own models, and test the results. There isn't ever a meaningful market reaction after the latest forecast is announced, but once it is, the chatter runs fast across trading platforms and in chat rooms across the financial markets. This measure has gained a great deal of attention in recent months, and is an essential part of every economic newsletter on the Street today. If you're looking for a quick forecast before running out to a trade show, a business meeting, or a cocktail event, you better know what the latest Atlanta Fed GDPNow is projecting.

## The Best Representation of U.S. Economic Activity

The Federal Reserve Bank of Philadelphia has created a measure of overall economic growth that combines the two economic approaches estimated by the Bureau of Economic Analysis (BEA), gross domestic product (GDP) and gross domestic income (GDI). The measure, GDPplus, provides a dual perspective that uses the parts of economic activity that are not capable of detection in the gross

**EXHIBIT 2.7** Atlanta Fed GDPNow Forecast

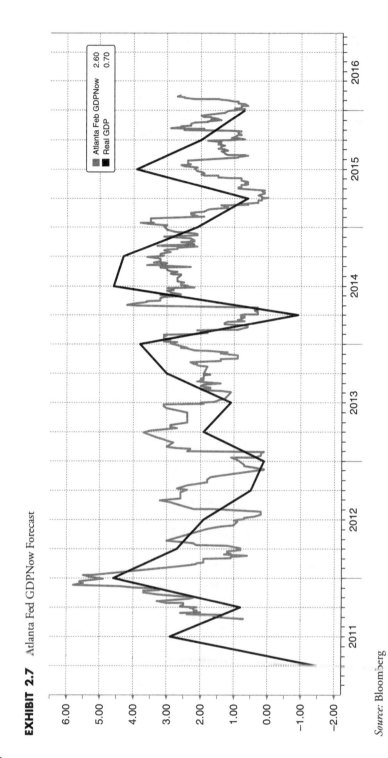

| Atlanta Feb GDPNow | 2.60 |
| Real GDP | 0.70 |

*Source:* Bloomberg

**EXHIBIT 2.8** Philadelphia Fed GDPplus and Real GDP

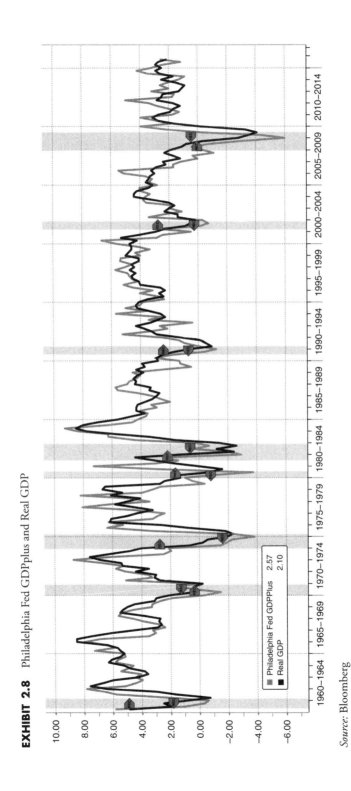

*Source:* Bloomberg

33

domestic product report. Many goods and services are undetected by simply summing up the products in the economy (the expenditure approach), which is how the GDP report is estimated. It's simply quite difficult having to identify and count all of the items in such a massive economy. By adopting the BEA's lesser followed approach of gross domestic incomes—that is, summing up all of the incomes earned in the economy—we can achieve a better representation of the total amount of economic activity in the economy. Basically, the GDI report measures the amount of money paid for the goods and services, so some services may not be calculated, but the exchange of income for those services will be.

Exhibit 2.8 shows the relationship between the year-over-year trend in the Philadelphia Fed's GDPplus and the same change in the BEA's real GDP. It is no surprise that these two are closely correlated since GDPplus is simply a modified version of the GDP report.

This is not a market-moving release, and economists do not forecast this index. But it is an excellent gauge and is often used in macroeconomic modeling and forecasting since it is a more robust measure encompassing additional information and is somewhat less volatile. GDPplus is a relatively new indicator, having arrived on the scene in November 2013.

## Test Yourself

Answer the following multiple-choice questions:

1. The organization responsible for the determination of the business cycle is called the:
   a. National Bureau of Economic Research.
   b. Federal Reserve.
   c. Federal Open Market Committee.
   d. National Association of Business Economists.
   e. Council of Economic Advisers.

2. Economic indicators basically represent one of three phases with respect to the business cycle:
   a. Initial, middle, and end stage.
   b. First, second, and third.
   c. Recession, depression, economic collapse.
   d. Leading, coincident, and lagging.
   e. None of the above.

3. To determine a recession, economists:
   a. look at a number of economic series to identify a downturn.
   b. look only for a minimum of two consecutive quarters of negative GDP growth.

   c. look only at total real GDP.

   d. look at the budget of the United States.

   e. All of the above.

4. Economists look at the yield curve as a predictor of economic activity by:

   a. adding the yield of the Fed funds rate and the 10-year Treasury note together.

   b. dividing the 10-year Treasury yield by the Fed funds rate.

   c. multiplying the Fed funds rate by the yield on the 10-year Treasury note.

   d. taking the difference between the yield on the 10-year Treasury note and the Fed funds rate.

   e. noting any yield curve reading of 3.0 or higher suggests recession.

5. The Federal Reserve Bank of Philadelphia's GDPplus index is a measure of economic activity using:

   a. GDP plus the components of the coincident index.

   b. GDP plus some measures of the GDI report.

   c. GDP plus some measures in the CPI index.

   d. GDP plus all 85 indicators in the Chicago Fed's National Activity Index.

   e. None of the above.

## Answers

1. a
2. d
3. a
4. d
5. b

# CHAPTER 3

# Gross Domestic Product (GDP)

The quarterly gross domestic product (GDP) report is the most comprehensive of all the top-tier economic statistics and is considered the benchmark for the overall state of affairs in the U.S. economy. Essentially, all of the economic indicators used on Wall Street are employed with the intention of predicting or estimating the trends in the quarterly GDP report. When the growth rate in national GDP contracts for a period of usually—but not always—two consecutive quarters, the economy is said to be in recession. Conversely, when times are prosperous and GDP advances, the economy is considered to be in an expansionary phase.

GDP is defined as the sum of the market values of all final goods and services produced by the resources (labor and property) of a country residing in that country. When economists refer to final goods, they mean those goods produced for their final intended use—that is, as end products, not as component or intermediate parts in another stage of manufacture.

The other important term in the GDP definition is produced. Resales are not included in the accounts. Rightfully so, the BEA has determined that because the pace of reselling is not indicative of the current pace of production, it shouldn't be included in the output figures.

Tracking the developments in an economy as large and dynamic as that of the United States is not easy. But through constant revision and upgrading, a relatively small group of dedicated economists at the BEA accomplishes this huge task every quarter.

Each quarterly report of economic activity has three versions, all available on the BEA website, www.bea.gov. The first, the advance report, comes one month after the end of the quarter covered, hitting the newswires at 8:30 a.m. ET. Since all the data are not available during this initial release, the BEA must estimate some series, particularly those involving inventories and foreign trade.

As new data become available, the BEA makes the necessary refinements, deriving a more accurate estimate for GDP. The second release arrives two months after the quarter covered—one month after the advance report—and reflects the refinements made to date. The last revision, also referred to as the third or final report, is released three months after the relevant quarter and a month after the second report.

Annual revisions are calculated during July of every year, based on data that become available to the BEA only on an annual basis, such as state and local government consumption expenditures.

Every five years, the BEA issues a so-called benchmark revision of all of the data in the NIPAs. This has typically resulted in considerable changes to the five years of quarterly figures.

Benchmark revisions are different from annual revisions in that they generally contain major overhauls to the structure of the report, definitional reclassifications, and new presentations of data. New tables need to be created to account for products that are developed.

The headline figure that the Street focuses on is the annualized quarterly growth rate of real GDP (Exhibit 3.1); similar to most indicators, strong positive postings are a sign of a thriving economy, which is good news for the drivers of activity (investment and employment), corporate profits, and stock market valuations. Conversely, fixed-income asset prices tend to sell off during stronger-than-desired postings in GDP since a rapidly rising economy can carry higher rates of inflation, which erodes the value of bond prices, resulting in higher yields.

The data tell the story of how the economy performed—whether it expanded or contracted—during a specific period, usually the preceding quarter. By looking at changes in the GDP's components and subcomponents and comparing these with changes that have occurred in the past, economists can draw inferences about the direction the economy might take in the future.

Of all the tasks market economists perform, generating a forecast for overall economic performance as measured by the GDP data is the one to which they dedicate the most time. In fact, the latest report on GDP is generally within arm's reach of most Wall Street economists. Because several departments in a trading institution rely on the economist's forecasts, this indicator has emerged as the foundation for all research and trading activity and usually sets the tone of all of Wall Street's financial prognostications.

## Composition

There are two measures the BEA employs when estimating the size of the U.S. economy, gross domestic product (GDP) and gross domestic income (GDI). GDP is calculated by the aggregate demand, or expenditures approach, while GDI is the aggregation of costs and incomes in the associated output. This chapter

**EXHIBIT 3.1** GDP Breakdown—History

GDP$PCE Index (GDP Dollar Level Personal Consumption Expenditures)
GPDITOT Index (US Gross Private Domestic Investment Total Nominal SAAR)
GPGSTOT Index (US GDP Govt Purchases & Investment Total Nominal SAAR)
GDP$NETX Index (GDP Dollar Level Net Exports of Goods and Services)

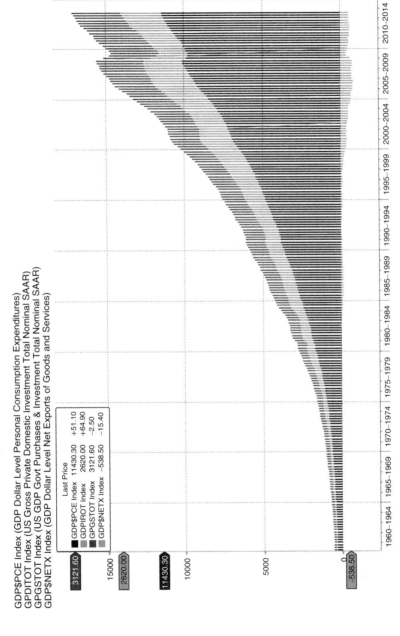

*Source:* Bloomberg

39

focuses on the expenditures approach, since that is the more common of the two estimates on the Street. GDI will be presented briefly in the end of this chapter.

To calculate GDP, the BEA uses the aggregate-expenditure equation:

$$GDP = C + I + G + (X - M)$$

where, $C$ is personal consumption expenditures, $I$ is gross private domestic investment, $G$ is government consumption expenditures and gross investment, and $(X - M)$ is the net export value of goods and services (exports minus imports). The identity expressed in this equation is probably the most widely cited of all economic relationships and appears in virtually all introductory macroeconomic texts.

The largest component of GDP is consumption expenditures, usually accounting for about 70 percent of total output (Exhibit 3.2). Investment spending in the economy is roughly 16 percent of GDP, while the government expenditures accounts for 18 percent. These three components add up to a bit more than 100 percent, but once the level of net exports is considered, which subtracts about 3 to 5 percent from the total (in recent years the United States has experienced a trade deficit because it imports more than it exports), the sum is 100 percent.

The GDP report contains a wealth of information about the nation's economy. Each of its components tells a different story about a particular group, sector, industry, or activity. Not surprisingly, then, market participants look at different sections and draw their own respective inferences. Retail analysts, for instance, focus mostly on consumer spending trends. Those covering housing, construction, or real estate investment trusts (REITs) concentrate on the residential activity in investment spending. Defense-industry analysts focus on the national defense spending component of government consumption expenditures and gross investment. Fixed-income analysts and investors, ever wary of the eroding effects of inflation, concern themselves with the GDP deflators and GDP growth rate. Traders, who are always on the lookout for possible market movers, watch for numbers that contradict expectations, which they track carefully, often

**EXHIBIT 3.2**   GDP Component Composition, %

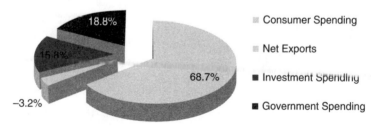

*Data Source:* BEA, a/o QII–2013

jotting them down in notebooks kept at their desks for quick reference when the real figures are announced.

## Nominal and Real Values

The data reported in the GDP release are presented in two forms, nominal and real. Nominal, also known as current-dollar GDP is the total value, at current prices, of all final goods and services produced during the reporting period. Real, or constant-dollar, GDP is the value of these goods and services using the prices in a specified base year. Economists tend to prefer the real figures to the nominal measure. To understand why, consider a two-good economy that produces bottles of Chanel perfume and chocolate-covered fortune cookies.

If during Year 1, our somewhat peculiar economy produces 2,000 bottles of perfume and sells them at $100.00 each and 10,000 fortune cookies at $1.00 each, its nominal GDP will be $5,200:

$$\text{Year 1: } 2,000 \times \$100 = \$200,000 + 10,000 \times \$1 = \$210,000$$

Next year, the same country produces only 1,250 bottles of Chanel perfume and 8,000 fortune cookies, but the prices of perfume and cookies change to $160 and $1.25, respectively, we once again get a nominal GDP of $210,000:

$$\text{Year 2: } 1,250 \times \$160 = \$200,000 + 8,000 \times \$1.25 = \$210,000$$

Is the economy larger during the second year? Did it produce the same amount? The difficulty in answering these questions illustrates the problem with nominal values. Economists have no way of telling whether it was the price or the quantity produced that increased, or by what magnitude. As more goods and services are considered, the problem obviously gets bigger.

Real GDP is a more accurate indicator of changes in production. Referring to a base year eliminates the uncertainty of whether an increase in the value of the goods and services produced was the result of increased prices or of higher production.

Let's estimate real GDP in year two using the prices of year one.

Year 2: $1,250 \times \$100 = \$125,000 + 8,000 \times \$1.00 = \$133,000$, or a decline of $77,000 (37 percent) from the previous year. Not a very good year for our odd economy.

Basically, the difference between real and nominal GDP is the level of inflation. Exhibit 3.3 depicts the year-over-year rates of change in real and nominal GDP since 1949. The spread between the two lines is the inflation rate. When the gap widens like in the 1970s, inflation is high. Conversely, for narrow gaps like in the 1990s through today, inflation in the economy is low.

**EXHIBIT 3.3** Real and Nominal GDP (Y/Y%)

GDP CYOY Index (GDP US Chained 2009 Dollars YoY SA)
GDP CURY Index (US GDP Nominal Dollars YoY SA)

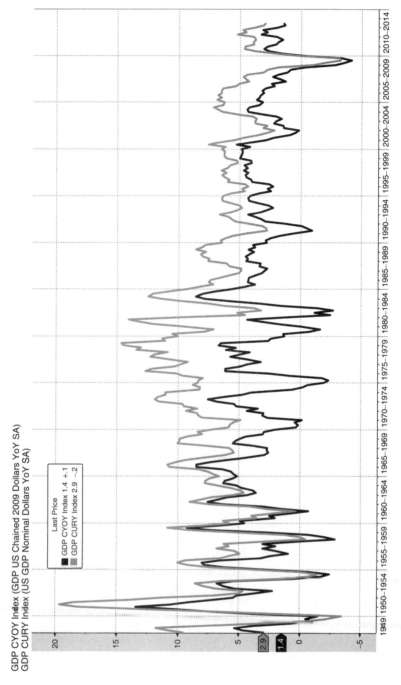

*Source:* Bloomberg

Although the annualized quarterly figure is important, many economists prefer to look at the year-over-year change in GDP. The longer perspective makes it easier to spot turning points in the economy, such as an approaching recession or an acceleration of activity.

As Exhibit 3.4 shows, major downturns in the four-quarter growth rate of real GDP are recessions (red shaded areas). On average, the year-over-year growth rate in GDP starts slowing four to five quarters before a recession. Not all slowdowns, however, result in recession. By the time the warning signals appear, government policy makers have usually put in place measures to avert an economic downturn. Still, watching changes in year-over-year changes in real GDP growth can be useful for short-term forecasts: very rarely do trends reverse immediately. It takes a great deal to knock a $16 trillion economy like that of the United States off kilter. Luckily for those in the financial markets, several "leading" indicators usually send alerts when the behemoth GDP is running out of energy.

## Consumption Expenditures

As the consumer goes, so goes the U.S. economy. And this old saw may be more truthful than ever before. It is believed that the consumer's utter resilience to disruptions such as war, terrorist attacks on U.S. soil, widespread corporate malfeasance, 8 of the top-10 corporate bankruptcies in U.S. history, and presidential impeachment proceedings is the reason for the underlying strength of the economy and the mild recessions in 1990–1991 and 2001 (Exhibit 3.5).

But when conditions turn calamitous and the economy is in upheaval like in 2007 to mid-2009, which was the cumulative result of the banking and financial crisis, the housing bubble, and a synchronous global economic recession, then the consumer will toss in the towel. And surrender, it did.

Consumer spending is the total market value of household purchases made during the accounting term, and is detailed by three basic components: durable goods, nondurable goods, and services. Durable goods are those with shelf lives of three or more years. Examples include motor vehicles, air conditioners, furniture, ovens, and stoves. In addition, there are less bulky items like dishes, jewelry, and luggage. Since these are big-ticket items, and not frequently purchased, expenditures tend to be volatile. During the second quarter of 2013, durables accounted for roughly 11 percent of total spending.

Nondurable goods are those with shorter lifespans, or as a former professor once remarked, "Nondurables would disappear within three years if you left them in the backyard for up to three years." Included in this category are food, beverages, prescription drugs, magazines, and gasoline. This was about 23 percent of total spending in mid-2013.

Services spending is historically the largest consumption category, comprising nearly 66 percent of all expenditures—the United States is definitively a

**EXHIBIT 3.4** Real GDP (Y/Y%) versus Recessions

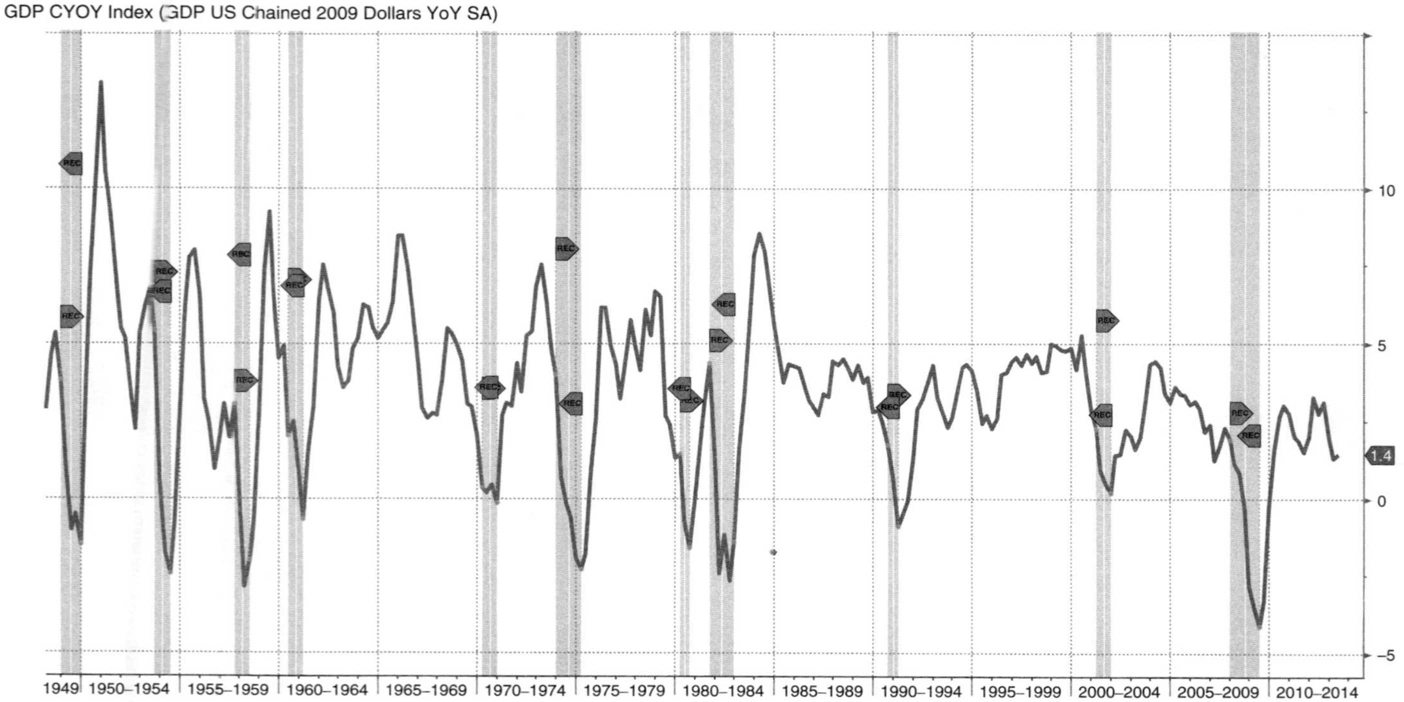

GDP CYOY Index (GDP US Chained 2009 Dollars YoY SA)

*Source:* Bloomberg

**EXHIBIT 3.5** Personal Consumption Expenditures

GDPCDUR Index (GDP US Personal Consumption Durable Goods)
GDPCNDR Index (GDP US Personal Consumption Nondurable Goods)
GDPCSRV Index (GDP US Personal Consumption Services)

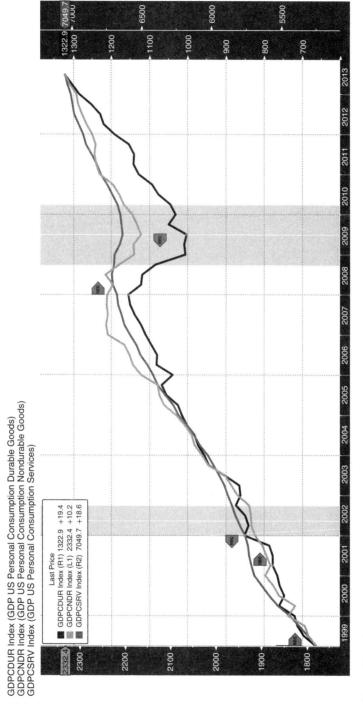

*Source:* Bloomberg

45

services-based economy (82 percent of those employed in America are in the services sector). This is a sizable increase from a mere 33 percent in 1950. Purchases in this massive component include casino gambling, restaurant spending, health care, movies, airline tickets, and hairstyling—for those fortunate to have hair necessary of styling.

A more detailed summary of personal consumption expenditures is available on a monthly basis in the BEA's Personal Income and Outlays report, which is the direct source of data for this component of the GDP report. Personal income and outlays are discussed in Chapter 4.

Generally, a drop in the growth rate of consumer spending is a surefire sign that the economy is on the verge of petering out. When people are feeling uneasy about the economic climate—perhaps unemployment is on the rise, or inflation is eroding the dollar's purchasing power, or individuals are just feeling tapped out—it shows in their spending habits.

## Investment Spending

Gross private domestic investment encompasses spending by businesses (on equipment such as computers, on the construction of factories and production plants, and in mining operations); expenditures on residential housing and apartments; and inventories. Inventories, which consist of the goods businesses produce that remain unsold at the end of a period, are valued by the BEA at the prevailing market price. This value fluctuates greatly from quarter to quarter, making the level of gross private domestic investment quite volatile (Exhibit 3.6).

Accordingly, economists often look at fixed investment—gross private domestic investment minus inventories. This, in turn, has two major components, residential and nonresidential. The latter, which is also referred to as capital spending, includes expenditures on computers and peripheral equipment, industrial equipment, and nonresidential buildings such as plants and factories. The former comprises spending on the construction of new houses and apartment buildings and on related equipment.

Capital equipment comprises all the industrial and technological items used to produce other goods and services for sale. The amount of money companies invest in this equipment is thus a good predictor of future economic activity. It indicates whether corporate profitability is accelerating or decelerating, how managers view future economic conditions, and how strong or weak the economy is.

As explained earlier, the Street tends to focus on fixed investment—gross domestic investment minus inventories. Of the two categories of fixed investment, residential and nonresidential (or capital spending), the former is by far the smaller, accounting for just 18 to 20 percent of the total. One shouldn't underestimate the influence of residential business investment, however. It represents roughly 3 percent of total economic output, but housing construction

**EXHIBIT 3.6** Investment Spending

GPDIFXIC Index (US Gross Private Domestic Investment Fixed Chained 2009 SAAR)

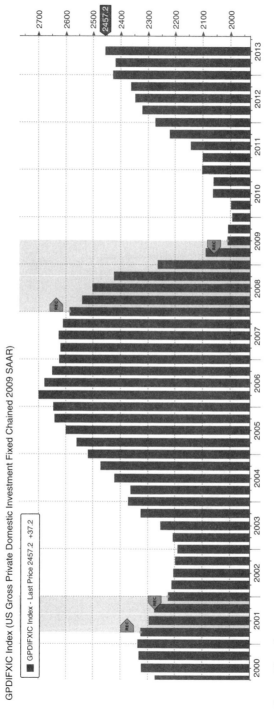

*Source:* Bloomberg

has a tremendous multiplier effect on the economy: once a house or apartment building has been built, personal consumption expenditures usually receive a big boost as owners head out to paint, decorate, and furnish their homes.

That said, analysts and economists tend to pay close attention to nonresidential investment. In part, this is because of the component's size—it accounts for about 80 percent of total fixed investment. It also provides a great deal of insight into how the corporate sector views economic conditions. Finally, many equity traders, especially those active in the Nasdaq and on the lookout for the next Microsoft or Intel, are particularly interested in technology investment, which falls into the nonresidential category.

A certain amount of nonresidential fixed investment is always required, regardless of the overall state of the economy. Equipment and machinery, for example, constantly need to be refurbished, updated, and repaired. Every year the auto industry shuts down its plants for about two weeks to allow engineers to retool machinery for upcoming new car models. Weather, overuse, and just plain wear and tear cause capital equipment to break down. During booming periods of technological advances, some capital equipment becomes obsolete. Upgrades often help a business raise its level of productivity, which, in turn, helps the company's bottom line.

Rising capital spending is generally associated with periods of solid corporate profitability and economic prosperity. For businesses to invest in new capital equipment, they need sufficient profit growth. After all, they can't spend what they don't have. (Actually businesses can spend or invest by borrowing via issuance of bonds. But if the company doesn't have respected profit growth, then the ability to obtain the financing is hampered. With a poor financial history, companies are saddled with low credit ratings and are forced to pay higher returns for borrowing those needed funds.)

Management also needs to be positive about the economic outlook. If conditions are soft and consumer demand unpromising, they will be less inclined to purchase new machinery and equipment. If, however, the economy is expanding at a respectable pace, economic fundamentals are conducive to continuing growth (low interest rates, low inflation, firm labor market growth), and consumers are spending, then businesses will be more likely to pick up the pace of their investment.

Some of the companies that are involved in capital equipment expenditures include Caterpillar, Paccar, Deere & Co., Boeing, Illinois Tool Works, and Danaher Corp.

During the benchmark revision of 2013, the BEA added a new category called intellectual property products. This nonresidential component includes spending on related items like research and development, and ownership rights on entertainment, literary, and artistic originals.

## Inventories

The level of inventories has a tremendous influence on the investment component of GDP. The amount of inventories a company holds are influenced by many factors, but ultimately, the expected demand for their goods is the primary determinant.

Exhibit 3.7 shows the quarterly change in private inventories with recessions highlighted. Obviously businesses slash stockpiles during periods of extreme weakness or recessions—more appropriately, they refrain from adding aggressively during these sullen times and permit consumers to draw down existing inventories.

In recent years supply chain management has helped businesses maintain a proper level of inventories. But sudden and extreme changes in demand can cost a business dearly. Too much inventory on the precipice of recession would force a company to discount goods and crush profitability in the process. Similarly, too little inventory around a period of strong demand can send would-be buyers to go to competitors for products and cost the company lost revenues. Inventories are therefore very important in the determination of business cycles.

## Government Spending

Government consumption expenditures and gross investment covers all the money laid out by federal, state, and local governments for goods (both durable and nondurable) and services, for both military and nonmilitary purposes. The category includes spending on building and maintaining toll bridges, libraries, parks, highways, and federal office buildings; on compensation for government employees; on research and development, spare parts, food, clothing, ammunition; and on travel, rents, and utilities. Government expenditures and investment typically account for 20 percent of total GDP. During the second quarter of 2013, government consumption expenditures and gross investment accounted for about 19 percent of total economic activity (Exhibit 3.8).

Wall Street doesn't generally pay much attention to government consumption expenditures and gross investment. One reason is that number's stability. Since 1947, government spending and investment has accounted for about 15 to 20 percent of total economic output. Only during periods of profound economic weakness or military conflict does the percentage rise, as the government picks up the pace of spending to boost economic growth or to support a war effort. In the post–World War II era, a peak of 24 percent was registered in 1953, at the end of the Korean War.

**EXHIBIT 3.7** Change in Private Inventories

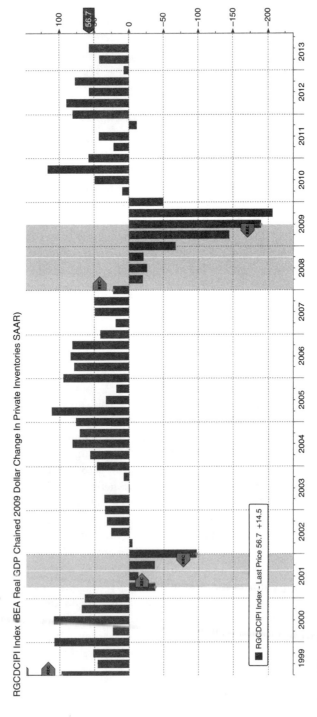

RGCDCIPI Index (BEA Real GDP Chained 2009 Dollar Change In Private Inventories SAAR)

*Source:* Bloomberg

**EXHIBIT 3.8** Government Spending

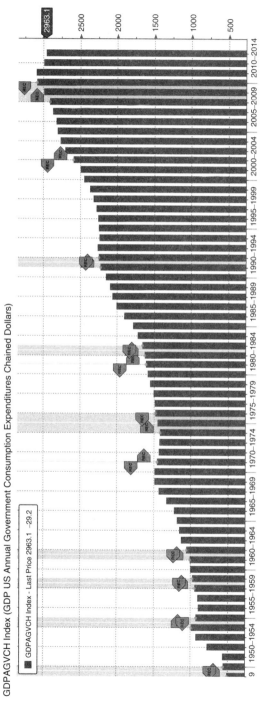

GDPAGVCH Index (GDP US Annual Government Consumption Expenditures Chained Dollars)

*Source:* Bloomberg

Within the government data, however, is one item to which some economists do pay attention, especially in recent times. That item is national defense spending. The long-term trend in national defense spending as a percentage of total government spending since the end of World War II has been consistently downward. Still, increases (in some instances, slight) have occurred when the government has ramped up purchases for military conflicts such as the Korean War in the early 1950s; Vietnam, in the mid-1960s to early 1970s; Desert Storm, in 1990; and most recently, the wars in Afghanistan and Iraq.

Stock analysts responsible for the defense contractors and aerospace companies, such as Northrop Grumman Corporation, Lockheed Martin Corporation, General Dynamics Corporation, Curtiss-Wright Corporation, find the detail on national defense expenditures in the report a treasure trove. The category is broken down into spending on aircraft, missiles, ships, vehicles, electronics and software, ammunition, petroleum, and compensation. If the government bought it, it is recorded here.

## Net Exports

Net exports of goods and services, the last component in the equation, is simply the difference between the dollar value of the goods and services the United States sends abroad (exports) and the dollar value of those it takes in across its borders (imports). Because the country generally imports more than it exports, this figure is usually negative, thus acting as a drag on economic growth. During the second quarter of 2013, net exports subtracted 3.0 percent from total economic activity.

When the United States imports more than it exports—as has been the case for the better part of the past three decades—the net ex-port balance is said to be in deficit. This reduces the level of GDP produced in a given period. Conversely, when exports outweigh imports, the trade balance is said to be in surplus. This results in an addition to economic activity. Such an outcome stands to reason, as U.S. export goods are produced by plants located in the United States, whereas imports are produced by foreign workers and sent to the United States. Exhibit 3.9 represents the value of net exports as a percentage of GDP. Imports needn't have a negative connotation, however. A number of resources are not as abundant in the United States as they are outside its borders. One obvious example is crude oil. The United States has domestic sources of oil but not enough to fuel its consumption. For that reason, it has to import about half its crude oil from foreign countries. Should we consider these imports disapprovingly? Probably not. The mere fact that the United States consumes so much crude is testament to its economic vitality. Its plants and factories need a great deal of oil to produce what is the largest output in the world, employing millions of people and creating an economic climate that permits its citizens to prosper like no others on Earth. Spending on imports to heat our homes, run our transportation

**EXHIBIT 3.9** Net Exports as a % of GDP

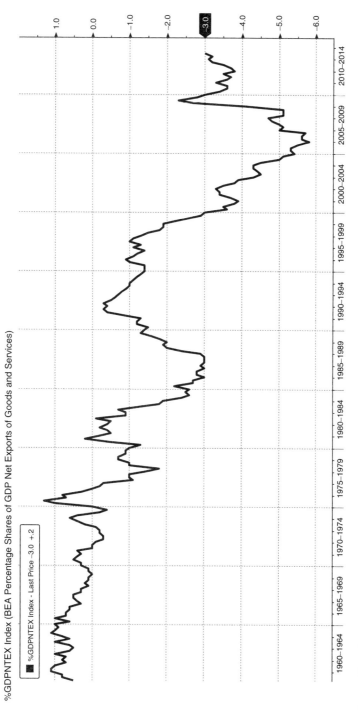

%GDPNTEX Index (BEA Percentage Shares of GDP Net Exports of Goods and Services)

*Source:* Bloomberg

system, and conduct business should not be considered a drag on prosperity but an enhancement.

As with government expenditures, the trading community has little reason to get excited about the net export balance. It's true that the business community frowns on widening trade deficits because increasing imports slow U.S. GDP growth. But rising imports also mean that U.S. businesses and households are consuming more goods and services that they deem attractive (Exhibit 3.10). Nobody forces consumers to purchase Italian wine, Japanese cars, or Canadian lumber.

U.S. businesses and households purchase foreign-made goods for any number of reasons including price, quality, size, and taste. The ultimate force behind demand for foreign-produced goods is simply desirability.

Furthermore, several foreign-produced goods tend to be cheaper. Because many countries in the world, particularly China, India, and several Asian-Pacific nations, have relatively low-cost labor, they are capable of producing goods at lower costs. These low-priced products are usually sent to the United States, which influences the prices of similar U.S.-produced goods. This globalization has led to a lower inflation rate here in the United States—especially since the mid-1990s.

Perhaps the major reason investors ignore the trade data is the data's minor influence on total economic activity. Over the past 55 years, the net export position has averaged a mere half a percentage point of total economic output.

**EXHIBIT 3.10**   U.S. Imports and Exports (Y/Y%)

## Deflators

If GDP growth is the most important number in the release, the GDP deflators run a close second. As indicators of inflation, these deflators are preferred
to the Consumer Price Index (CPI), the Producer Price Index (PPI), and other
commodity price gauges by many traders and economists, including those at the
Federal Reserve.

Why have the deflators superseded the other inflation measures? For starters,
policy makers, traders, and investors in general want to see overarching economic
trends, not smaller, more targeted ones like those dedicated to only prices on
the retail (CPI) or wholesale level (PPI). GDP deflators reflect price activity in
the broader economy. A fuller explanation of price activity and the core rate of
inflation will be presented in Chapter 10.

Traders focus on movements in the personal consumption expenditure
excluding food and energy deflator, commonly referred to as the core PCED.
This inflation gauge is preferred to most of the others as it measures the core,
excluding food and energy, rate of inflation that consumers face. Because prices
of food and energy can fluctuate greatly during the month, economists like to
view price trends without these noisy readings.

The difference between nominal GDP and real GDP is essentially inflation. It
is therefore possible to compute an economy's inflation rate from this difference.
The result of the computation is called an implicit price deflator.

Exhibit 3.11 shows the history of the annual change in the implicit price
deflator since 1950. Notice how prices tumble during the highlighted recessions.
During economic downturns, companies recue prices in order to attract business
from a customer that has diminished incomes and salaries.

Policy makers fear when the price level actually contracts on a year-over-year
basis. This phenomenon, known as *deflation,* hasn't occurred much in the United
States since the 1950s, and that was only a temporary dip. During the Great
Depression, a contracting price level crippled the economy, businesses, and the
stock market. Since the mid-1980s, inflation has not been an economically compromising influence.

Every GDP report contains implicit price deflators for the headline GDP
number and also for many of its subcomponents, such as consumption expenditures, government spending, and gross private domestic investment. Economists
at the BEA calculate the GDP implicit price deflator using the formula:

$$\text{Implicit deflator} = (\text{Nominal value})/(\text{Real value}) \times 100$$

Plugging in the entities for the second quarter of 2013:

$$= (\$16,661.0/\$15,679.7) \times 100$$

$$= 106.258$$

**EXHIBIT 3.11** GDP Deflator (Y/Y%)

GDP DYOY Index (GDP US Implicit Price Deflator YoY SA)

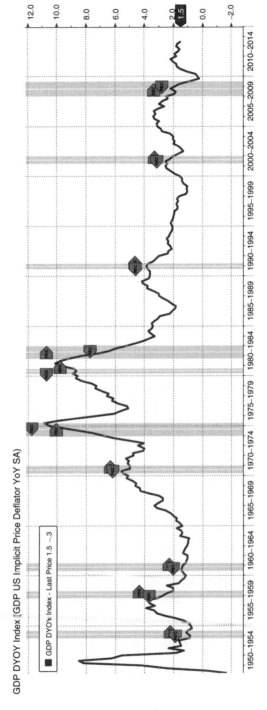

■ GDP DYOY Index - Last Price 1.5 ··3

*Source:* Bloomberg

To compute the annualized inflation rate for GDP during the second quarter 2013, economists take the GDP deflators from the first quarter 2013 (106.105) and the second quarter (106.258) and plug them into the following formula:

Annualized inflation rate

$$= (((\text{Current quarter}/\text{Previous quarter})^4) - 1) \times 100$$

$$= ((106.258/106.105)^4 - 1) \times 100$$

$$= ((1.001442)^4 - 1) \times 100$$

$$= (1.00578 - 1) \times 100$$

$$= 0.0578 \times 100, \text{ or } 0.578 \text{ percent, or approximately } 0.6 \text{ percent.}$$

## Final Sales

Included in the addenda in the GDP report are three measures little noted by the financial media but closely scrutinized by the investment community because of the insights they provide into the underlying spending patterns in the GDP numbers. These three indicators are the final sales of domestic product, gross domestic purchases, and final sales to domestic purchasers.

Final sales of domestic product is a measure of the dollar value of goods produced in the United States in a particular period that are actually sold, rather than put into inventory. To calculate this figure, the BEA first computes "the change in private inventories" by comparing the current level of inventories with that of the previous period. This indicates how many goods have been added to businesses' storage and thus how much of current production has remained unsold. This change in private inventories is then subtracted from GDP to give final sales. This is an important number, because it paints a more accurate picture than GDP of the current pace of spending in the economy. Economists say *current pace* because the quarterly figure excludes inventories that have been produced in previous quarters. Many times, economists will compare the growth rates of GDP with those of final sales to determine whether economic growth is being driven by new production or by the consumption of goods that were previously produced and stored as inventories.

Gross domestic purchases measures all the goods U.S. residents have bought, no matter where the goods were produced. This figure is obtained by subtracting net exports from GDP. There is indeed a difference between GDP and gross domestic purchases. GDP is a measure of domestically produced goods and services, whereas gross domestic purchases is a measure of all the goods domestically purchased. Strong quarterly increases in gross domestic purchases generally imply solid demand by U.S. consumers, as only those purchases of domestic goods are calculated.

Final sales to domestic purchasers is the level of gross domestic purchases less the change in private inventories. It depicts the desire of Americans, both households and businesses, to spend, no matter where the goods or services are produced. Some economists consider it a good indicator of overall economic well-being. Slumping final sales to domestic purchasers suggests that U.S. consumers may be tapped out.

As Exhibit 3.12 illustrates, every time since 1948 that the year-over-year change in real final sales of domestic product has fallen below 2.0 percent, the economy has ultimately slipped into recession. The circled points depict the onset of recession. Whether or not this recession-predicting ability continues remains to be seen. Still, this is an excellent warning signal for all market watching economists.

It should come as no surprise that changes in the growth rate of the economy (as measured by the year-over-year percent change in real GDP) possesses a strong correlation with the change in jobs as measured by nonfarm payrolls. Holding productivity constant, the greater the need for output (increased GDP), the greater is the need for workers. Conversely, as the economy cools, so too does the demand for employment.

Exhibit 3.13 shows this tight relationship. The most recent observations include the 1990–1991 and 2001 recessions, which were mild—barely falling below zero—and the corresponding drop in employment wasn't too troubling. However, the extreme downturn in real GDP of 4.0 percent in 2007–2009

**EXHIBIT 3.12**   Real Final Sales of Domestic Product (Y/Y%)

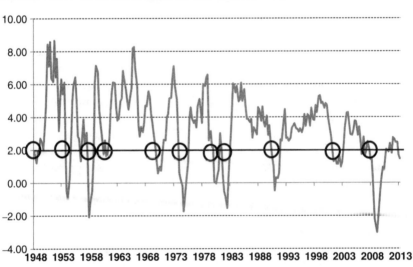

**EXHIBIT 3.13** GDP versus Nonfarm Payrolls (Y/Y%)

GDP CYOY Index (GDP US Chained 2009 Dollars YoY SA)
NFP TYCH Index (US Employees on Nonfarm Payrolls Total Net Change SA From Year Ago)

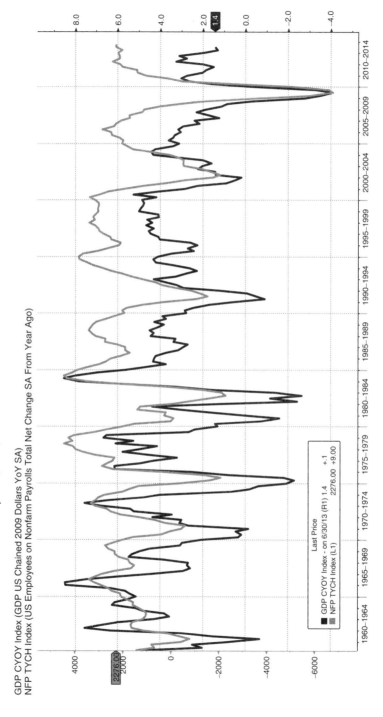

*Source:* Bloomberg

resulted in a steep loss of employment and weighed on the economy's recovery efforts for quite a while. It is this reason that so many economists refer to this downturn as a depression.

## Corporate Profits

The GDP report refers to several types of corporate profits. Pretax profits, also known as book profits, are what companies earn before paying taxes and distributing dividends to shareholders. Applying the IVA and CCAdj to this total results in profits from current production, termed operating profits in the business community. This is the corporate profits figure used in computing national income. Subtracting companies' tax liabilities from book profit gives after-tax profits.

The corporate profits data are obtained from IRS tabulations, as well as from the Census Bureau's quarterly survey of corporate profits and publicly available corporate financial statements.

Not every GDP release reports corporate profits. Because corporate earnings reports are scattered throughout the quarter and IRS processing of corporate tax returns is rather lengthy, accurate tallies are only possible months after the end of the quarter. The most complete presentation of corporate profits is usually provided in a year's final report of GDP.

Exhibit 3.14 shows the year-over-year trend in corporate profits after tax. While it is true that all recessions have coincided with declines in corporate profits, not all profit downturns result in recessions. Three distinct periods (1967, 1986, and 1999) had contractions in profits without an associated recession. The best explanation for this may be these were profit recessions—that is, not a change in the business cycle but simple contractions in the pace of U.S. corporate profits.

This inability to count on the stock market as a reliable economic indicator has led to a famous comment accredited to Nobel Laureate Paul Samuelson: "The stock market has predicted nine of the last five recessions."

As with most of the other measures discussed, a rise in corporate profits indicates a healthy business climate. The economy's growth cycle really starts with a lift in corporate profits. When businesses are successful, their incomes exceed costs, and they make profits. This permits them to invest in new capital equipment or hire additional employees, which in turn engenders greater economic activity and kicks off another round of investment and hiring.

Beginning in early 2001, the stock market bubble of the late 1990s burst, wiping out trillions of dollars in personal wealth. Widespread accounting scandals and egregious corporate impropriety also hammered investors' confidence, stalling the financial markets. For the first time in more than 50 years, the United States was attacked on its own soil, virtually paralyzing the economy. Hundreds

**EXHIBIT 3.14** U.S. Corp Profits after Tax YoY%

CPFTATYY Index (US Corporate Profits Without IVA and CCA Profits After Tax YoY)

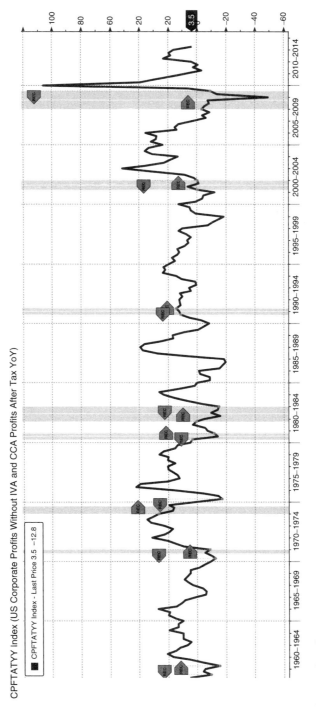

*Source:* Bloomberg

of thousands of businesses closed for weeks, and the borders were sealed. Fear of anthrax attacks was widespread. As if all of this weren't enough, U.S. armed forces became engaged in military conflicts in Afghanistan and Iraq. Yet despite all these profoundly negative influences in a relatively short period, the economy managed to avoid a deep or prolonged recession. Perhaps the ultimate sign of resiliency is that consumer spending never fell during this downturn. So, be careful when comparing the stock market, profits, and economic turning points.

The output gap is the difference between the economy's actual and potential levels of production. This difference yields insight into important economic conditions, such as employment and inflation.

The economy's potential output is the amount of goods and services it would produce if it utilized all its resources. To determine this figure—the trend level—economists estimate the rate at which the economy can expand without sparking a rise in inflation. It is not an easy—or exact—calculation, and it yields as many different answers as there are economists with different definitions of the maximum level of output, productivity, hours worked, and so on. Luckily, a widely accepted estimate of potential output is reported relatively frequently, about once a quarter, by the Congressional Budget Office (CBO). The CBO's website, www.cbo.gov, contains information about its methodology and underlying assumptions in computing the trend level, as well as a detailed historical data set.

A negative output gap exists when actual GDP growth is below its estimated potential. This suggests that the economy isn't utilizing all its labor and capital resources. Such periods of underutilization are usually characterized by high unemployment and low inflation, with plants and factories closing down, workers furloughed, and machinery idled. Exhibit 3.15 shows that in 1990–1991 and 2001–2002, periods of profound economic weakness, the actual growth rate of real GDP was considerably below its potential.

When GDP growth exceeds its calculated potential, creating a positive gap, the economy is pushed to its limit. All plants and factories are running at capacity, the labor force is fully employed, and economic output is skyrocketing.

Economists sometimes express the output gap in the form of a ratio derived by dividing the difference between actual output and potential output by potential output. When this ratio falls below zero, conditions are said to be soft, or sluggish; when it rises above zero, conditions are expansionary.

Because the output gap provides such telling economic insight into a whole host of economic relationships, it is a favorite of policy makers. The Federal Reserve, for example, considers it in determining where to set the federal funds rate. If the gap is negative, indicating that the economy is growing below its potential, the Fed may try to spark activity by lowering the overnight rate. This results in a decline all along the interest rate maturity spectrum, making it easier

**EXHIBIT 3.15** Output Gap

CBOPGAPN Index (Nominal Output Gap)

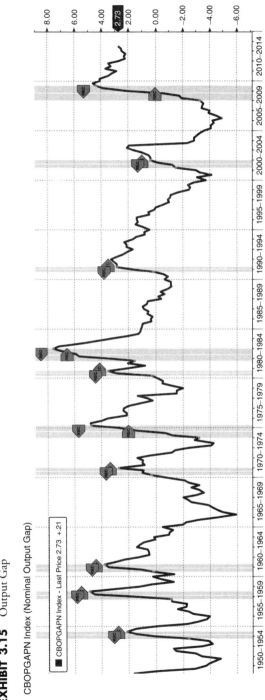

*Source:* Bloomberg

for companies to fund capital projects. It also spurs individuals' spending by rendering loans to purchase interest rate sensitive items such as automobiles and homes more affordable. Conversely, when the gap is positive, indicating that the economic party is getting a bit out of hand, the Fed may take away the punch bowl by increasing its overnight target rate, thus discouraging consumers and businesses from spending and investing.

## Gross Domestic Income

As mentioned earlier in this chapter, there are two approaches to estimating total economic activity, gross domestic product (GDP)—the sum of the final goods and services produced for sale in the economy—and gross domestic income (GDI)—the sum of the incomes received by the factors of production involved in that process.

In theory, these two measures should be the same—businesses receive incomes in the form of rent, profits, interest, wages, and so on for sales of these produced goods and services, and households receive payment for their services in the production process, mostly in the form of compensation. (Recall the circular flow diagram from your Intro to Economics text.) Add up the incomes received and they should total the value of the expenditures.

In reality, however, GDI and GDP are not the same, primarily since they are derived from many different and volatile sources. The Bureau of Economic Analysis reports the difference between these two measures in the "statistical discrepancy" of the release. Nevertheless, the two entities are closely related. Like GDP, the year-over-year trend in GDI also identifies turning points in the economy's performance (Exhibit 3.16).

There are seemingly never-ending arguments as to which is the better measure; some claim that the four-quarter change in gross domestic income is preferred measure since it better captures the severity of downturns or the strength of recoveries. Conversely, there are issues with the GDI estimation, particularly with respect to adjustment factors and statistical assumptions. Ultimately, it's more likely that the jury is still out on this argument.

Some economists argue that since GDI includes government transfer payments like food stamps and unemployment benefit insurance, the trends might be a flawed indicator. If the economy is advancing largely because of government assistance is that a true measure of economic vitality?

Also, since illegal activity is not recorded—well, it doesn't happen, right?—then discrepancies may surface from incomes exchanged for illicit goods. Similarly, incomes may be unreported for any number of reasons—think of tax evasion—so there are mismeasures there as well.

Another issue with GDI is that it is delayed. The advance estimate for GDP is released one month after the reported quarter. For example, the third-quarter

**EXHIBIT 3.16** Gross Domestic Income (Y/Y%)

GDI CHNG Index (US Gross Domestic Income SAAR YoY Percent)

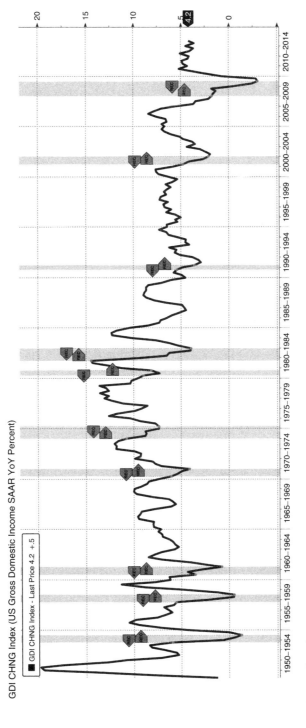

*Source:* Bloomberg

GDP report is released in late October. The GDI data for the same quarter isn't known until a month after that. Issues also surface in the collection of the GDI data as the sources are not updated for years after the fact. This is then captured in benchmark revisions, which may result in different trends.

## Test Yourself

Answer the following multiple-choice questions:

1. The Bureau of Economic Analysis estimates GDP based on which of the following equations?
   a. Consumption expenditures + Investment spending + Government spending + Net exports.
   b. Consumption expenditures + Investment spending + Government spending + National imports.
   c. Consumption expenditures + Inventories + Government spending + Services exports.
   d. Consumption expenditures + Interest spending + Government spending + National exports.
   e. none of the above.

2. The largest component of gross domestic product is:
   a. consumption expenditures.
   b. interest expenses.
   c. government spending.
   d. national exports.
   e. a and b only.

3. The largest component of consumption expenditures is:
   a. durable goods.
   b. nondurable goods.
   c. services.
   d. motor vehicles.
   e. residential investment.

4. Traditionally, a recession signal is triggered when the year-over-year pace in real GDP is:
   a. above 5.5 percent.
   b. from 2.0 percent to 5.5 percent.
   c. below 2.0 percent.
   d. below −2.0 percent.
   e. none of the above.

5. The difference between nominal GDP and real GDP is:

    a. the underlying pace of inflation in the economy.

    b. an indicator of interest rates in the economy.

    c. imports and exports.

    d. all of the above.

    e. a and c only.

## Answers

1. a

2. a

3. c

4. c

5. a

# CHAPTER 4

# The Labor Market and Employment

In the United States, you are identified by what you do for a living; when you walk into a bar the first thing you may say to start a conversation is, "What is your name?" The follow-up question is generally, "What do you do?" In fact, employment is so important to a person, people have adopted surnames based on their professions—that's how we have Millers, Bakers, Carpenters, and Smiths.

Economically speaking, employment breeds confidence, boosts spirits, and provides a wage and salary. With this income, consumers spend on goods and services, engendering more hiring as those companies benefit from increased sales and profits and head out to hire more people to facilitate that increase in demand. Then the cycle continues until the economy hits a speed bump, causing a slowdown or recession.

Conversely, the loss of a job can have many undesirable consequences. It isn't surprising that unemployment—particularly prolonged joblessness—can be a leading cause of mental anguish, marital strife, divorce, depression, suicide, and crime. Obviously, this indicator has as many economic as social properties, which also play into the trends of an economy's performance.

Therefore, it is easy to see why the labor market situation is so critical to economists and investors alike. Of all the economic releases covered in this book, none is more important than the employment report.

## Employment and the Business Cycle

The most comprehensive and primary survey of labor market conditions is the monthly Employment Situation published by the Bureau of Labor Statistics (BLS). This chapter will be largely dedicated to the key barometers contained in that report, while additional measures from other sources will be presented at the end of the chapter. Since the economy is so deeply dependent on workers, and people need a source of income in order to live and prosper in society, trends in hiring are strongly correlated with changes in economic output. This makes sense; as the economy advances you require more workers to create the additional output—holding productivity constant. Alternatively, as an economy weakens and growth decelerates, businesses tend to furlough workers until the cycle bottoms and the need to rehire those idled workers surfaces. This close-knit relationship between these two gauges is one of the strongest of all major indicators, which is why the Conference Board chose to include nonfarm payrolls as its largest (weighted) component in its index of coincident indicators (Exhibit 4.1). In addition, it is also used as a determinant in business cycle changes by the National Bureau of Economic Research.

When unexpected increases in the unemployment rate occur, equity investors generally sell off stocks. The same occurs when nonfarm payrolls decline by a particularly large amount. Because employment determines income and spending, and consumer spending accounts for the largest portion of economic activity, traders like to see solid employment growth—usually 170,000 or more jobs a month. When the unemployment rate declines and jobs are being created, stock prices tend to rise.

Things are different in the fixed-income market, which is sensitive to inflation threats. Increasing nonfarm payrolls and a falling unemployment rate spark inflation expectations amid fears of an overheating economy, which can, in turn, cause a sell-off in bonds, depressing prices, and raising yields.

## Two Measures of Employment: Payrolls and Households

The monthly employment report is based on two separate surveys: the Current Population Survey (CPS), also known as the household survey, and the Current Employment Statistics survey (CES), referred to as the establishment, or payrolls, survey. The household data are aggregated and disseminated in the "A" tables found in the first half of the report; the establishment survey information is presented in the "B" tables (Exhibit 4.2).

The employment report contains several headliners, but top billing is generally shared by two figures: the unemployment rate and the monthly change in nonfarm payrolls. Average hourly earnings, hours worked, overtime hours worked, and the monthly change in manufacturing jobs also command a great deal of Wall Street's attention. Unlike many other economic releases, the Employment Situation report takes a great deal of time to digest.

### Household Survey

Officially called the Current Population Survey, the household survey contains the responses of a sample of about 60,000 households to questions about work and

**EXHIBIT 4.1**   NFP versus Real GDP

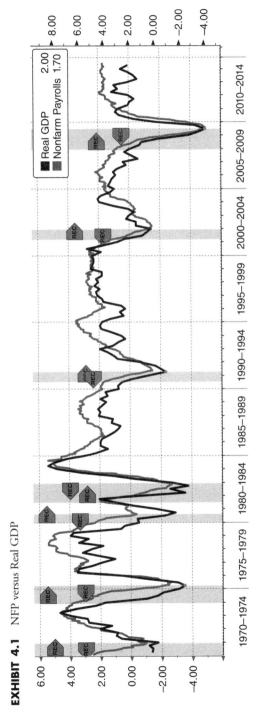

*Source:* Bloomberg

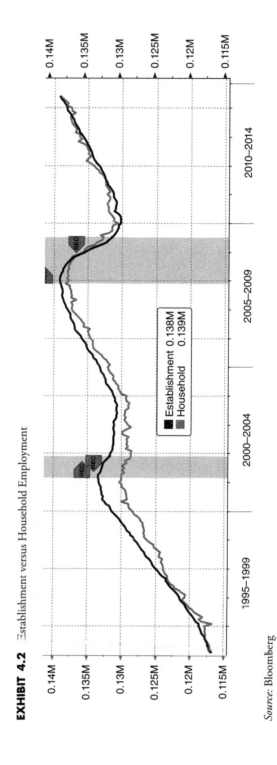

**EXHIBIT 4.2** Establishment versus Household Employment

*Source:* Bloomberg

job searches. It is generally conducted during the week containing the nineteenth day of the month. This is known as the survey week. It addresses employment conditions during the week containing the twelfth of the month, which is known as the reference week. The statistics gathered are compiled and presented in the "A" tables of the report that include the labor force, participation rate, number of employed, unemployed, unemployment rate, duration of unemployment, and reason for unemployment.

## Establishment Survey

The establishment survey is based on a sample of about 160,000 businesses comprising some 400,000 individual work sites. Like the household survey, it is conducted with respect to a reference week, which is the pay period containing the twelfth day of the month.

Nonfarm payrolls fall into two categories: goods-producing and services-providing. The goods-producing category includes manufacturing jobs, which account for 64 percent of the category total; construction jobs, accounting for 31 percent; and jobs in natural resources and mining, accounting for 5 percent. The majority of manufacturing positions are in the production of transportation equipment, mostly motor vehicles. Other big manufacturing sectors are food, fabricated metal products, computer and electronic products, machinery, and chemicals. The majority of construction jobs are with specialty trade contractors, such as tradesmen engaged in practices like drywall and insulation, framing, roofing, siding, electrical, masonry, and painting.

The largest component of the services-providing payrolls category is education and health (22 percent), followed by professional business (20 percent), retail trade (16 percent), leisure and hospitality (15 percent), finance (8 percent), wholesale trade (6 percent), other services (6 percent), and information (3 percent). There are other smaller categories that round out the total.

Economists pay particular attention to the growth rate of nonfarm payrolls since it is closely tied to so many other top-tier economic indicators. Exhibit 4.3 identifies the association that job growth has with final sales in the economy. As underlying labor market conditions worsen, consumers become increasingly aware of how difficult it is to find a job: increased chatter of friends, neighbors, and family members losing their jobs. Also, relatives call asking about any available positions. Daily reminders in the newspapers and evening news only increase the gloom. These conditions aren't exactly conducive to greater consumer spending and positive economic growth. Anyone that has been unemployed knows all too well that when you have lost your job, or fear for the loss of employment, you don't spend money.

The two primary categories of the establishment survey are goods and services type jobs. Exhibit 4.4 identifies the clear path that the U.S. economy has taken over the last 60-plus years. In 1950, the U.S. economy was predominantly

**EXHIBIT 4.3** Final Sales versus Nonfarm Payrolls

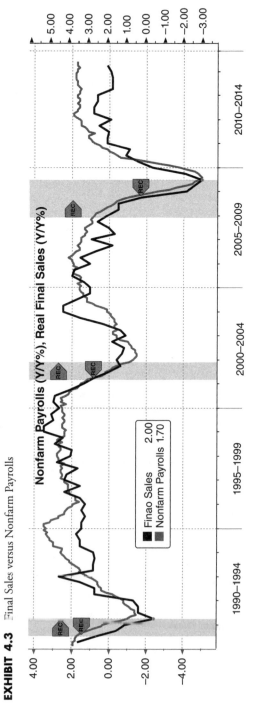

*Source:* Bloomberg

**EXHIBIT 4.4** Composition of Employment: Services, Goods

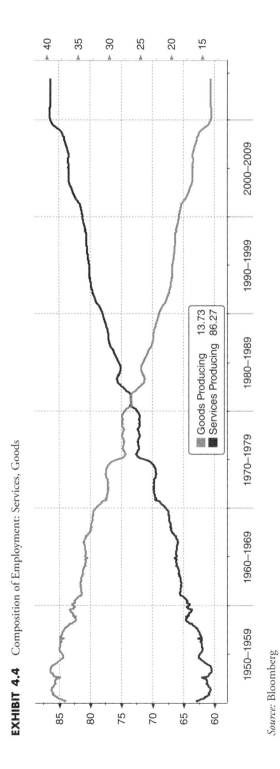

*Source:* Bloomberg

a manufacturing behemoth with roughly 40 percent of the people employed in manufacturing. One in three workers held a union card in the mid-1950s.

This trend isn't disturbing or unsettling; it's simply the way American commerce has changed. We no longer have to make "stuff" in order to be a thriving economy. Gone is the mentality of the *Happy Days* era when the motto was, "As GM goes, so goes the economy."

The level of manufacturing workers is the same today as it was in 1941! We no longer need a massive manufacturing workforce in order to have a vibrant level of factory output. This is in large part due to productivity and labor-saving technologies. Rather than have an assembly-line of 150 workers, we may only require five employees to operate the robotics or computerized machinery, which now do the work of 145 laborers.

Today, the U.S. economy is services-dominant; upwards of 86 percent of all people in the U.S. economy are employed in this sector! We design, develop, engineer, create, invent. That's what we do. We created the iPhone, iPad, and countless other items; we let other countries fabricate them. This doesn't make us less competitive or weaker. It's simply the case of a different composition of labor.

## Unemployment

Although the report doesn't make this distinction, economists identify several types of unemployment. Seasonal unemployment results from short-term cyclical changes in the labor market; examples include the yearly layoffs of retail staff who were added to take care of the Christmas shopping rush and the winter furloughs of construction and landscaping workers in regions where harsh weather makes such activity virtually impossible.

Frictional unemployment refers to the situation of workers in the process of changing occupations who are temporarily between jobs.

Structural unemployment is the result of economic restructuring caused by new technologies or other innovations, such as when the invention of the automobile put buggy-whip makers out of a job.

Finally, cyclical unemployment, the most relevant type for Wall Street economists, occurs when jobs are eliminated as part of the business cycle because of declining demand and the consequent drop in production.

Economists are constantly attempting to determine whether the job losses in the post 2007–2009 economic downturn were cyclical or structural (Exhibit 4.5).

The BLS has identified several definitions of the unemployment rate, which are traditionally presented in Table A-15 of the release as follows:

- U-1: persons unemployed 15 weeks or longer, as a percent of the civilian labor force

**EXHIBIT 4.5** Unemployment Rates — Various Measures

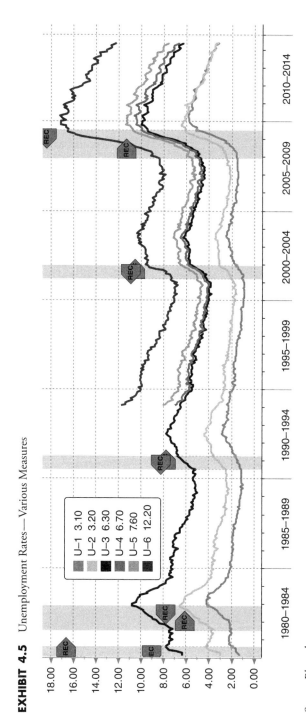

*Source:* Bloomberg

- U-2: job losers and persons who completed temporary jobs, as a percent of the civilian labor force
- U-3: total unemployed, as a percent of the civilian labor force (official unemployment rate)
- U-4: total unemployed plus discouraged workers, as a percent of the civilian labor force plus discouraged workers
- U-5: total unemployed, plus discouraged workers, plus all other persons marginally attached to the labor force, as a percent of the civilian labor force plus all persons marginally attached to the labor force
- U-6: total unemployed, plus all persons marginally attached to the labor force, plus total employed part time for economic reasons, as a percent of the civilian labor force plus all persons marginally attached to the labor force

The most recognized as the nation's civilian unemployment rate, U-3, is calculated by dividing the number of unemployed workers by the civilian labor force, the figures for which are listed in the household survey. During May 2014, for example, the unemployment rate was computed to be 6.3 percent: 9.799 million unemployed persons divided by the 155.613 million-person labor force.

## The Labor Force

To be included among the unemployed, a person must have made an effort to find work. Those who have given up looking, believing their skills, qualifications, or geographic area preclude finding a job, are regarded as discouraged workers. Increasing numbers of discouraged workers usually signal a weak economy.

Discouraged workers and others who don't fit into either the employed or unemployed groups are classified as "not in the labor force." The percentage of the employable population that is in the labor force is known as the labor force participation rate. The employment-population ratio is the percentage of employed persons in the total population. It is usually lower than the participation rate. The labor force participation rate is simply the proportion of the population that is in the labor force (Exhibit 4.6).

In recent years, the labor force participation rate has slumped from some historically elevated levels in a relatively short period of time. For much of the 1990s through 2008, the range in the labor force participation rate was 66 to 67 percent. Then, in 2009, this rate fell below 66 percent and proceeded to fall below 63 percent by early 2014. Many economists on the Street attempted to say that people simply became so disheartened by the state of affairs in the labor market that they've become discouraged and have given up looking for work. Assuredly, this was the case during the immediate aftermath of the 2007–2009 downturn. But there is something else—well telegraphed—that can explain the sudden decline.

**EXHIBIT 4.6** Labor Force Participation Rate

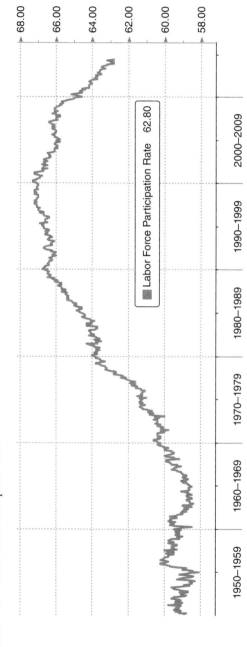

*Source:* Bloomberg

Anybody who has ever studied the U.S. economy knows that the boomer generation has been the ultimate determinant of all things economic, particularly spending. And anyone who understands demographics appreciated this trend ultimately had to end. Unfortunately, investors and pundits conveniently forget that boomers retire. It shouldn't be that shocking.

This reminds me of the annual family picnic where, every year, Mom tells you to take a plate of bar-b-que to your sick Uncle Nick since he's not feeling well and cannot get food for himself. For years, decades in fact, you continue this practice of taking your elder a plate of the family's fine fixin's because he is so ill. Then the family is shocked to learn of Uncle Nick's passing; "He died! I cannot believe it." Really? For 15 years, he was frail and too ill to attend the family gatherings—and now he dies and everyone is surprised? It's no different for the retiring boomer generation—we knew these pig-in-the-python boomers were going to commence retirement in 2009 and fall out of the labor force.

## Hiring of Temporary Workers

One interesting indicator that Street economists watch is the growth rate in employment at temporary help services companies—a subcomponent of the Professional and Business Services category. These positions tend to be reduced when the economy takes a turn for the worse and escalate rather sharply when the economy is emerging from its sunken state of affairs. As Exhibit 4.7 shows, there is a growth rate of about 10 percent during expansions for temp service positions. Temporary workers provide businesses with great flexibility.

If economic conditions, demand, and profitability deteriorate, management reduces the number of workers on the payroll. Among the first people to get pink slips are temporary, or contingent, workers. The tasks they perform are generally not critical to the day-to-day performance of the company—otherwise, they likely would have been employed full time. Furthermore, temporary workers usually aren't unionized, so they can be cut most easily and cheaply during downturns. Temporary workers aren't usually entitled to severance or unemployment insurance. Conversely, in the initial stages of recovery, companies are not sure of future demand, so rather than go through the costly process of hiring full-time workers, they add temporary ones.

Knowing that businesses operate in this fashion, economists keep a close eye on the goings-on in the temporary-services sector by reading the Bloomberg Orange Book of CEO comments of the temporary staffing and recruiting agencies. Many companies, such as Kelly Services Inc., Manpower Inc., and Robert Half International Inc., provide a great deal of information regarding industry trends, statistics, and forecasts. Trade organizations such as the American Staffing Association provide timely outlooks and related publications on temporary help and flexible staffing.

**EXHIBIT 4.7** Temporary Staffing

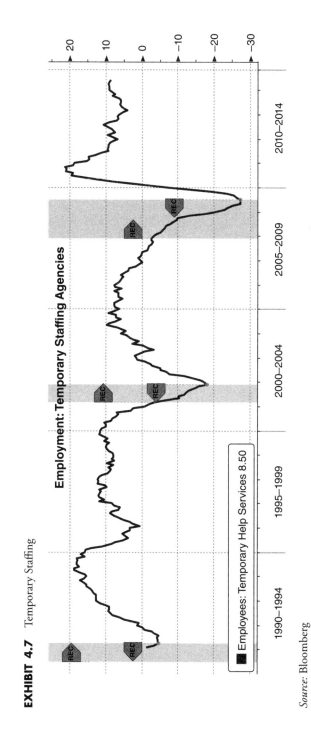

*Source:* Bloomberg

## Employment Trends of Various Age Cohorts

Economists like to look at trends in some of the detailed data for possible turning points in a specific industry. For example, if you are an equity analyst for one of the teen-apparel retailers like Abercrombie & Fitch, American Eagle, Aeropostale, or Urban Outfitters, or some of the fast fashion teen retailers like Zara, H&M, or Forever 21, you might want to incorporate some representation of the teen unemployment rate (both sexes, 16 to 19 years) into your models or analysis. Similarly, if you'd like to see the relationship of a larger, more macroeconomic indicator like new home sales activity, it would be wise to follow employment trends for those of first-time home-buying age.

Traditionally, this has been ages 25 to 35, since it takes a while for high school graduates to find a job and accumulate funds sufficient for the necessary down payment (Exhibit 4.8). College-age grads often have a larger paycheck, but a great hurdle in the way of student loans, which would need to be repaid before they head out and purchase a home.

The prolonged period of joblessness following the 2007–2009 depression may have pushed that range out to 40 years old as the ability to afford a home (and place 20 percent down) was hampered: jobs were not plentiful, higher-paying positions were extremely competitive, incomes were weak, and many savings accounts were decimated by the associated stock market slump. Remember, this economic depression was associated with a housing crisis, which was largely a function of too many homebuyers falling short of the required incomes, jobs, and assets necessary for a home purchase. After the crisis, lenders tightened up those loose standards and made sure that some sort of collateral was available before a loan was granted.

## The Duration of Unemployment

The duration of unemployment—the number of weeks that people remain unemployed after being furloughed—can provide an investor or economist with the understanding of how challenging labor market conditions are for the nation (Exhibit 4.9).

There is no specific figure that signals tough times, but it is safe to say that elevated levels like those registered after 2009 placed a great deal of hesitancy on the household sector. When you are unemployed, the family budget is placed under serious constraints. Purchases are generally limited to necessities like food or rent. Many times, people need to borrow from their savings in order to make ends meet. This is simply not an environment conducive for a desirable pace of economic activity. In fact, during these periods of lofty unemployed

**EXHIBIT 4.8** Unemployment Rate Ages 25–34 versus New Home Sales

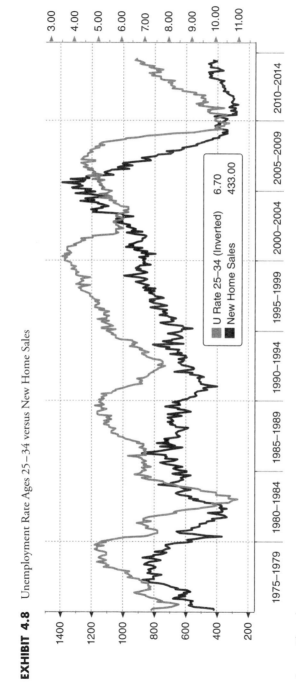

| | |
|---|---|
| U Rate 25–34 (Inverted) | 6.70 |
| New Home Sales | 433.00 |

*Source:* Bloomberg

**EXHIBIT 4.9** Median Weeks Unemployed

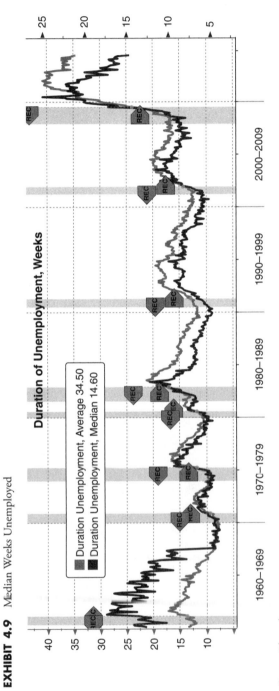

**Duration of Unemployment, Weeks**

Duration Unemployment, Average 34.50
Duration Unemployment, Median 14.60

*Source:* Bloomberg

duration, stock prices of companies that sell discretionary—nonessential goods and services—tend to suffer.

## Part-Time and Full-Time Employment

There are times economists look to the composition of employment (full-time, part-time, and part-time for economic reasons) to see whether there are any changes in store for the business cycle.

Full-time employees work 35 or more hours per week. If businesses are confident that the outlook is positive, they like to know that there's a sufficient skilled staff to meet their needs as the economy expands and demand for their goods or services rises along with that pace of activity. Full-time employment is therefore considered to be a better, more desirable source of work since it is a confidence-boosting, steady stream of income.

Part-time employment (typically employees who work 1 to 34 hours per week) is not always as desirable. Many people don't have the flexibility or certainty of the hours, which may lead to volatile weekly paychecks. In addition, part-timers may not have a wage that is as desirable.

Being employed part-time for economic reasons is associated with weekly work between 1 and 34 hours, for—according to the BLS—an "economic reason" such as the inability to find full-time work, a seasonal downturn in economic activity, or unfavorable business conditions. Essentially, the person took the part-time job simply because this is all he or she could get given the surrounding economic climate.

Part-time employment for noneconomic reasons—by far the largest of all part-timers—occurs when people choose to work on an abbreviated (1 to 34 hours per week) basis due to personal or family obligations, child-care issues, or education. They have a commitment and opt to forgo working on a full-time basis.

During expansions of the business cycle, full-time employment and part-time employment for noneconomic reasons advances. When conditions turn for the worse, they both tend to fall rather precipitously (Exhibit 4.10).

Conversely, when the going gets tough, part-time employment for economic reasons rises. This is generally due to the inability to find full-time work. A part-time job is better than no job during a recession.

## Price of Labor and Earnings

The Street places average hourly earnings (AHEs) atop its watch list when the Employment Situation is released. This is the most-watched measure of inflation

**EXHIBIT 4.10** Part-Time, Full-Time Employment

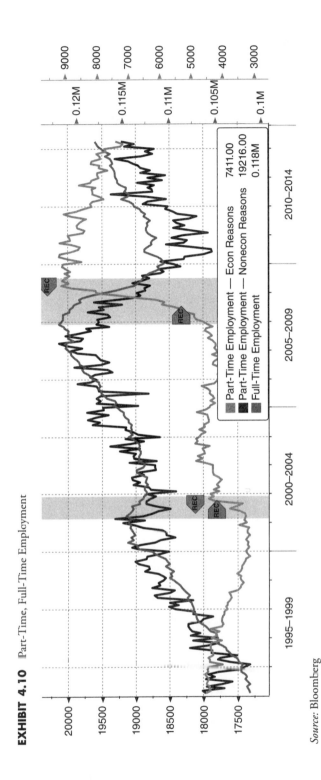

*Source:* Bloomberg

in the report—the price of labor—and those investors in the fixed-income market have a history of rapid reactions to abrupt changes (positive or negative) since inflation can erode the value of fixed-income securities.

Observing the 12-month trend in the average hourly earnings is the most ideal approach since it can smooth out extreme month-to-month fluctuations. During periods of expanding economic activity, earnings rise, since businesses benefit from greater demand for their products or services and tend to pay workers a higher wage for their efforts. Alternatively, when activity is softer, the demand for workers is diminished and businesses may reduce wages before opting to furlough a worker (Exhibit 4.11).

One of the most important issues in this series is that it is not adjusted for inflation. So a reported 2.0 percent pace in AHEs might not be as strong as it sounds. If the prevailing inflation rate is 2.0 percent or more, the "real" rate is actually flat or even negative. This can be a stifling condition. Consumers may be running in place and not making any advancement in purchasing power. This can dampen consumer confidence, reduce the level of spending in the economy, and ultimately result in a weaker growth rate of total economic output.

Notice how exceptionally inflationary readings in wages (say, larger than 4.5 percent) in the 1970s through the mid-1980s were disruptive to overall economic activity. Businesses paid their wages, which ate into profit margins, reducing their stock market valuations. There were four recessions during that time span. When the prevailing inflation rate is as high as it was, businesses pay higher wages. Conversely, when the inflation rate remains low (at or below 4.0 percent), as it has for the near three decades hence, the economy experienced fewer recessions and enjoyed prolonged periods of expansion.

## Hours Worked

Because economic activity is basically a function of the number of people employed and the amount of time they are working, economists have discovered that the level of hours worked can have some predictive ability regarding the underlying trends of the labor market and the economy at large.

As Exhibit 4.12 identifies, there has been a long-term, downward trend in the average hours worked in the United States. There are several possible causes for this deceleration, with the largest being productivity-enhancing technologies over the last 50-plus years. Computers, the Internet, supply chain management, and RFID technologies have all helped businesses operate more efficiently, and thereby reduced the number of hours—and to some extent number of employees—needed to produce goods and services.

Consider something as unique as GPS systems—now available for free on our mobile phones as an app. One can't help but wonder about how much time

**EXHIBIT 4.11**   Average Hourly Earnings

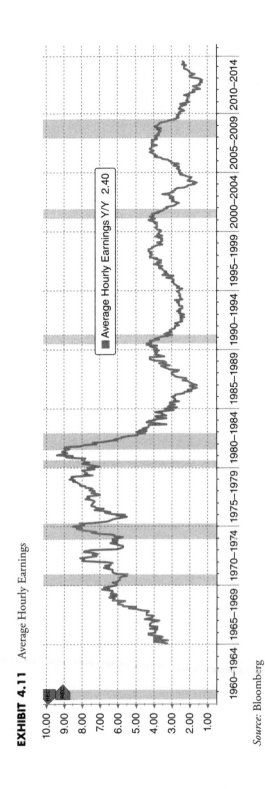

*Source:* Bloomberg

**EXHIBIT 4.12** Average Weekly Hours

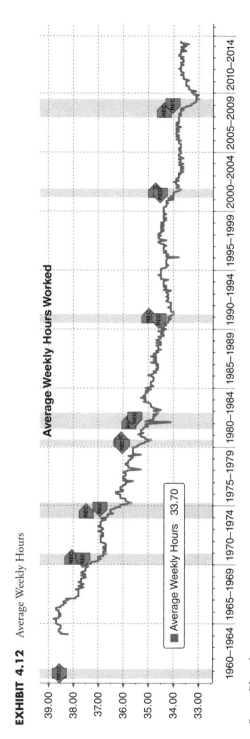

*Source:* Bloomberg

89

the ability to immediately determine your whereabouts can save in travel, delivery, and transit in general. Think of a cab driver that has to head out to the suburbs in the wee hours of the dark morning to pick up a client or a truck driver making a delivery of groceries. These advances that are often taken for granted today clearly have saved an incredible amount of time.

When economic conditions begin to sour, employers first reduce the number of hours worked before they choose to eliminate staff. That way, if economic activity recovers, they can ramp up production quickly by merely adding hours, rather than having to spend time and money finding and training new hires. This makes the average hours worked, in some degree, a leading indicator of economic growth.

## Leaving the Labor Force

The number of persons not in the labor force is a telling indicator. This might not seem to be interesting or relevant to every economist or analyst out there, but if your field of study is that of taxation, fiscal policy, or population economics, this is a vital statistic for use in your toolbox.

The BLS classifies a person as not in the workforce as anyone of the civilian labor force employed or employed, with any of a number of explanations of their job search history.

The bulk of those not in the labor force are retirees. And as the baby boomer generation (those born between 1946 and 1964) begins to retire, the ratio of those not in the labor force to those in the labor force will climb (Exhibit 4.13). In fact, the ratio last stands at 0.58, clearly an increase from the 0.50 to 0.51 range set in place prior to 2009.

This could conceivably be a worrisome trend as those retirees depending on government collected tax revenues from those employed in the work force increase.

Policymakers should look at this disturbing trend and implement some sort of policy prescription to help alleviate the burden that appears to be coming down the pipeline. One possible plan could be to raise the retirement age.

When Social Security was set up in the mid-1930s amidst the Great Depression, life expectancy of an American averaged 61.7 years.[1] This was below the 62–65 years of age that applicants traditionally collect. More recently, thanks to the adoption of medical and technological advances, a better-informed public regarding health, diet, and exercise, and improvement in workforce conditions, the average life expectancy has surged to 78.7 years (2010).

---

[1]Life Expectancy at Birth by Race and Sex, 1930–2010, Infoplease.com, http://www .infoplease.com/ipa/A0005148.html#ixzz34f6ZBQMO.

**EXHIBIT 4.13**  Ratio of Total Persons Not in Labor Force versus Total Labor Force

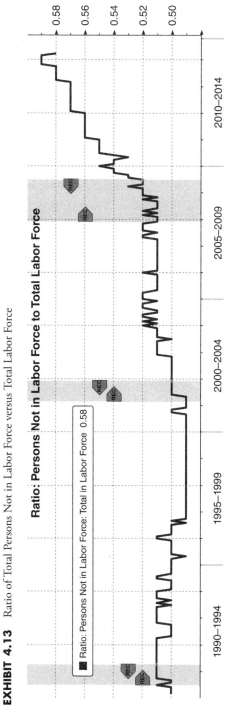

**Ratio: Persons Not in Labor Force to Total Labor Force**

Ratio: Persons Not in Labor Force: Total in Labor Force  0.58

*Source:* Bloomberg

## Employment Diffusion Indexes

Each month, the BLS provides diffusion indexes for 1-, 3-, 6-, and 12-month periods, both for private nonfarm payrolls, which comprise 264 industries, and for manufacturing payrolls, which represent 81 industries. Economists tend to gravitate to the one-month indexes, as they are not as noisy as the others.

The diffusion indexes are derived from establishments' responses to questions about whether they intend to add or eliminate workers or leave payrolls unchanged. To calculate the indexes, the percentage of responses indicating an intention to add workers is added to half the percentage of the unchanged responses. When the indexes are above 50, indicating that a greater percentage of industries intend to add workers than to lay off workers or keep employment levels stable, employment conditions are strong. High readings are usually accompanied by economic expansions. When the indexes fall below 50, industries are leaning toward cutting their payrolls. That situation is typical of recession. As shown by Exhibit 4.14, most of the recessions designated by the National Bureau of Economic Research coincide with sub-50 postings in the BLS diffusion indexes.

## Related Measures

There are several labor market indicators not included in the BLS Employment Situation report that garner a great deal of attention by the Wall Street community. Economists never look at one series or report to determine the underlying trends in the economy. Looking at a wide variety of measures permits the analyst to support (or refute) a specific conclusion like is the labor market turning around or are jobs difficult to find.

High on that list is the Labor Department's weekly claims for unemployment benefit insurance, more popularly referred to as *jobless claims* on the Street.

As Exhibit 4.15 suggests, there's a strong correlation between the level of first-time claims for unemployment benefits (inverted scale) and the trend growth rate of real GDP. This shouldn't be surprising—the stronger the economy advances, the less likely businesses will be to dismiss workers. Conversely, weaker periods result in higher levels of unemployment claimants.

The most attractive quality of this report is that it is released every Thursday; it is considered to be the most important of the high-frequency reports. Economists focus on the activity of claims during the week containing the twelfth day of the month—the survey week for the Employment Situation report—in order to capture possible insight into the monthly nonfarm payrolls report.

**EXHIBIT 4.14** Diffusion Indexes

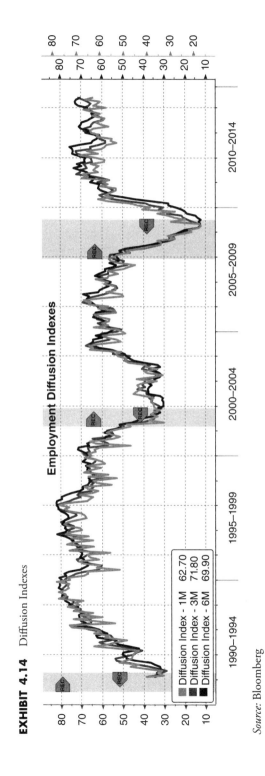

*Source:* Bloomberg

93

**EXHIBIT 4.15** Claims versus Real GDP

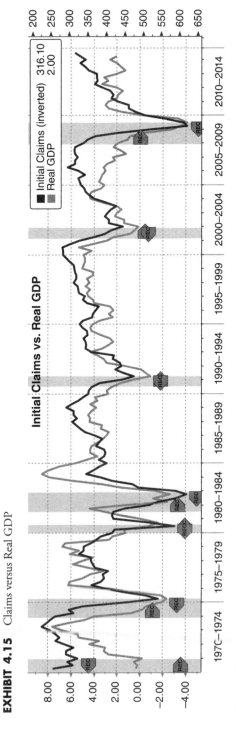

*Source:* Bloomberg

While the weekly release makes this a desirable indicator, it also makes for extreme volatility and is prone to revisions. For that reason economists like to look at the four-week moving average (Exhibit 4.16). This tends to depict a more accurate picture of the employment situation.

There's a rule of thumb on the Street with respect to jobless claims: when the four-week moving average rises above 300,000, then concerns of a recession surface. Of course, this level is not set in stone, but the historical view suggests that investors should begin to worry about economic weakness at that level.

Despite the welcomed insight of benefits claims, there are a number of issues regarding claims as a top-tier indicator. Granted, it's a safe bet that as the number of recipients declines, more people are employed, but there is no direct manner to understand how many. This stat tells us nothing about the pace of hiring.

Second, not everyone is entitled to apply (and receive) unemployment insurance, so there are a large number of people that will not be identified as unemployed. For example, during March of 2014, there were 10.5 million unemployed persons. Meanwhile, there were only about 2.6 million receiving unemployment benefit compensation around that time.

This divergence may be especially exacerbated today where a great deal of people are employed in the service sector as consultants or temporary contract workers, who are probably not entitled to benefits. In years past, people were predominantly employed in manufacturing, particularly for a large, unionized, goods-producing company. When their position was downsized, they could easily apply and receive compensation (benefits) from the government.

Another measure of the labor market situation is the ADP Employment Report produced by Automatic Data Processing (ADP) and Moody's Analytics. The estimates are of private nonfarm payroll employment based on payroll data demand derived from ADP and its 411,000 U.S. clients, which employ roughly 24 million U.S. workers.

The ADP survey is released on the Wednesday prior to the BLS's Employment Situation report, which is released on the following Friday.

Exhibit 4.17 depicts the solid relationship between the ADP survey of private payrolls and the BLS total nonfarm payrolls estimated from its establishment survey.

Additional detail is contained in the survey and characterized by size of firm small (1–19, and 20–49 employees), medium (50–499 employees), and large businesses (500–999, 1,000+ employees). The data are also presented by sector (goods- or services-producing) as well as by industry (construction, manufacturing/trade/transportation/utilities, financial activities, professional/business services).

**EXHIBIT 4.16** Four-Week MA Initial Claims

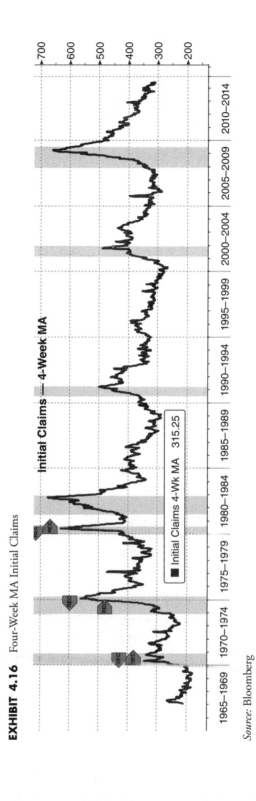

*Source:* Bloomberg

**EXHIBIT 4.17**  ADP, Nonfarm Payrolls

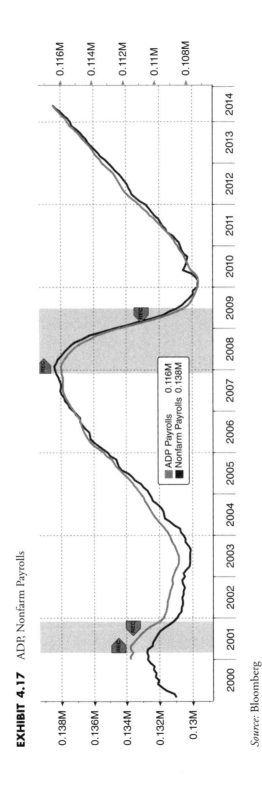

*Source:* Bloomberg

97

The Job Openings Labor Turnover Survey (JOLTS) is another jobs-related report that captures the attention of Wall Streeters. The data are reported monthly and the focus is largely on the level of job openings and the number of hires. There are several measures of rates (hires and openings); however, the investment community mostly ignored them.

Knowing the level of job openings is helpful for a number of reasons; it tells you to what degree employers are willing to take on the expensive cost of hiring. The last thing businesses want to do is add to their payrolls if they are concerned about the economic outlook. Also, there are many additional costs other than a wage or salary to consider when hiring a person (health care, insurance, taxes, training, and other business-related expenses like travel, computer, and phone costs). A company doesn't want to have to incur these expenses if the economy or demand for their product doesn't warrant this exorbitant expense.

The number of unemployed workers per job opening explains a great deal about the state of affairs in the labor market. When times are economically challenging, there are more unemployed workers per opening. As Exhibit 4.18 highlights, the long jobless recovery of 2001–2003 saw a near threefold increase in this ratio. During the depression of 2007–2009, the level soared to a staggering 7.0 unemployed persons per opening. Although this statistic had fallen from a dangerously elevated level, it took several years to return to a relatively livable 2.5 unemployed workers per available job opening (Exhibit 4.19).

Economists have been known to incorporate the level or pace of announced job cuts into their labor market models. Since the announcements are somewhat of a leading indicator—intentions to furlough workers are traditionally realized one to three months down the road—they tend to have a slightly predictive ability. For this, the benchmark on the Street is the Challenger, Gray & Christmas Job Cut Announcements survey (Exhibit 4.20). Each month, a few days prior to the BLS Employment Situation Report, Challenger releases the details of announced cuts. These data are not seasonally adjusted, and the year-over-year is generally considered to be a much better depiction of the trend in job cut announcements.

This survey contains a great deal of information, including the level of announced job hires. Combining announcements on hires and fires can be quite helpful when forecasting the payrolls figures by industry, since the monthly payroll jobs figures are on a net (hires – dismissals) basis.

Wall Street analysts also look at these hire and fire announcement data to decipher trends in their respective industries, since these announced cuts and hires are summarized by industry. In recent months, the biggest hiring industries have been telecommunications, automotive, computer, aerospace, and

**EXHIBIT 4.18** JOLTS Openings, Hires

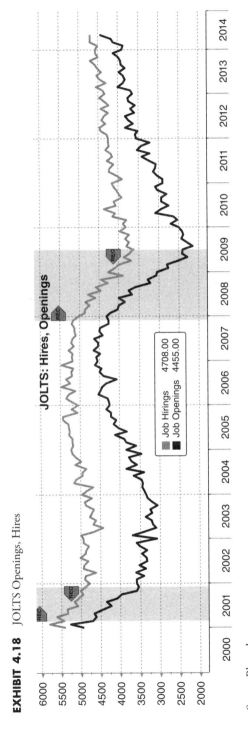

*Source:* Bloomberg

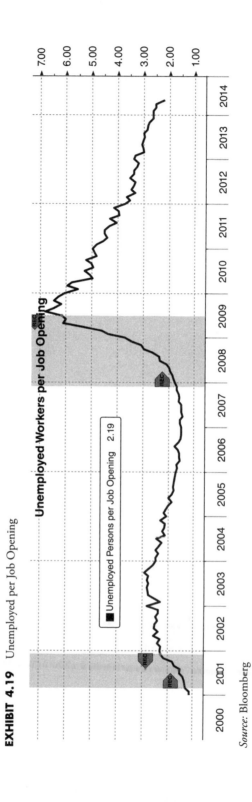

**EXHIBIT 4.19** Unemployed per Job Opening

*Source:* Bloomberg

**EXHIBIT 4.20** Challenger Layoffs Survey

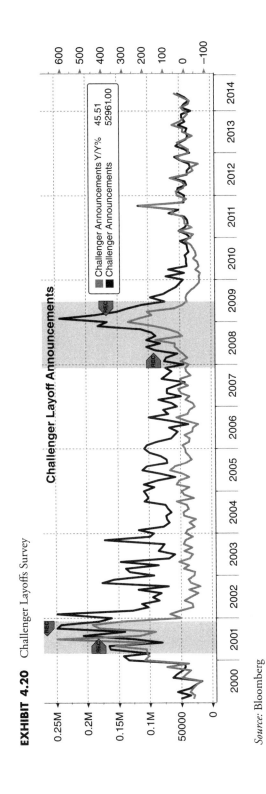

Challenger Layoff Announcements

| | |
|---|---|
| Challenger Announcements Y/Y% | 45.51 |
| Challenger Announcements | 52961.00 |

*Source:* Bloomberg

health care. The greatest job-cut announcements included: telecommunications, health care, entertainment, government, industrial goods, consumer products, commodities, and transportation.

## Test Yourself

Answer the following multiple-choice questions:

1. The goings on in the labor market matter because:
   a. they reveal social as well as economic conditions.
   b. employed people account for almost 95 percent of the total population.
   c. every company has to report its unemployment rates.
   d. a and b only.
   e. none of the above.

2. What is the largest portion of the U.S. labor force?
   a. manufacturing positions.
   b. construction workers.
   c. services jobs.
   d. all of the above.
   e. a and b only.

3. Watching the trends in employment at temporary help services companies can identify:
   a. changes in the diffusion indexes.
   b. changes in demand for retail workers.
   c. a and b only.
   d. turning points in the economy.
   e. none of the above.

4. Why might the weekly initial claims for unemployment benefit insurance *not* be the best data to watch to forecast employment?
   a. It tells us nothing about hiring.
   b. Not everyone is entitled to unemployment benefits.
   c. Only 300,000 people are entitled to benefits at any one time.
   d. All of the above.
   e. a and b only.

5. If you want to see the price of labor, you should observe trends in:
   a. temporary payroll jobs.
   b. average hourly earnings.
   c. the labor force participation rate.
   d. all of the above.
   e. a and b only.

## Answers

1. a
2. c
3. d
4. e
5. b

# CHAPTER 5

# Retail Sales

Since the consumer is King in the U.S. economy, much may be gleaned by observing trends in buying habits. The level and movements in retail sales data are quite telling with respect to the state of current and future macroeconomic affairs.

The Census Bureau's monthly report on sales for retail and food services is one of the more closely watched indicators on the Street and possesses great market-moving potential. The two best features of this report are its prompt release and detail.

The advance retail sales report hits the tape at 8:30 a.m. ET around the fifteenth day of the month and is based on estimates obtained from roughly 5,000 retail and food establishments. The results are weighed and benchmarked to embody activity at more than three million retail businesses.

The two primary considerations of the Wall Street community are the headline retail and food services figure and the total level of sales excluding motor vehicle and parts dealers.

Both measures move pretty much in sync since the only difference between the two is automotive sales. Generally speaking, if consumers are feeling confident enough to buy a costly item like a car, they may also be inclined to purchase other big-ticket items like a refrigerator, washing machine, or flat-screen television.

Ultimately, the object of watching the trends in retail sales activity is to decipher turning points in the economy (Exhibit 5.1). When economic conditions are strengthening—that is, employment is rising, incomes and wages are advancing, and the underlying level of inflation is low—consumers feel confident and are prone to increase spending. Conversely, when it is difficult to find steady work, wages and salaries are depressed and inflation is eating away at those less than desirable earnings, consumers retrench and limit purchases to only the necessities—shelter, food, and fuel (gasoline).

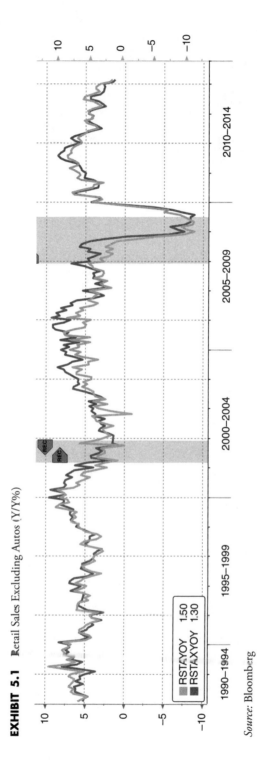

**EXHIBIT 5.1** Retail Sales Excluding Autos (Y/Y%)

*Source:* Bloomberg

Unfortunately, spending on durable items like motor vehicles can lead to distortions. Some months are more conducive to auto sales than others, interest rates—a primary determinant of more expensive purchases—change by the day, and of course dealer incentives vary by manufacturer, model, and month. In order to smooth out the volatile influences of motor vehicle sales, economists look to the sales trends excluding autos.

In addition, the year-over-year pace of retail sales is the preferred perspective of trends since month-to-month readings can fluctuate greatly. Notice the lack of any distinguishable trend when the month-over-month changes are charted for total retail sales (Exhibit 5.2). The lone exceptions are the spike in October 2001 when auto dealers introduced 0 percent financing immediately following the 9/11 attacks on the United States—the Keep America Rolling Campaign. Conversely, in 2008 and 2009 there were deep monthly declines largely the result of economic depression and the freezing up of the credit markets.

The year-over-year percentage change in the headline retail sales report is an excellent economic barometer. In recent recessions, however, the trend of retail trade hasn't been a leading indicator, and has adopted more of a coincidental movement with the business cycle.

## Composition

There are 13 major subsectors in the advance report, including electronics and appliance stores, food and beverage (grocery, supermarkets, delicatessen-type, etc.), and general merchandise stores. Those groups are detailed even further a month later, when additional data are received (Exhibit 5.3). For example, electronics and appliance stores would have up-to-date data regarding sub-categories of appliances, TV, and camera stores and computer and software store sales.

The largest group in the retail sales release is motor vehicles and parts, representing about 18 percent of the entire level of sales. This group is followed by food and beverage stores and general merchandise stores—each accounting for approximately 13.0 percent of the total amount of sales.

Some economists observe just the trends in auto sales since it takes a great deal of confidence in overall underlying economic conditions to make such a major purchase. It also takes an optimistic outlook with respect to one's own situation, including the jobs climate, the pace and level of income growth, and the cost of a new vehicle.

One problem focusing solely on auto sales is that trends are difficult to decipher and may take several months to surface. Since the purchase of an auto is generally made once every decade—the average age of a lightweight vehicle is roughly 11 years and is usually replaced in that time frame—sales have a tendency to whipsaw and distort the overall level of spending on any given month.

**EXHIBIT 5.2** Retail Sales Month-to-Month

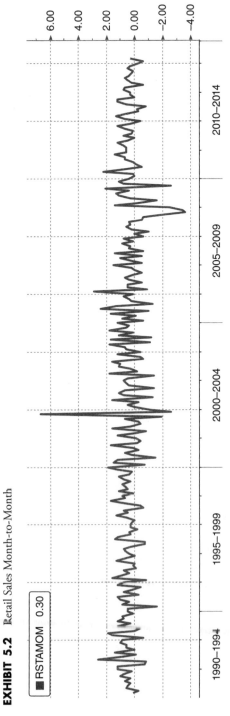

*Source:* Bloomberg

**EXHIBIT 5.3** Retail Sales Composition

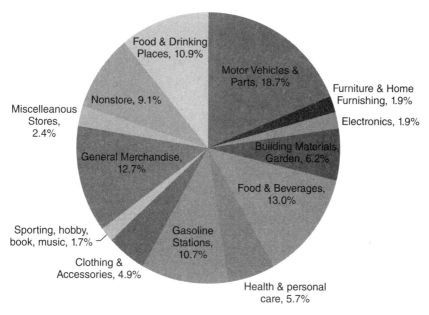

*Data Source:* U.S. Bureau of Census

## Different Perspectives

Just as there is rare agreement among economists on virtually every topic under the sun, there is a definitional issue with regard to the ideal measure of retail sales. Should economists and analysts watch trends of retail sales with auto sales included, or should they watch only sales of autos? What about the sales of restaurants and drinking places—should we include that in our studies? For these reasons, economists have adopted several representations of monthly retail sales.

For a less volatile depiction, most economists agree that big-ticket sales of motor vehicles and parts should be excluded from the headline figure. Taking this adjustment one step further, Wall Streeters have created a view of retail sales called the *control group*, which excludes sales at auto dealers, building materials stores, as well as those at gasoline stations. By eliminating these peripheral purchases, it is believed that a more accurate picture of consumer buying trends is revealed.

Some may argue that excluding sales at building material stores in the measure means removing so-called "hardline" retailers like Lowe's and the Home Depot, which might not be an accurate measure since activity in this category often includes big-ticket items like carpeting, air conditioners, generators, and lawn mowers. These are all legitimate home purchases and should be represented in a measure of total retail sales.

Essentially, there are two types of retailers, *hardlines* and *softlines*. The hardlines include those that sell household appliances, housewares, furniture, electronics, sporting goods, and jewelry—hard goods. The softline retailers distribute "softer" products like clothing, apparel, and footwear. Of course there are several stores that sell a combination of hard and soft goods, which are usually the big department stores.

One of the older, more respected representations is *GAFO*, an acronym for sales of General merchandise, Apparel (clothing and clothing accessories), Furniture and home furnishings, and Other sales, including office supply, stationery, and gift stores. Sales of electronics and appliances, sporting goods, hobby items, books, and music also make into the GAFO calculation.

Charting this series against U.S. per capita disposable personal income—on a year-over-year basis—depicts a solid relationship, which makes sound economic sense (Exhibit 5.4). The more money an individual has (adjusted for taxes and inflation), the more likely they are able to spend.

## Anecdotal Evidence

You don't need to be a Wall Street economist to know about how the consumer or American economy is faring. New York Yankee legend Yogi Berra once said, "You can see a lot by just looking." Nowhere does this approach work better than in the retail sector.

If you want to take the temperature of the American consumer, just walk through malls, shopping centers, discount outlets, or any individual retail establishment. If traffic is heavy and people are carrying bags, then there's a good chance economic conditions are solid. If, however, there is abundant parking lot space, empty stores, no lines at the checkout area, and heavily discounted merchandise, then economic conditions are probably a bit more challenging.

Essentially, every Wall Street analyst covering companies in the retail space perform *channel checks*—routine visits to stores to view parts of the distribution channel like inventory levels on the shelves, pricing, staffing, and general demand for a specific product. Sometimes they are performed with a manager, often they are unaccompanied and unknown to store employees. Either way, information obtained from store tours or mall crawls is invaluable, and all individual investors or economists should conduct similar research in their own attempt to ascertain economic conditions.

Combining anecdotes obtained through various observations and conversations with actual sales data can provide a solid foundation for a forecast for the retail industry as well as a macroeconomic projection.

**EXHIBIT 5.4** GAFO per Capita Disposable Income

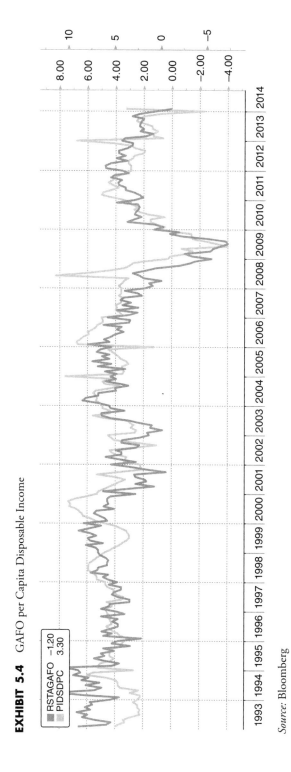

*Source:* Bloomberg

111

## Luxury Sales

There is a very strong correlation between the level of stock market activity and the sales pace at luxury retailers like Saks, Bloomingdale's, and Nordstrom. This is somewhat obvious, since it takes a very wealthy person to afford a $4,500 Hermes handbag, a $3,500 Prada dress, or a $1,500 Louis Vuitton wallet. It takes money to spend money at the high-end retailers.

Comments made during conference calls or investors and analyst meetings like those contained in the Bloomberg Orange Book often provide clues about the determinants and drivers of sales activity. Karen Katz, the CEO of luxury retailer Neiman-Marcus, said in a November 28, 2012, earnings call, "As you know, our customers are very attuned to the fluctuations of the markets both here and abroad. They also closely followed the election and continue to weigh news from Washington and Congress regarding the economy, the debt crisis and possible changes to the tax laws."

The associated chart depicts the solid relationship between the stock price change in Tiffany's and Nordstrom with that of the overall S&P 500 Index (Exhibit 5.5).

Former Saks CEO Steve Sadove frequently chatted about the value of the dollar and its counterparts when determining sales, particularly travelers visiting the Saks flagship store in midtown New York City. In a November 13, 2012, earnings call, Sadove told investors:

> If I looked at our overall tourism trends, what's happened is that...the tourism trends are not very much out of line with our overall trends. But what we're seeing is an uptick of the Chinese, the Brazilian, Russian customers, more than offsetting the decline that we're seeing in some of the European customers. So I clearly see an opportunity with the international tourist, largely the Chinese, the Russians, the Brazilians continuing to shop. Focused activity against the Chinese customer is an opportunity and you're continuing to see the traffic building with that customer.

Sadove also echoed the Neiman Marcus chief executive officer's comments: "Our customer, we've said for a long time, is very much driven by how do they feel about their net worth and what are they feeling about where the markets are. There's a little bit of volatility in the markets today."

These anecdotes become quite helpful, especially to a microeconomic or industry approach to forecasting trends in the luxury market. Any economist or analyst attempting to project sales, spending, or value of the company should incorporate some measure of wealth in their analysis, whether it is stock prices or incomes.

**EXHIBIT 5.5** Retail Luxury versus S&P500

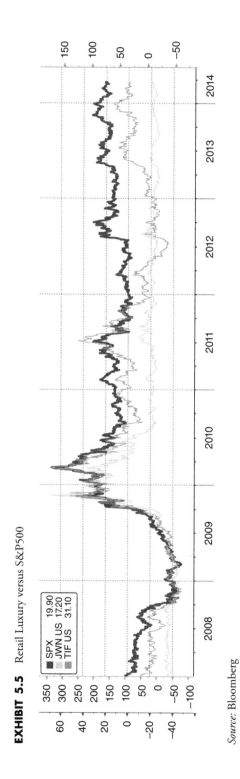

*Source:* Bloomberg

113

## Shortcomings

There is a drawback to the monthly retail sales report that can be somewhat misleading. All of the data are reported in nominal terms. That is, they are not adjusted for inflation. This can make interpretation difficult. Economists have no way of knowing how much of a gain at a particular sales channel was due to higher prices of the goods in that sector or increased volumes. That's why prices are closely scrutinized when interpreting these data.

Consider sales at gasoline stations. It looks as if this component may be the easiest to forecast since sales at gasoline stations are traditionally so closely correlated to the price of gasoline. If you know the price at the pump for the current and previous month, it is a safe bet that you could guesstimate, fairly accurately, the monthly change in sales at gasoline stations. And since retail sales of gasoline stations account for a good 11 percent of all sales, significant movements in gasoline prices have the ability to greatly influence the overall report (Exhibit 5.6).

In order to get a feel of movements in gasoline prices prior to the posting of the monthly retail sales report, economists look to the U.S. Energy Department's Energy Information Administration's website (http://www.eia.gov) for the weekly retail price of regular grade gasoline (Exhibit 5.7).

Clothing and clothing accessory retailers may also experience sizable month-to-month fluctuations due to price changes. Analysts often follow the price trends in cotton since so many of the stores in this group use this commodity. Heavy discounting and promotional periods like Christmas, Easter, and back-to-school have been known to greatly influence monthly sales activity, particularly at apparel and footwear stores. It's very important to know what retailers are doing with the prices of their goods when attempting to forecast this component. Industry analysts look to see whether businesses are in a promotional environment—widespread sales, discounts, or offers of *buy-one-get-one* (BOGO)—when forecasting retail trends. Generally, when businesses slash prices, it's a sign of economic weakness. Retailers have to attract consumers, and in troubling times, the best way to accomplish this is through lower prices or couponing.

The third most price-sensitive sector in the retail sales report is building materials and garden equipment supply dealers. Price changes in industrial commodities and materials like metals, copper, pigments, and lumber change the sales performances of related goods like fencing, wiring, piping, tubing, paints, drywall, plumbing fixtures, and cabinetry. Industrial commodity prices are always in an economist's toolkit.

There is also a noticeable price influence on grocery store sales. When prices of food and beverages rise, there's a good chance that retail sales at grocery stores have increased as well. Here again, if you know the trends in prices of food and beverages, there's a good chance you will be able to eyeball the trend in sales of this category.

**EXHIBIT 5.6** Retail Sales Gas versus Gas Prices

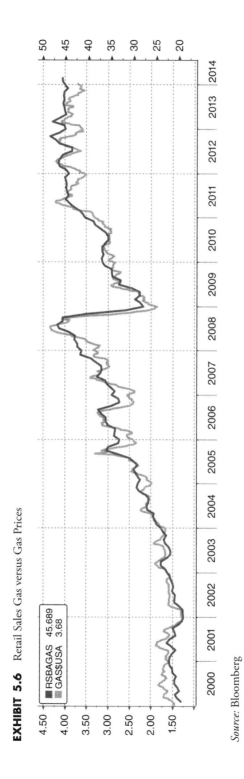

*Source:* Bloomberg

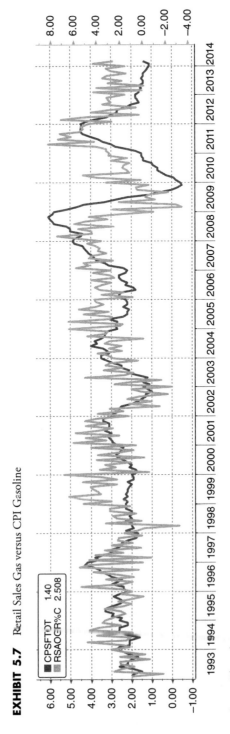

**EXHIBIT 5.7** Retail Sales Gas versus CPI Gasoline

*Source:* Bloomberg

## Corrections

There is a way to adjust the retail sales data for the price discrepancy, albeit an imperfect procedure. Economists at the Federal Reserve Bank of St. Louis adjust the headline retail sales report by deflating the level using the consumer price index (CPI-U), the Bureau of Labor Statistic's measure for prices on the retail level.

This process is a crude attempt to adjust the nominally based data for inflation.

Here is how you "deflate" an economic series like retail sales:

1. Get the data you wish to adjust, retail sales: $412,403 million
2. Find a comparable measure of inflation, like CPI-U for the same month: 231.025
3. Divide the series by the inflation measure: $412,403 / 231.025 = $178,510

This is a back-of-the-envelope approach and is not a precise adjustment, since many of the components in the Consumer Price Index are not represented in the retail sales report including health care, household energy (natural gas, electricity, etc.), and shelter.

When this series is charted (Exhibit 5.8), a few important trends arise; during periods of prosperity or economic expansion, the 12-month pace of real retail trends advances in a range of about 2 to 5 percent. This is unsurprisingly similar to the growth rate of total consumption expenditures and the trend growth rate of real GDP over the same period.

When real retail sales exceed 5.0 percent, as in 1994, 1999, and 2005, the Federal Reserve fears that the economy may be overheating and attempts to cool things down by ratcheting up its benchmark overnight borrowing rate.

The range of 0 and 2 percent growth in real retail sales growth is traditionally associated with periods experiencing weak economic conditions. This may best be described as the thin-ice scenario—any lower and the economy could fall through the cracks and slip into recession.

Of course subzero rates of growth are generally accompanied by recession.

## Recent Trends and Influences

There are a number of transformations in the economy that have resulted in meaningful changes in the way economists should interpret the monthly retail sales report. The most obvious is where people shop.

The arrival of the Internet may be the biggest development to the retail sector since the expansion of the shopping mall in the early 1950s.

Since the purchasing process on the Internet is conducted with such ease— and many items are similar and relatively interchangeable—bricks-and-mortar

**EXHIBIT 5.8** Real Retail Sales

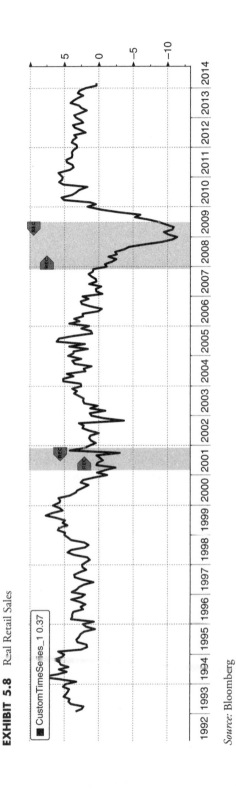

*Source:* Bloomberg

118

stores have come to be regarded as mere showrooms. Why battle traffic and escalating prices at the pump when most purchases can be made in the convenience of one's home, office, or essentially anywhere on Earth via mobile device?

*Omni-channel retailing* (the integration of sales activity at bricks-and-mortar stores, kiosks, the Internet, catalog, television, warehouses, and mobile devices) is a relatively new and emerging part of the retail business, and references are commonplace in the industry and during conference calls. This process can reduce inventories—always a concern for retailers—and promote sales for an ever-demanding consumer.

*Showrooming* (the practice of visiting traditional bricks-and-mortar stores and purchasing desired merchandise on the Internet or other venue) is a growing trend among the retailing community. This can, and has, had a meaningful influence on some components in the retail sales report. For example, **general merchandise** or **department stores** may not experience the same amount of activity as they once did, while other categories become a beneficiary of the trend (Exhibit 5.9).

Department store sales as a percentage of total retail sales excluding autos has tumbled from 11 percent in the early 1990s to barely above 4.0 percent today. Clearly the acceptance of online shopping is responsible for this deterioration of department store sales activity. There is little reason to believe that this downward trend will reverse course any time soon.

Amazon.com, the world's largest online retailer, was founded in 1994 and commenced online sales in 1995. It was around this time that the share of department store sales began to wane. Once other retailers joined the community and wrinkles regarding payment systems, security, shipping, and distribution were ironed out, the Internet began to soar in acceptance and sales appreciated considerably (Exhibit 5.10).

Internet spending is captured in the monthly retail sales report under *Nonstore Retailers*. This group also includes sales made during infomercials, direct-response merchandising, mail-order houses, portable stalls (street vendors), paper and electronic catalogs, and direct-sale items like newspapers. Roughly 80 percent of the $40 billion nonstore retail sales (early 2013) are composed of electronic shopping and mail-order house shopping.

The growing popularity of the Internet as a thriving sales channel is having profound macroeconomic effects. If the demand for physical stores is diminished, then the need for retail workers should also be expected to decline. Since some goods are omnipresent and are not going to vary by store, a salesperson might not be as necessary as they once were.

Consider the purchase of a book, any book. Let's use Gary Koop's *Analysis of Economic Data* as an example. (It is an excellent introductory econometrics book for those looking for a primer on the topic, and not anticipating the field

**EXHIBIT 5.9** General Merchandise Percentage of Total Retail Sales Excluding Autos

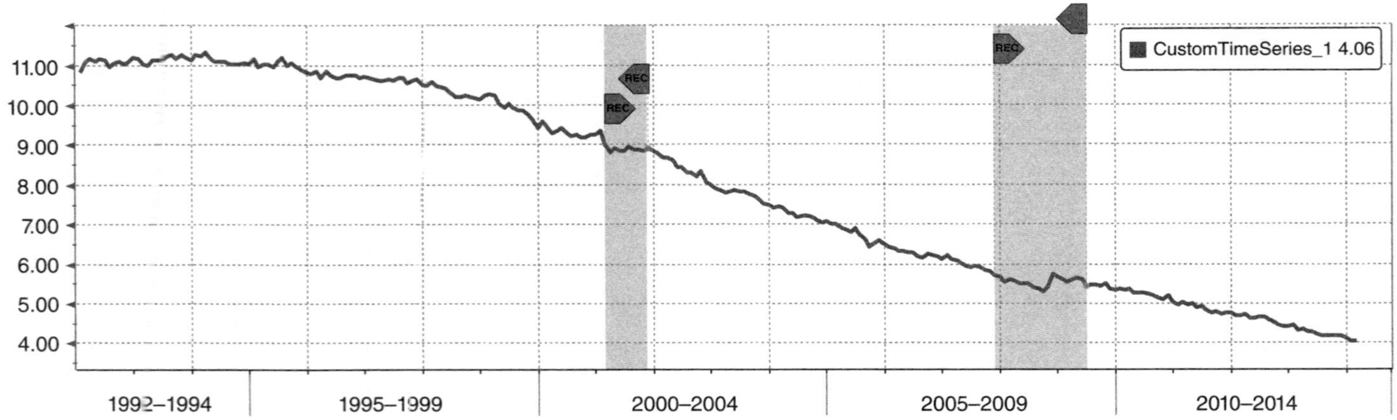

*Source:* Bloomberg

**EXHIBIT 5.10** E-commerce Sales

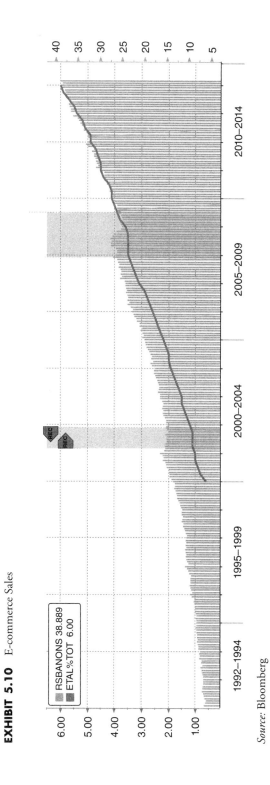

*Source:* Bloomberg

121

of econometrics as a career. Any and all students would benefit by having it on their shelf.)

This book may be purchased in a store or online. It will not vary in size, shape, weight, or color. It is the same whether purchased in either venue. The would-be buyer knows this information, and will determine where to purchase it with respect to price and convenience. In many instances, purchases on the Internet may be made tax-free, shipped without cost, and at a heavy discount. This practice is intensified around the holidays as traffic, weather, parking, and crowds reduce the desire to scurry off to shopping centers, malls, and stand-alone stores.

The more ubiquitous an item is, the more likely the purchase will be made on the Internet and not at a physical retail store. As the market realizes this trend, establishments selling those products will close and furlough those workers.

The level of people employed at sporting goods, hobby, book, and music stores has basically been unchanged for the last 15 years (Exhibit 5.11). In fact, the level now appears to be declining. Why? Because the Internet is hitting those bricks-and-mortar establishments that sell goods like hockey sticks, guitars, model trains, or electronics. It is no wonder that some stores like Circuit City, Borders, and Linens 'n Things have been forced to file for bankruptcy protection.

For some goods, particularly apparel and footwear, consumers actually have a need to visit stores to examine their would-be purchases. Unlike a book, an electronic devise, or a vacuum cleaner, clothing is not a ubiquitous item. Colors are very different, brands carry varying fabrics, and sizing is inconsistent for everything from boots to blouses. So there is a need for a salesperson and a store.

Employment at apparel and clothing accessories stores has actually increased by 15 percent over the last decade and a half.

So called *big-box* retailers—megastore retailers that sell a wide variety of goods and services in massive buildings (like Wal-Mart, Target, Costco, BJ's Wholesale Club, and Best Buy) are pressured by the trend in showcasing or showrooming and the move to online shopping. Although many of these chains offer Internet sales, the need to have large commercial buildings full of goods is diminished. It can be quite costly to heat/cool, stock, clean, insure, staff, and provide security for a mere showroom where people are less inclined to visit. Many companies are rethinking this big-box approach.

The commercial real estate sector is also getting hurt by the growing popularity of the Internet. If there is a lessened need for bricks-and-mortar stores, then retail construction will not flourish, and hiring in that important sector will not increase either. During November 2012, the level of private construction spending on commercial projects was the same level as it was in 1995. Similarly, the level of mall vacancies had increased to record highs in 2011 and lingered at those lofty levels throughout 2012. When malls are vacant, state and local municipalities lose revenues (tax receipts) and they become strained as well.

**EXHIBIT 5.11** Level of Employment in Apparel and Sporting Stores

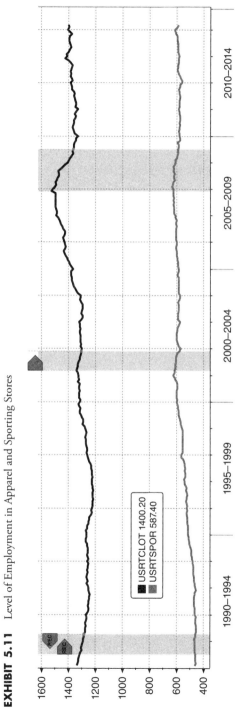

*Source:* Bloomberg

123

Often times, they would be forced to cut workers and spending. So it's clear that the comeuppance of the Internet has many profound influences on the macroeconomic landscape.

## The Retail Calendar

America is a retailing dream. Every month has a handful of events or holidays widely celebrated and benefit many of the major retailing categories. A recent (2012) survey conducted for the National Retail Federation estimated the order of the biggest retail holidays/events. The largest by far was the winter holidays, which contain Thanksgiving, Christmas, Hanukkah, and Kwanzaa. This was followed by back-to-school, Valentine's Day, Easter, Mother's Day, Father's Day, the Super Bowl, Halloween, and St. Patrick's Day (Exhibit 5.12).

**EXHIBIT 5.12**   Retail Calendar

|  | Holiday(s)/Driver | Traditional Goods/Services Trends |
|---|---|---|
| January/ February | New Year's, Super Bowl | "white" sales, gym memberships, diet plans, food & beverages, gift cards |
| February | Valentine's Day | candy, jewelry, electronics, perfumes, cosmetics |
| March | St. Patrick's Day, NCAA Basketball | apparel, building materials, gardening, food services & drinking places |
| April | Easter | gardening, apparel, footwear |
| May | Easter, Mother's Day, Memorial Day | apparel, footwear, food & beverages, building materials |
| June | Proms, graduations, Father's Day, weddings | appliances (air conditioners), food & beverages, sporting goods, hobby |
| July | Weddings, Independence Day | food & beverages, travel, gasoline, health & personal care |
| August | Back-to-school | apparel, footwear, health & personal care, gasoline, electronics, travel |
| September | Labor Day | office supplies, apparel, footwear |
| October | Columbus Day, Halloween | candy, health & personal care |
| November | Thanksgiving | food & beverages, just about every category |
| December | Christmas | food & beverages, just about every category |

It's important for economists to know the state of affairs in the major categories during each holiday season. Anecdotes from industry executives can tell a great deal about the strength or weakness of a given month's retail sales report. In February, for example, listening to the comments made by jewelry, chocolate, florist, and restaurant professionals can be quite telling about the underlying economic climate. If spending on those items pale in comparison to year-ago levels, then the consumer may be exhibiting some exhaustion, which may be a signal of slower economic times ahead.

This information may also be gathered by individual conversations with smaller/local business people or by listening to executives on earnings or analyst conference calls. Many retailers give monthly sales updates, which are well worth dialing in to.

## Holiday Retail Sales

Estimating the size of the holiday sales season is obviously very important. There are several approaches to take. Some economists look to the level of sales by the "control group" during November and December. Others simply look at the December ex-autos retail sales figure.

One widely accepted measure is to add the GAFO values for November and December of each year (Exhibit 5.13). Since retailers begin some sort

**EXHIBIT 5.13**   Holiday Sales (GAFO November and December) (Y/Y%)

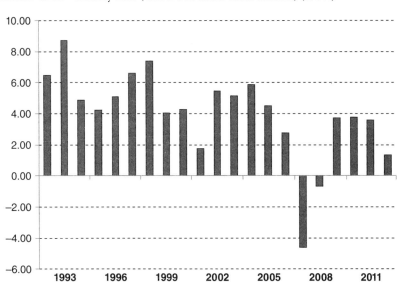

*Data Source:* Department of Commerce

of pre-holiday marketing as early as the day after Halloween (October 31), consumers often get a head start on purchases in the beginning of November. The use of GAFO firm sales assures the volatile groups like gasoline station sales and motor vehicles will not influence the measurement, thus providing a more accurate depiction of holiday-related activity.

The associated chart shows the year-over-year change in holiday sales as measured by adding the November and December values of GAFO retail sales. Lackluster growth rates are obviously associated with a crummy economic climate and are known as weak holiday spending periods. The outright contractions in 2008 and 2009 are associated with the tremendous downturn in aggregate demand and employment during those years.

A popular holiday present in recent years has been the gift card. Many find it a more convenient purchase, at the same time being a bit more personable than cash. Moreover, economic conditions in the United States have been somewhat trying in recent years, and the thought of giving presents that the receivers potentially won't use, discard, or "regift" is not a wise choice, so the gift card has surfaced as a smart option.

Like so many other recent innovations, gift cards have had a meaningful impact on consumer buying trends. These are often purchased in November or December and usually disseminated in mid- to late-December. One major influence to keep in mind when analyzing holiday sales is that the sales of the cards themselves do not count in the retail sales figures. They are counted only when redeemed at the associated retailer with a purchase. Given that these cards come so late in the month, there's a good chance that they will not boost sales in December, but in January or even February. And since so much merchandise is discounted after the holidays, consumers tend to wait for sales to surface before redeeming the cards. Even more favorable to sales activity, consumers rarely limit purchases to the value of the card—exceeding that value seems to be the rule, not the exception.

It used to be the case that once January arrived, retailers would furlough workers and cut back on hours worked. Now, as gift cards in effect extend the holiday season, trends related to labor, inventory, price, and production have all shifted down the calendar.

The beginning of the holiday season traditionally begins on the day following Thanksgiving, known as *Black Friday*. The explanation for this varies, but a reasonable argument is that all retailers operate "in the black," or profitably on that day. Some have claimed it's the first time of the year that some retailers turn into the black. Recently, some stores have attempted to alter that commencement by opening doors during the evening of Thanksgiving. Nevertheless, the unofficial beginning of the holiday shopping season is the day after Turkey Day.

Economists and analysts like to count the number of days that lie between Thanksgiving and Christmas. Since Thanksgiving is celebrated on the fourth Thursday of the month, the earliest date for Thanksgiving in the United States is November 22. Therefore, the most days between Thanksgiving and Christmas is 32 (8 in November plus 24 in December), while the least is 26 days, from November 29 to December 24. The theory behind counting shopping days is, the more time consumers have to shop, the more shopping they will do. Some trade organizations publish the busiest shopping days of that period, which interestingly is not Black Friday. Americans tend to wait until the last moment, which usually results in a mad dash to the mall on the weekend prior to Christmas.

## The Crucial Indicator

One of the little secrets in the Retail Sales report is to watch the level of sales at food service establishments and bars. Other than the sizable 10 percent contribution to total sales, there is something to be said about watching sales at these familiar institutions. The economic explanation of this concept is rather simple; when times get tough, consumers don't head off to Morton's Steakhouse or the Cheesecake Factory. There might be an immediate desire for a visit to the local saloon, but for the most part, spending on a somewhat extravagant, nonessential purchase is not usually the first thought after one loses a job or faces an uncertain outlook.

History shows that spending at food services and drinking places, the Commerce Department's formal name for the category, advances in a range between 4 and 8 percent during periods of prosperity (Exhibit 5.14). Yearly growth rates of below 4 percent are usually seen as sluggish or as conditions that are associated with questionable economic performances. Since these data are not adjusted for inflation, and the 60-year average inflation rate for "food away from home" is 4.0 percent, it's easy to see how lower than 4.0 postings are a warning signal for economic activity.

From time-to-time, there will be surges in the level of sales at Miscellaneous Store Retailers. This category contains sales at florists, pet and pet supply stores, and other establishments with unique characteristics. One of the more interesting components is used merchandise, or sales at consignment stores. Since many of the group's components are safely assumed (e.g., February, May, and June are probably favorable for flower shops due to demand for Valentine's Day, Mother's Day, and graduations, respectively, while pet store sales are relatively constant), unforeseen fluctuations are probably due to movements in the used goods, or thrift store component. Strong gains in the miscellaneous category may then be signaling subdued economic circumstances

128

**EXHIBIT 5.14** Retail Sales for Food Services and Drinking

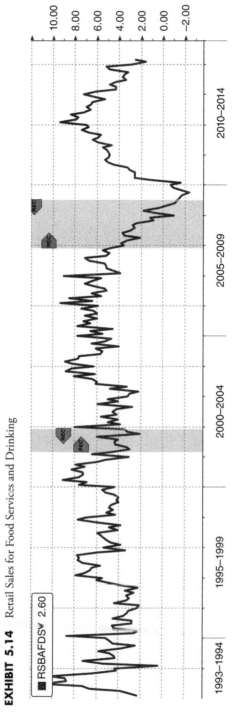

*Source:* Bloomberg

since more people are frequenting these retailers. It's also a good idea to watch the trends and comments coming from discounters such as TJX Companies and Ross Stores.

## Related Measures

There is another measure of retail sales—a separate report from the Commerce Department's monthly retail sales release—that the Street focuses on, and it's the level of company *same-store sales*. Every month, some retailers would report the comparative, or *comp*, sales at stores that have been open a year or more. The reason for only including sales at those stores is to determine whether the growth is coming via acquisition of new businesses or from existing stores.

At one point in time, there were several chain stores that would contribute this desirable economic information, making it an excellent economic indicator. Unfortunately, at the current time there is a trend away from divulging too much information on a monthly basis, so the ability to decipher any meaningful relationships from the limited data has essentially evaporated.

## Recent Trends

During late 2012, fears and uncertainty surrounding the U.S. fiscal situation imposed fear into households. It wasn't until the last moment that Congress came to a solution—albeit temporary. Consumers had no idea what they would be paying in taxes or whether government programs would still be funded. Similarly, businesses were not sure of their tax requirements, or what the government spending situation would be.

Essentially, every company executive made mention of this critical influence. Dollar General CEO Rick Dreiling said:

> . . . I think there's a change taking place in the customer environment right now. I think the customer is fatigued, they're tired, they're scared. Every time you turn on the television, there's a bunch of guys in suits who are frowning, telling you that the world's going to go over the fiscal cliff. And as that happens, I think the competitive environment heats up in response as we all try to hold onto the sales that are out there.

So retailers obviously recognized the problem and were clinging to any and every sale they can make. The issue for the retailer became, how do I get sales in an environment where heavy promotion and discounting is the norm? Nobody bought anything without a coupon, discount, BOGO offer, or a promotion of some sort.

With this mentality so ingrained in the American consumer's psyche, it's nearly impossible to change. In fact, the only thing that actually does change is for the consumer's economic condition to improve—job prospects have to increase, incomes and wages needed to rise, the stock market and housing investments need to boost overall wealth, and so on. Unless that improves, couponing becomes a near-impossible habit to break.

Consumers will simply refrain from purchasing until they see "Sale" or percent-off signs, or they receive discount coupons by mail or email. And only if and when things improve for them will they will be more accepting (or tolerant) of paying higher prices for goods and services.

## Test Yourself

Answer the following multiple-choice questions:

1. Why do economists like to look at the pace of retail sales excluding autos?
   a. The U.S. auto industry is so weak.
   b. Most of the autos sold are in China.
   c. The level of auto sales can be very volatile.
   d. All of the above.
   e. a and b only.

2. Black Friday is:
   a. the day when all retailers sell out of their wares.
   b. the day after Thanksgiving.
   c. the day after Christmas.
   d. all of the above.
   e. a and b only.

3. The second largest spending holiday or season behind the "winter holidays" is:
   a. Valentine's Day.
   b. the Super Bowl.
   c. Back-to-school.
   d. Easter.
   e. Halloween.

4. Which of the following is a shortcoming of the retail sales report?
   a. Data are not adjusted for inflation.
   b. Auto sales are not included in the report.
   c. Sales at gasoline stations are not included.
   d. All of the above.
   e. a and b only.

5. When the 12-month pace of real retail sales rises above 5.0 percent:

   a. the economy slips into recession.
   b. the Fed has a tendency to increase rates.
   c. the Treasury Department issues more bonds.
   d. all of the above.
   e. a and b only.

## Answers

1. c
2. b
3. c
4. a
5. b

# CHAPTER 6

# National Federation of Independent Businesses (NFIB) Small Business Economic Trends

The most underappreciated segment of the U.S. economy is that of the small business sector. Representing 99.7 percent of all employer firms, 98 percent of firms exporting goods, 64 percent of net new private-sector job creation, and 46 percent of private-sector employment, small businesses essentially have only one major economic indicator, the National Federation of Independent Business (NFIB) Optimism Index.

These powerful economic qualities make the goings on in this industry—as well as the expectations of its contributing members—some of the most meaningful and accurate forward-looking indicators available today. Each of the report's many indicators deserves a place in the economist or analyst toolkit.

The NFIB's report on small business economic trends began in the 1970s.

Surveys were initially conducted for reporting during the first month of the quarter. The NFIB adopted a monthly estimation in 1986. The number of survey responses for the first month of the quarter range from 1,500 to 2,500 businesses, while the monthly surveys between the quarterly average about 500 respondents.

Each month the Survey of Small and Independent Business Owners is released on the Tuesday of the week including the tenth day of the month at 6:00 a.m. ET.

Oddly, this series doesn't move the market as much as some of the government's economic releases. Perhaps equity analysts don't see the benefits of

133

observing reported trends in companies that are a fraction of the size that they are accustomed to following. But since small business activity impacts such a large and diverse amount of the economy, the dozens of components in this monthly report should be scrutinized and considered in the determination of the current and forward-looking economic outlook. On a scale of importance, this series should be rated high, as it is considerably more significant to understanding the underlying tone of the economy than a measure of manufacturing activity, which accounts for only 15 to 20 percent of the economy. It may be more accurate than some of the more volatile measures like durable goods or high frequency initial claims.

An extensive commentary by the NFIB chief economist William Dunkelburg accompanies each monthly release. The comments and analysis are quite colorful and always insightful.

Definitions of a *small business* vary, depending on the source. The NFIB claims that its typical member employs five people and reports median gross sales of about $350,000 annually, and that these figures closely resemble the national small employer profile. The Small Business Association—a U.S. government agency created in the 1950s and not related to the NFIB—has several definitions depending on industry, but its Office of Advocacy generally defines it as "an independent business having fewer than 500 employees."

## Composition

The NFIB's headline Small Business Optimism Index is estimated by utilizing responses to 10 of the key survey indicators:

1. Plans to increase employment
2. Plans to make capital expenditures
3. Plans to increase inventories
4. Expectations of economy to improve
5. Expectations of real sales to improve
6. Current inventory
7. Current job openings
8. Expectations of credit conditions
9. Now a good time to expand
10. Earnings trends

Optimism on the small business level is critical in the determination of the direction of the U.S. economy for several reasons.

Economic trends may first be identified in the NFIB data. Smaller institutions can make quicker decisions and react to changes in the business climate than their larger counterparts. At the first sign of higher prices, greater demand, softer sales, or any turn in the outlook, the smaller, independent business can identify and adjust their strategy and implement their plan expeditiously.

Big, multinational corporations usually have a great deal of red tape to struggle with before hiring, raising prices on their goods or services, or committing funds to projects or expansion. An airline can't quickly slash capacity by cutting flights and idling planes if the economy sours; government regulations and unions impede many of those decisions. Similarly, if the economy is advancing and a business would like to expand operations, some companies may have to get approval from a board of directors or investors. Smaller businesses traditionally aren't as formal.

Also, small businesses provide a perspective to the overall economic landscape since they tend to engage in some interaction of commerce with larger businesses—as well as those their own size.

## The Business Cycle and the Headline NFIB Index

The headline Small Business Optimism Index has an excellent history predicting business cycle turning points. It also possesses a solid correlation with trends of many top-tier indicators. It should come as no surprise that when a signal is sent from this group of indicators, Wall Street economists take great attention and start to look for other signs of economic turning points in this data series as well as others.

A reading of 95–96 seems to be the level at which concerns are first signaled, with recession forming soon after those levels are breached (Exhibit 6.1). At the onset of the last five recessions in the United States, the average level of the Optimism Index was 96.22 (the first month). The average level registered during the last five recessions was 93.2. Clearly, it doesn't take a sizable slump for the headline NFIB Index to make meaningful waves in the determination of economic cycles.

It's clear how weak the small business sector had been in the aftermath of the 2007–2009 depression with the optimism index remaining below that 95.0 level for several years.

The relationship between the small business sector and the overall economy may better be appreciated by charting the Optimism Index against the Conference Board Coincident Economic Index (CEI). Expansions continue (increasing values in the CEI) as long as the NFIB Optimism Index is above 95–96. Levels above 100 are generally associated with very strong and solid expansions in the U.S. economy (Exhibit 6.2).

One notable trend of the headline index was the string of sub-96 readings after the 2007–2009 depression. Notice how the economic growth rate in the overall economy advanced despite the despondent attitudes registered in the small business sector.

136

**EXHIBIT 6.1** NFIB Optimism Index with Recessions

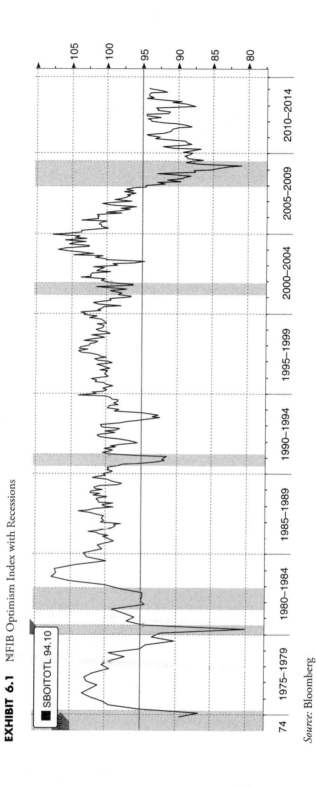

*Source:* Bloomberg

**EXHIBIT 6.2** NFIB Optimism Index versus Index of Coincident Indicators

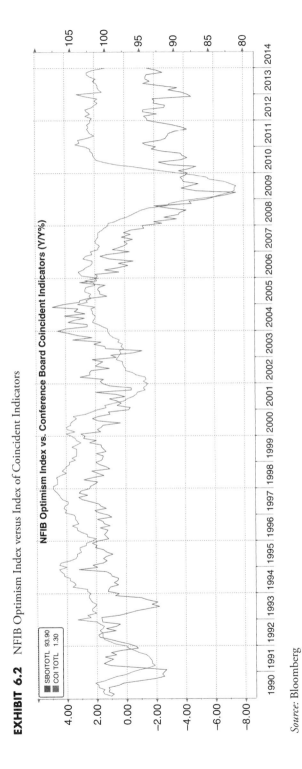

*Source:* Bloomberg

137

This could be explained by the bifurcated economy. Larger firms received the attention of policy makers in the initial stage of the crisis and therefore carried the economy, while smaller businesses—at least early in the recovery process—were denied access to credit; or they had little-to-no incentive to borrow since their businesses were decimated by the severe economic contraction and associated credit crisis. Why would these companies bother expanding operations if activity was dead? The construction, retail, finance, and manufacturing industries struggled greatly when the economy first emerged from the deep, prolonged downturn. This toil was experienced by a greater degree among small business than their larger counterparts.

## The Crucial Indicator: Hiring Intentions

One of the more popular and widely followed indicators from the NFIB Survey is its Hiring Plans Index. This figure represents the net percent of "increase" responses minus the "decrease" expectations regarding hiring plans over the next three months (Exhibit 6.3). The association with the Labor Department's unemployment rate is rather strong. Economists on the Street use the NFIB Hiring Plans Index in many of their forecasting models for employment, confidence, and overall economic conditions.

This strong relationship may be a function of the data source of the unemployment rate, which is the *Household Survey*. This is estimated by making phone calls to households and asking questions regarding employment status. Since this is a more personal, grassroots-oriented process than the alternative *Establishment Survey*, which entails asking business establishments to submit information regarding the number of employed persons on their books, the results are more likely to resemble the goings on in the small business arena.

It appears as if a recession is signaled when the Hires Index falls below a reading of 10.

Other employment-related measures in the NFIB Survey include Job Openings, Actual Employment Changes, and Qualified Applicants for Job Openings. These measures tend to provide insight into the health of the labor market, rather than predict or project the direction of employment.

According to the Small Business Association, from 1993 to 2011, 11.8 million of the 18.5 million net new jobs, or 64 percent, were jobs created by small businesses. Since this is such a sizeable share, and employment is the most important of all indicators, the NFIB Hiring Index is considered the *crucial indicator of this entire survey*.

## Small Business Investment Spending

The decision to invest in new plants, factories, or even to add new equipment is a function of many variables: Are economic conditions currently solid? What is the

**EXHIBIT 6.3** NFIB Hiring Plans Index versus Unemployment Rate

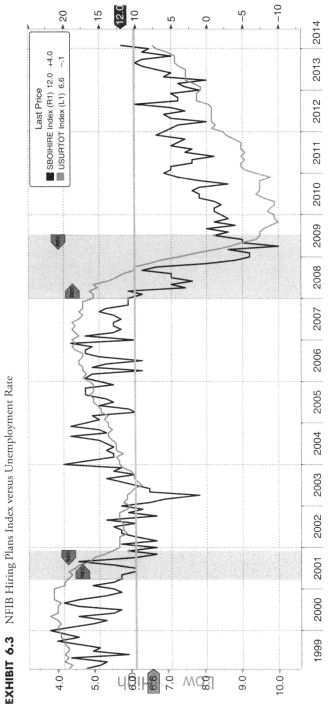

*Source:* Bloomberg

outlook for growth? Is it expected to advance at a solid pace in the next couple of months or years, or are there disconcerting issues looming? Will there be enough business coming through the door to justify my capital expenditures? Are interest rates at appropriate levels? Do I really need to make such a large investment? These are just a few of the dozens of questions business owners must ask themselves prior to committing funds to these particular projects.

In order for a businessperson to invest, they had better have the right responses to these and several other questions. They must also be assured of their expectations. Only when they are confident that their actions will give a desirable return on their investment will they move forward and commit those funds. That is why Capital Expenditures Plans is such a wonderful indicator. If the outlook is bleak or less than positive, then businesses will not invest. If expectations are bright, an upbeat assessment should be projected, especially for business equipment and services spending.

In Exhibit 6.4, we compare the NFIB's Small Businesses Capital Expenditure Plans Index against the year-over-year change in U.S. nonresidential fixed investment, and one of its major sub-components, business equipment spending. There is obviously a solid correlation, especially when economic conditions flourish as they did from 2002 through 2006. In 2007, the Index began to slide, and investment measures followed in time.

The two series diverge in early 2009, as capital spending in the U.S. escalated and small business intentions to invest remained at or below those levels traditionally associated with recession. This had a great deal to do with the ability to access funds.

Financing is crucial to the proper functioning of trade and commerce for any company, but more so for those in the small business sector. Large, multinational publicly traded corporations like Macy's, Coca-Cola, and Wal-Mart have easier access to the capital markets. They can issue equity-backed securities or long-term debt. Small businesses don't have that luxury.

And since the credit crisis of 2007–2009, many small firms have suffered from the inability to borrow. Anecdotal reports of small retailers financing operations and inventories using personal credit cards—amid lofty interest rates—were commonplace.

Unfortunately, it appears as if enacted policies had little influence on the small business community. In the Monetary Policy Report of February 26, 2013, the Federal Reserve noted, "Borrowing conditions for small businesses continued to improve over the second half of 2012, but as has been the case in recent years, the improvement was more gradual than for larger firms. Moreover, the demand for credit from small firms apparently remained subdued." This might be either a function of banks unwilling to lend to an historically riskier, less solid borrower, or smaller businesses not willing to take on debt that might not be able to be repaid.

**EXHIBIT 6.4** NFIB Small Businesses Capital Expenditure Plans Index versus Non-residential Fixed Investment

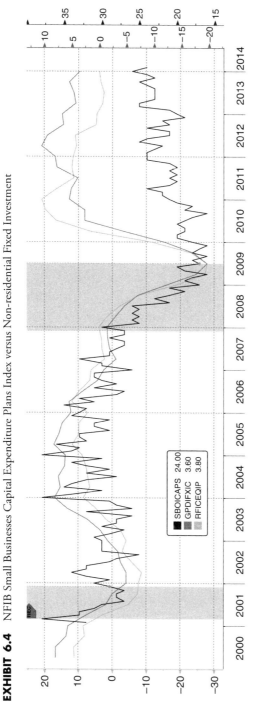

*Source:* Bloomberg

141

A similar measure to the Capital Expenditures Index is the NFIB's Good Time to Invest Index (Exhibit 6.5). Knowing whether conditions and underlying economic fundamentals are conducive to expansion is critical for those studying the overall pace of economic activity, or determining the state of affairs for new business formation and start-ups. This has always been a favorite indicator. What could be more telling than the confidence level that the economic drivers of the economy, small businesses, have regarding the desire to expand their businesses.

Since this series has an expectations element, it assumes a bit of a leading quality. In fact, prior to each of the last two recessions, the Good Time to Expand Index fell, on average, 12 months before the initial downturn in the economy. The warning signal in this series seems to be flashed when the Index hits 14.0.

Readings below 14.0 are often associated with troubling times for the small business sector and, unsurprisingly, the overall macroeconomy. The year-over-year growth rate in real GDP is about 2.0 percent when the Good Time to Expand Index approaches 15.0, which is often a recession signal. With one exception since 1948, when the four-quarter change in real GDP slips below 2.0 percent, the economy eventually has fallen into recession.

In 2003, the Index plunged to 7 yet no recession ensued. Many economists on the Street had expected a so-called *double-dip recession* since many indicators had fallen to levels traditionally associated with an economic downturn.

In early 2007, the Good Time to Expand Index fell from 18.0 to 12.0, then nine months later, the U.S. economy entered depression.

## The Outlook Index and the Economic Performance

The NFIB Outlook for General Business Conditions Index may be the least foretelling index for overall macroeconomic conditions in this otherwise valuable set of economic barometers. There appears to be few predictive abilities regarding U.S. recessions or recovery phases. Steep declines as in 1992–1993, 2003, 2005, 2011, and 2012 called for possible declines in economic output, but were unanswered as the economy expanded for several years after each signal of weakness projected by the Outlook for Business Conditions Index (Exhibit 6.6).

It is more likely that issues centric to the small business sector were less favorable and therefore resulted in these lowly readings.

There is little doubt that the 20-plus-point collapse in the Business Outlook Index in mid-2012 was related to the uncertainties surrounding the Affordable Care Act, which imposed a penalty on all businesses (with 50 or more people working 30 or more hours per week) that didn't offer employees health care insurance. Commentary included in the NFIB monthly reports confirmed these fears.

**EXHIBIT 6.5** NFIB Good Time to Invest Index versus GDP Y/Y%

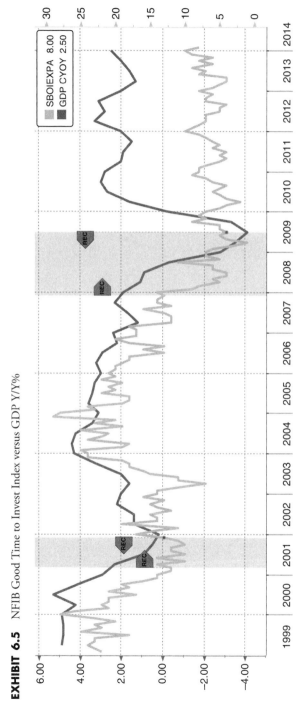

*Source:* Bloomberg

143

**EXHIBIT 6.6** NFIB Outlook for General Business Conditions Index *versus* Coincident Economic Indicator

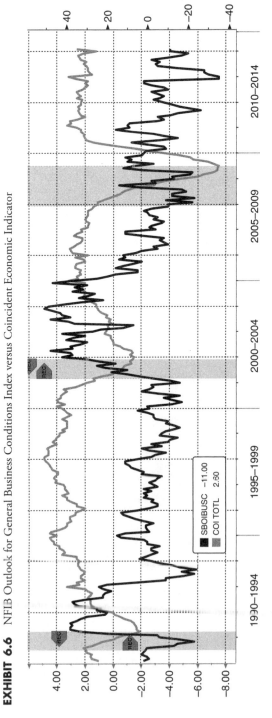

*Source:* Bloomberg

## The Credit Market and the Small Business Sector

The NFIB has a barometer that measures a small business's perspective on credit conditions. The Credit Conditions Availability of Loans Index is a measure of the net percent ("easier" minus "harder") responses regarding the credit environment compared to three months ago. Deeply negative readings (−16, −14, −12) suggest difficulty borrowing, while less negative values (−5, −6, −7) imply an easier ability to get financing. This closely parallels the trends in the Federal Reserve's Net Percent of Domestic Respondents Reporting Stronger Demand for Commercial and Industrial Loans from Small Firms (Exhibit 6.7).

These are excellent gauges regarding the desire for firms to borrow and banks' willingness to lend to the critical small business sector.

The general price level in the U.S. economy is closely correlated with the NFIB's Higher Price Index. Households and businesses (small and large) alike, possess a great ability to project the underlying rate of inflation. Since consumers are always and everywhere familiar with expenditures, the appreciation for costs is an everyday and often immediate occurrence.

## Small Businesses and Inflation

How many times do you hear people complaining about paying too much for food, clothing, or gasoline? Similarly, businesses can identify changes in prices since many of the goods and services they consume are similar. Energy prices, for example, are a considerable portion of a company and individual consumer's budget. Consumers are familiar with higher prices at the pump, or heating and electricity prices for their homes. Similarly, businesses must know transportation and shipping costs, as well as the price to heat and run air conditioning in their stores, warehouses, showrooms, and manufacturing facilities (Exhibit 6.8).

Expectations of sales matter a great deal to business health and the macro-economy. The NFIB Small Business Sales Expectations index is a measure of the net percent responses (that is "higher" minus "lower") regarding the outlook of sales during the next three months. Sales are the lifeblood of a business; poor sales growth can topple a company, while strong activity can turn a small business into a goliath. From small things, big things one day come.

During expansionary periods, the Sales Expectations Index lingers in the 10 to 30 range, with occasional breakouts of five points in either direction (Exhibit 6.9). But when times get tough, small businesses dramatically curtail their expectations, and the associated Index sinks to zero or lower. Sustained periods of depressed sales expectations could beget reduced staffing, lower rates of investment, and spending cuts. If deep enough, as in 2008–2009, a poor sales environment could force widespread store closures, bankruptcy filings, and general economic malaise.

**EXHIBIT 6.7** NFIB Credit Conditions Availability of Loans Index versus Net Percent of Domestic Respondents Reporting Stronger Demand for Commercial and Industrial Loans from Small Firms

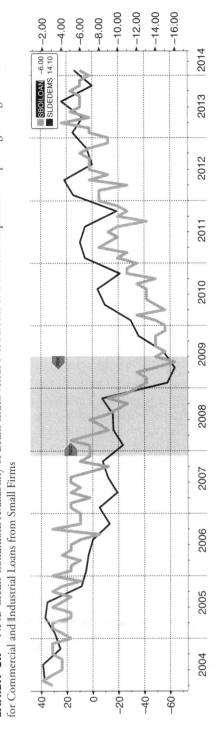

*Source:* Bloomberg

**EXHIBIT 6.8** NFIB Higher Price Index versus CPI Y/Y%

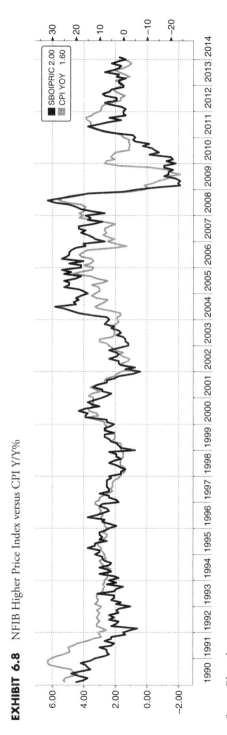

*Source:* Bloomberg

147

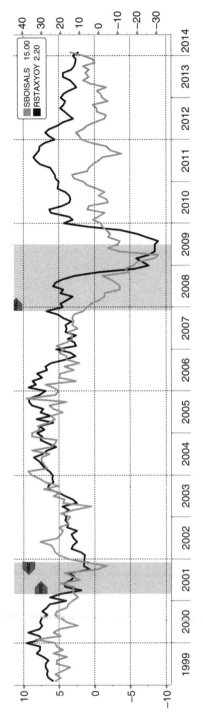

**EXHIBIT 6.9** NFB Sales Expectations Index versus Retail Sales Excluding Autos

*Source:* Bloomberg

The Sales Expectations Index is closely related to the 12-month trend in the Commerce Department's retail sales excluding autos. This is an excellent gauge of activity since so much of U.S. output is predicated on the consumer and the associated level of expenditures.

The NFIB's Actual Earnings Changes Index draws a solid relationship to the year-over-year change in personal income. Since both measures are related—earnings are essentially incomes—the Actual Incomes Index is a nice proxy for the viability and health of the small business sector (Exhibit 6.10). Just as incomes are necessary to facilitate trade and buoy spending, companies need actual earnings to advance their businesses via capital spending, hiring, and investment. The greater the amount of earnings, the more options the company has—whether that is for reinvestment into the business or distribution of profits to investors.

The NFIB also includes a table identifying respondents' thoughts of the most important reason for lower earnings, including "sales volume," "increased costs," "cut selling prices," "usual seasonal change," and "other."

Unsurprisingly, there is little difference between the small business confidence measures and the consumer attitude surveys. Many small businesses are single proprietorships, Mom and Pop establishments, or very small companies. According to the June 2013 NFIB Small Business Economic Trends Report, 10 percent of the companies participating in the survey had one employee, and 9 percent had two workers. Some 22 percent had three to five full- and part-time employees. Cumulatively, that's a bit more than 40 percent of the survey represented by companies with five or fewer workers.

Since small businesses are the closest to Main Street, we should expect views to be very similar to those of individuals. Exhibit 6.11 identifies the solid historical relationship between the University of Michigan's Consumer Sentiment Index and the NFIB's Optimism Index.

Both measures slide about a month or two before economic downturns, and emerge from recession about midway through the slump.

The signal for recession appears to be a level of 95.0 in the NFIB Small Business Optimism Index, which is associated with an 85.0 reading in the University of Michigan's Consumer Sentiment Index.

When you are feeling sick, the first question the doctor asks is: What's ailing you? It's a wise starting point for diagnosis and subsequently treatment. The NFIB asks its members a similar question: "What is the single most important problem facing your business today?" (Exhibit 6.12).

Rather than simply focus on a point estimate of sentiment, we can find out why the small business sector is not feeling too optimistic. With this knowledge, policy makers may prescribe policies to correct for the ailments, much like the doctor does. If inflation is the top issue, then the Federal Reserve knows it should adopt a more restrictive stance and combat rising prices.

**EXHIBIT 6.10** NFIB Actual Earnings Changes Index versus Actual Incomes Index

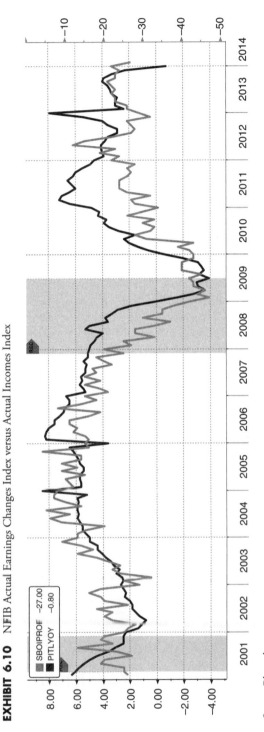

*Source:* Bloomberg

**EXHIBIT 6.11** NFIB Optimism Index versus University of Michigan Consumer Sentiment Index

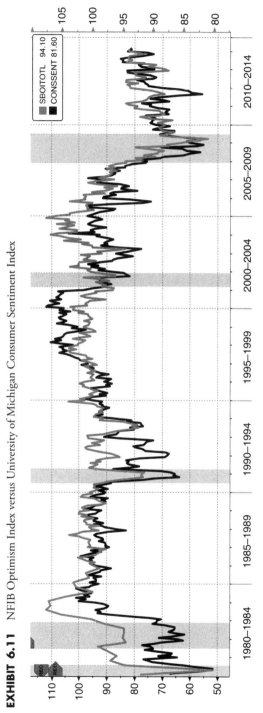

*Source:* Bloomberg

**EXHIBIT 6.12** NFIB Single Most Important Problem

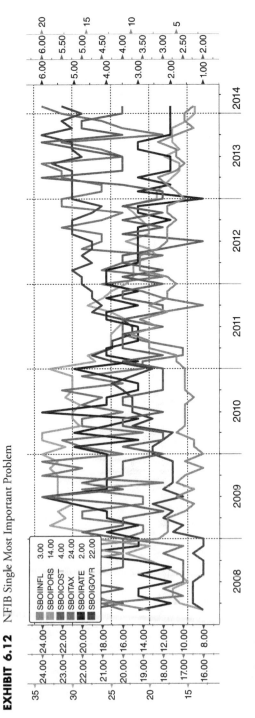

*Source:* Bloomberg

152

If interest rates are too high, then the central bank might want to consider reducing its overnight borrowing target rate.

Taxes always appear high on the worry list of the smaller business community—does anybody really want to pay taxes? This could be addressed by the federal, state, or local governments. (Investors are encouraged not to hold their breath too long for this solution.) Similarly, government regulations and red tape has climbed in importance over the last several years to be the top issue plaguing the small business sector. Again, our elected officials have sway over this issue. In fact, throughout most of 2012 and 2013, the top problem was either taxes or regulation. In other words, the government was considered to be the greatest obstacle to the recovery effort.

The NFIB's Small Optimism Index had enjoyed a very solid relationship with the top-tier manufacturing measures, industrial production and the Institute for Supply Management's (ISM) Purchasing Managers Index (PMI).

The relationship was considerably stronger prior to the 2007–2009 depression (Exhibit 6.13). Several reasons may explain the divergence: financing for the larger manufacturers was a priority during the credit crisis in 2008–2009. The financial markets were freezing up, and the Federal Reserve and Treasury Department's efforts were undoubtedly directed toward the biggest corporations, particularly those like General Electric, AT&T, Deere & Co, and International Business Machines. These multinational behemoths have extensive financing arms that were severely pressured, and it was believed that the financial system couldn't withstand a collapse of the money markets, including the commercial paper market, which these and many others contributed.

The July 2013 NFIB Small Business Economic Trends report found a mere 11 percent of respondents in the manufacturing industry. While this is a small representation, keep in mind that many businesses depend on, yet are indirectly related to, the manufacturing sector like retail, agriculture, financial services, and materials.

## Shortcomings

There aren't many disconcerting issues about the NFIB survey and its various components. This series is a sentiment index, so surveyed individuals may be upset or upbeat for any number of noneconomic reasons. Economists like to look at the indicators that actually measure stuff—like sales, hiring, and output.

The NFIB Indexes didn't forecast the 2001 recession in a timely matter as the headline index ranged from the mid-90s to 100 prior to the downturn. In defense of the survey, this downturn was a business equipment slump—an overbloated telecom equipment and business investment correction. It was not a not a consumer-driven recession, which the small business sector closely resembles. It was essentially the bursting of the dot.com bubble, which really

**EXHIBIT 6.13** NFIB Small Optimism Index versus Industrial Production versus ISM's Purchasing Manager's Index

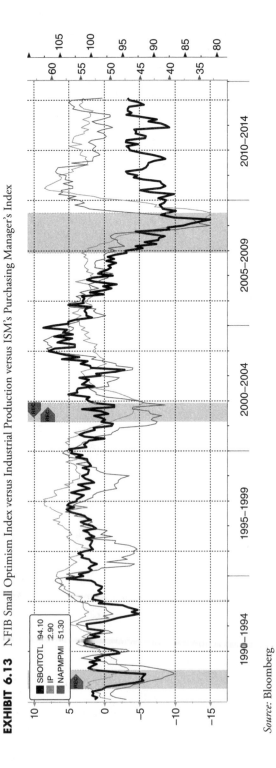

*Source:* Bloomberg

impacted those businesses that overinvested in Y2K buildup and associated technologies. And since most economic measures failed to predict the slump, we should give this a pass, too.

## Related Measures

There are no comprehensive and widely recognized measures of small business economic activity in use today that are better than the NFIB Survey. Any of the alternative indicators are decades shy of a meaningful history and have not yet been accepted by the Street.

The Federal Reserve Bank of Atlanta has a quarterly Small Business Survey that polls organizations (mostly area Chambers of Commerce, business alliances, economic development authorities, etc.) in its district (Florida, Alabama, Georgia, Louisiana, Mississippi, and Tennessee).

While this is a trusted source, the Federal Reserve, there are limits including limited geography and a history that dates back to 2010. It would be helpful if all the regional Fed banks followed this trend and established similar studies.

Wells Fargo/Gallup has a quarterly survey that appears to have commenced in the third quarter of 2004, which is encouraging since it has a history that experiences an economic downturn. Many of the questions deal with availability of credit, cash flow, and the company's financial situation.

## Test Yourself

Answer the following multiple-choice questions:

1. The U.S. Small Business Administration (SBA) estimates that:
   a. all small businesses have 99.7 percent of the profits.
   b. small businesses employ 99.7 percent of workforce.
   c. 99.7 percent of all employer firms are small businesses.
   d. 99.7 percent of all small businesses fail within the first year.
   e. none of the above.

2. Small business optimism closely mimics trends in consumer confidence because:
   a. small businesses are often sole proprietorships.
   b. the NFIB asks the same people the same questions that are asked by the Conference Board.
   c. consumers always have similar beliefs as business people do.
   d. all of the above.
   e. a and b only.

3. According to the Small Business Association, a small business usually employs:
   a. only 1 to 49 workers.
   b. between 50 and 100 full-time workers.
   c. 25 or fewer workers.
   d. 500 or fewer workers.
   e. none of the above.

4. Watching the NFIB'S Capital Expenditure Index gives us a clear reading into the future of the economy since:
   a. it always predicts financial crises.
   b. it tells us when companies need to raise capital spending.
   c. businesses need to feel confident with the economic outlook before investing capital.
   d. all of the above.
   e. a and b only.

5. Households and businesses possess an ability to appreciate the underlying inflation rate since:
   a. they frequently make purchases.
   b. prices rarely ever change.
   c. small businesses always know how much they will charge consumers.
   d. all of the above.
   e. a and b only.

## Answers

1. c
2. a
3. d
4. c
5. a

# CHAPTER 7

# Personal Income and Outlays

Incomes are the lifeblood of the U.S. economy, facilitating consumption expenditure, which, in turn, maintains the growth rate in output, engendering job creation and the promotion of the business cycle. When income growth is curtailed by a pay cut, higher inflation, or the loss of a job, serious negative economic consequences ensue; confidence deteriorates, spending slows, businesses reduce staff, and the economy often finds itself in recession. Watch the trends in the various measures of the monthly Personal Income and Outlays report, produced by the Bureau of Economic Analysis (BEA), it'll provide the best assessment of the U.S. consumer and economic landscape.

The BEA uses the spending data in this monthly report to compile the consumption expenditures portion of the quarterly GDP report. Consumer expenditures, as noted in Chapter 3, account for about 72 percent of all economic activity so it matters what the data look like. The income data, meanwhile, are used in the estimation of the income approach to measuring the economy's health. It provides insight into future spending and thus future economic activity.

The report is released about four weeks after the record month, on the first business day following the release of the gross domestic product (GDP) data, at 8:30 a.m. ET. For example, data for May will be released in late June, the day following the final GDP report. To some extent, this somewhat "dated" release is the least appealing quality of the report. But considering the critical nature of its contents, it's worth the wait.

Technically, both incomes and spending are considered coincidental indicators—that is they move in sync with the business cycle.

The Conference Board uses personal incomes less transfer payments in its Coincident Economic Index (Exhibit 7.1). However, conceptually it is easy to

158

**EXHIBIT 7.1** Personal Incomes

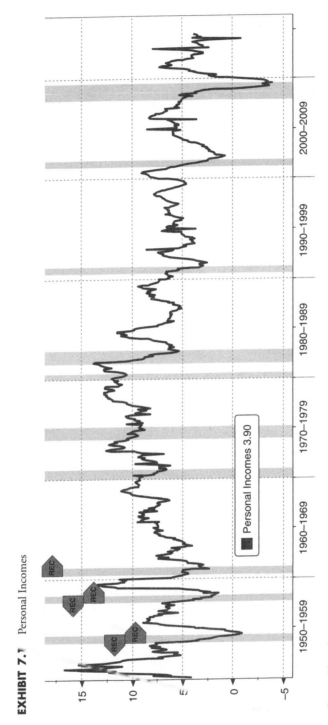

*Source:* Bloomberg

appreciate how rising incomes today will boost economic activity down the road. Ideally workers receive greater incomes influenced by lower taxes and inflation for a sustained period of time. In the event that conditions don't sour, and the underlying situation remains upbeat, consumers will spend. And when they spend—especially on nonnecessities—then the economy tends to advance. Conversely, if income growth is weak, or begins to stagnate, then consumers become apprehensive and tend to withdraw from more discretionary spending, limiting purchases to necessities like food, shelter, rent, and energy (electricity, gas, fuel, etc.).

We will see later in the chapter how detail in the consumer expenditures category can help investors and economists identify possible periods of strength or weakness.

The two top attention-getters from the income and spending report are the monthly percentage changes in nominal personal income and nominal personal consumption expenditures. This is odd since economists rarely, if ever, focus on nominal (non-inflation-adjusted) data. Since the Street is in a never-ending pursuit to forecast real GDP, the two most important gauges are real personal income and real spending, not the nominal figures that the business press likes to cite.

## Personal Income

The BEA calculates personal income by adding together income from several major sources and then subtracting personal contributions for government social insurance (Exhibit 7.2). The largest income source is wages and salaries, which accounts for about 50.6 percent of the total. The BEA obtains data for this category from Internal Revenue Service (IRS) reports. Supplements to wages and salaries, which includes employer contributions to pension and insurance funds, is about 12 percent. Transfer receipts—government disbursements such as Social Security payments, veterans' benefits, and food stamps—usually constitute about 17 percent of total income. The Social Security Administration and the Bureau of Labor Statistics supply the data for this category. The remaining 30 percent or so of total monthly income comes from personal income receipts on assets (interest and dividend income), which contributes 14 percent; proprietors' income, 9 percent; and rental income, 4 percent. (The actual percentages vary somewhat from month to month but remain relatively close to the aforementioned levels.)

By subtracting contributions for government social insurance and personal current taxes, as well as payments such as donations, fees, and fines from personal income, which total about 8 percent, you get the total level of personal income.

The financial media tend to pay less attention to income than to expenditures data. You are more likely to hear a business journalist comment on the monthly increase in services spending, for example, than on an unexpected gain in dividend

**EXHIBIT 7.2**   Calculating Total Level of Personal Income

|  | May 2014 in billions $ | Percent of Total |
| --- | --- | --- |
| Personal Income | $14,587.30 | |
| Wages & Salaries | $7,380.50 | 50.6% |
| Supplements to wages & salaries | $1,759.90 | 12.1% |
| Proprietors' income w/inventory and capital consumption adj. | $1,373.90 | 9.4% |
| Rental incomes of persons | $620.50 | 4.3% |
| Personal income receipts on assets | $2,069.20 | 14.2% |
| Personal current transfer receipts | $2,529.60 | 17.3% |
| | $15,733.60 | 107.9% |
| Less: Contributions for government social insurance … | $1,146.30 | 7.9% |
| Personal Income | $14,587.30 | **100.0%** |

income. The reason for this lack of interest is most likely due to the indirect effect of income on the economy. Income doesn't always have to be spent—it may be saved. Conversely, the spending data are quite telling about what consumers are actually doing with their income. Basically, spending data are simply sexier than the income data.

Another reason for the preference of expenditures data over income data is that stock market traders can directly determine what consumers are spending on. A surge in motor vehicle spending tells investors that the automakers are probably going to be performing better as a group. The income data don't provide market traders with such detailed information. That doesn't mean personal income data are less meaningful, however. On the contrary, they provide important insights into the financial health of consumers, a group that, as we have seen, has tremendous impact on all sectors of the economy.

By analyzing those details and the relationships between the personal income and expenditure figures, economists and investors are able to identify possible turning points and developing trends in the economy.

Real disposable personal incomes are simply incomes adjusted for taxes and inflation. It is in essence what is available for consumers to spend (or save), so it is generally considered a more useful measure of potential spending power. There is a close correlation between this indicator and real GDP.

Because some level of income is necessary for all economic activity, trends in income growth should theoretically permit inferences about future spending patterns—a leading measure. Unfortunately, theory doesn't always mesh with reality. As the chart in Exhibit 7.3 illustrates, real disposable personal income tends to move in sync with, rather than lead, consumer expenditures.

One reason for this synchronicity is that wages and salaries tend to get spent rather quickly. Some people live paycheck to paycheck, spending their earnings immediately and saving smaller and smaller amounts. In addition, personal income includes not only wages and salaries but also dividend and interest income and transfer payments, such as health insurance and unemployment benefits. These crucial disbursements of unemployment benefits are generally spent immediately on basic necessities, such as food and rent.

Because these payments are spent on necessities rather than on durable goods and services, they have relatively little influence on month-to-month changes in the macroeconomy.

## Personal Consumption Expenditures

The BEA defines personal consumption expenditures as the goods and services individuals buy, the operating expenses of not-for-profit institutions serving individuals, and the value of food, fuel, clothing, rentals, and financial services that individuals receive in kind. The primary source for these data is the Census Bureau's monthly retail sales report.

The relationship between real disposable personal income per capita and real consumer spending is presented in Exhibit 7.4. While the growth rate in per capita real disposable personal incomes is very volatile, there is definitively a solid relationship between the two. There are numerous reasons for this volatility; spikes may occur when companies announce large dividends or when the government provides assistance in a massive scale such as issuing transfer payments like food stamps or extending unemployment benefit programs.

The largest portion of consumer expenditures, accounting for 66.5 percent of the total as of mid-2014, is for services (Exhibit 7.5). The U.S. economy is service dominated. Approximately 80 percent of all workers in the United States are employed in a service profession. U.S. consumers spend incredible amounts on insurance, repair, transportation, investment advice, and medical care. Legal services are involved in virtually every aspect of American life, from buying a home to getting a divorce to writing a will. Other service expenditures include school tuition and spending on hotel and motel accommodations, sporting and theater events, and telephone and cable television services.

The second largest category, representing roughly 22.5 percent of total expenditures, is spending on nondurable goods. Nondurable goods are products with relatively short life spans. They are divided into four major groups: food; clothing and shoes; gasoline, fuel oil, and other energy goods; and the catchall "other," which encompasses products such as perfumes, cleaning preparations, film, and greeting cards.

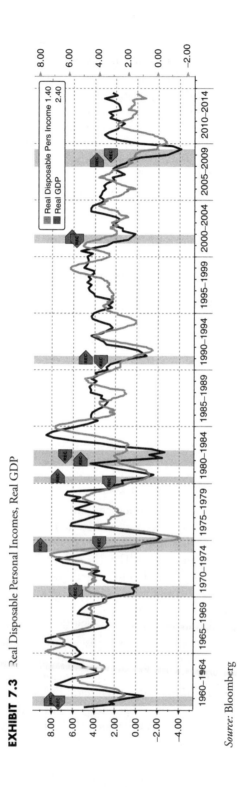

**EXHIBIT 7.3** Real Disposable Personal Incomes, Real GDP

*Source:* Bloomberg

162

**EXHIBIT 7.4** Real Disposable Personal Income per Capita, Real Consumer Spending

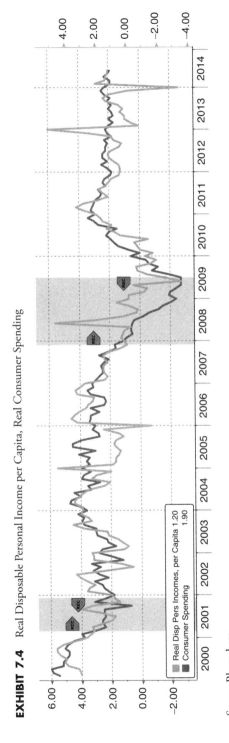

*Source:* Bloomberg

163

**EXHIBIT 7.5** Composition of Consumer Spending

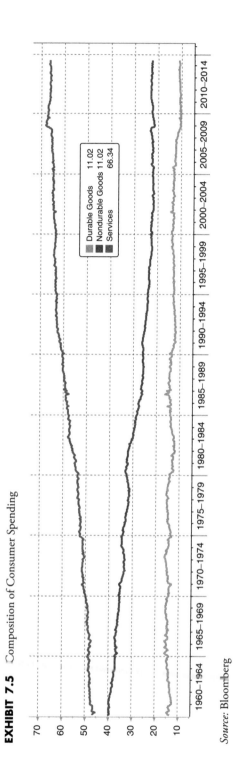

| Durable Goods | 11.02 |
| Nondurable Goods | 11.02 |
| Services | 66.34 |

*Source:* Bloomberg

Durable goods account for the remaining 11 percent of expenditures, are those intended to last a minimum of three years, and include automobiles, refrigerators, washing machines, televisions, furniture, and other big-ticket items, such as jewelry, sporting equipment, and guns. Because durables are expensive and (because of their "durability") are purchased infrequently, spending on these items as a percentage of total expenditures can vary considerably from month to month.

The connection between consumer expenditures and economic growth has already been well established. But not all spending is equally revealing of economic trends. Spending on nondurable goods such as food and home-heating fuel tends to be fairly constant, remaining positive even in trying economic times. In contrast, spending on durable goods, which are relatively expensive and long-lived, requires good economic conditions to flourish. In less flush times, consumers aren't going to head out to buy stereos, furniture, or new china. Therefore, of all the subcomponents in the Personal Incomes and Outlays report, durable goods spending might be considered the most effective in calling turning points in the economy.

Exhibit 7.6 illustrates the incredibly tight relationship between the growth rate of nonfarm jobs and the rate of consumer spending. This occurs for several reasons, but the two most obvious that come to mind include incomes and confidence. If you are gainfully employed, you receive a wage or a salary, granting you the wherewithal to spend. Also, if you have a job—more likely than not—you are upbeat and confident, so you are more likely to make purchases of goods and services.

Therefore, you can see that when the pace of job creation is advancing or sustained at a better than 2 percent pace, consumers tend to spend at a better than 5 percent pace (nominal dollars, noninflation adjusted). Of course, any time that nonfarm payrolls begin to slide, so too does spending. And if that pace in spending is precipitous, then the economy often finds itself in recession. Notice how the declines in payrolls and nominal spending are equal in magnitude.

Knowing that the level of employment is critical in the determination of spending, investors should always keep an eye on the pace of job creation. The stronger the rate of growth in employment, the stronger the pace of spending will be. Knowing what consumers are spending their incomes and salaries on can be a very telling indicator of current economic conditions, and may ultimately help forecast GDP.

## The Fab Five Indicators of Discretionary Spending

To be sure, there is no Holy Grail of economic indicators. Every economic statistic possesses flaws—some more than others. After decades, even centuries, of study and analysis of tens of thousands of indicators, the true gem of economic prediction would have been discovered by now . . . but it has not.

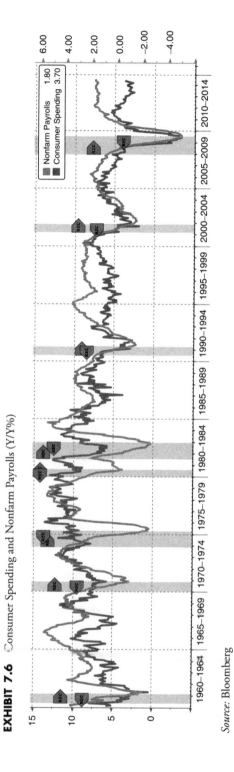

**EXHIBIT 7.6** Consumer Spending and Nonfarm Payrolls (Y/Y%)

*Source:* Bloomberg

I have identified the following five indicators as some of the most economically meaningful barometers, which I have dubbed over the last 20 years as the "Fab Five."

These are discretionary goods and services; that is, they are not likely to be consumed when economic conditions are deteriorating. Even these insightful measures are not without flaws. But when you look at the trends of these indicators collectively, and employ the commentaries of C-suite executives for the associated industries, you get a very powerful predictor of economic conditions.

When the going gets tough economically, the last place a disheartened consumer heads is to a restaurant. This notion makes dining out one of the best indicators to watch when forecasting the underlying strength of the U.S. consumer, and subsequently associated economic activity.

Imagine if there were layoff announcements at work or word of a few close friends or relatives having been recently laid-off. There's no doubt that those fears would somewhat take a toll on your thoughts regarding the economy. It would obviously hit home if you or a spouse lost your job. Either way, any of these events would influence your spending actions.

If you are remotely concerned with your employment situation, or the near-term prospects of hiring, you would not gather up the family and run off to the Cheesecake Factory.

Restaurateurs appreciate the underlying state of economic affairs in their businesses decisions. When consumers are less confident, whether due to an uncertain hiring climate, a period of weak income or salary growth, a higher inflationary environment, or just the stresses of a slower-paced economy, the consumer will become hesitant to frequent a dining establishment (Exhibit 7.7). Nearly every company in this industry will make mention of economic conditions affecting the household during their quarterly earnings conference calls. In fact, comments regarding the price of gasoline are the rule, not the exception when discussing their results—some will even mention the degree that higher prices at the pump reduced their earnings.

If conditions are truly bad, some restaurants might offer promotions in the form of discounts or coupons.

Inflation is an economic condition that can be very problematic to a restaurant. If the price of beef were to escalate for some reason (shortages, disease, etc.) then companies that offer beef products will need to make the adjustment to the menu either in the form of passing the higher price along or by reducing the size of the product. Rather than offer a 10-ounce hamburger, reduce it to 8 or 9 ounces. Any and all of these actions are adopted so as not to lose business, profitability, or possibly close stores. The sharp economist wants to know what exactly is driving (or not) the level of demand—prices, volumes, weather, or some other related issue.

Simply watching the trends of consumer expenditures on dining out or "meals at other eating places," as defined by the BEA, won't let you know ahead

168

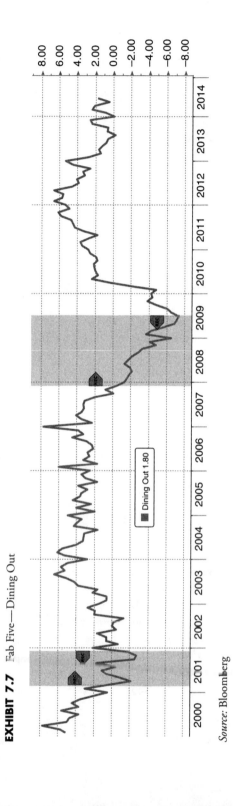

**EXHIBIT 7.7** Fab Five—Dining Out

*Source:* Bloomberg

of time if the consumer is ready to toss in the towel. Ultimately, you would want to know as soon as possible if the consumer is exhibiting signs of slowing. And since spending data are a little late in the data reporting cycle, you need to do a little extra homework.

This is best accomplished by reading the transcripts of restaurant companies. The Bloomberg Orange Book of CEO Comments has dozens of these businesses represented including the Cheesecake Factory, Ruth's Hospitality, Cracker Barrel, McDonald's, and Wendy's. Comments made by these executives will confirm, or refute, whether the data are sending erroneous signals.

Sometimes a decline in the trend of spending may not be a function of economic conditions. The weather can keep many consumers from visiting a restaurant. Snowstorms, floods, or heat waves can force store closures since personnel cannot get to those establishments to work even if consumers would be willing to brave the elements just to grab a dinner. This will only be announced in the conference calls, and not the data release.

Casino gambling is the second of the Fab Five indicators (Exhibit 7.8). This too makes sense; if you don't have the confidence that you'll be employed, you certainly won't head off to Las Vegas or Atlantic City. Only in Hollywood will they lead you to believe that a downtrodden, unemployed man found a quarter on the ground, placed it in a slot machine and won millions of dollars—that's not economic reality.

The fact is, if you are uneasy about your situation or the underlying economic environment, you look to cut discretionary spending—especially at casinos.

Again, simply observing the year-over-year trends is not enough to determine a change in overall consumer spending and the economy. This series tends to exhibit volatile fluctuations. Perhaps this is a function of data gathering and the various sources that are used in the estimation process. Nevertheless, contractions in the 12-month pace of spending tend to signal recessions.

Here, when we use anecdotes contained in the Bloomberg Orange Book of CEO Comments made by C-suite executives from related companies such as MGM Resorts International, Caesars Entertainment, Wynn Resorts, or Las Vegas Sands we may find certain influences in the data that may not be otherwise known. For example, several casinos reported elevated spending at U.S. establishments. However, a great portion of that was believed to have come from foreigners from 2009–2014. Some suggested that Chinese travelers were permitted to take more money out of the country than ever before, and many flocked to casinos as a tourist destination.

This welcomed activity—for company profits of the casinos and the tax revenues of the related regions—would not be a great representation of U.S. consumer spending conditions.

Unless you have a tremendous amount of money, you probably won't run out and buy a Rolex watch or a diamond tennis bracelet if the outlook is less than favorable. You certainly aren't buying a gold necklace if gold is lingering

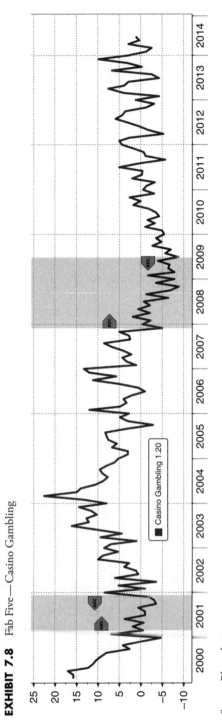

**EXHIBIT 7.8** Fab Five—Casino Gambling

*Source:* Bloomberg

around $1,500 an ounce. This makes keeping an eye on expenditures on jewelry and watches a relatively smart idea (Exhibit 7.9). Although this indicator has sent a few false signals in the recent past (early 2007, 2010–2011) it is a sound representative for the consumer's state of mind.

Consulting the Orange Book for this luxury group can provide incredible insight. The drawback of simply observing the data in this category is that we don't know if the consumer is spending on "bling" (high-valued baubles) or on costume jewelry comprised of beads, leather, or plastic lower-valued goods. Since we don't know, we may need to get the skinny from the companies themselves like Tiffany or Zale Corp. The larger department stores like Macy's, Dillard, JCPenney, or Nordstrom, will offer great insight that cannot be gleaned by solely looking at the data.

One interesting observation is that elevated spending on jewelry, particularly the high-end segment, is generally pretty solid, but this doesn't mean the economy is on solid ground and consumers on the whole are out ringing the cash registers on watches and rings.

During the 2007–2009 Great Recession, the income distribution in the United States bifurcated sharply between the "haves" (those at the higher end of the income spectrum) and the "have-nots" (those at the lower end). Truth be told, income inequality has always been an issue in America. This latest division was exacerbated by the severity of the economic downturn and the supplementing credit crisis. Countless consumers fell down a rung on the income scale. Many middle income earners fell to the lower end, while those at the lower end slipped into poverty. In fact, there were over 47 million people in the nation receiving food stamps. That occurred with a population of only 315 million persons.

The importance of knowing of this division is that merely looking at the data will tell you nothing about where it is being spent, and that matters.

Economists rarely look to the high end of the earnings spectrum to determine the health of the overall economy. As much as we would all like to be super-rich, this group doesn't drive economic activity. They contribute greatly, but the economy doesn't take off of deceleration solely with respect to this group's spending habits. If anything, there is a floor of growth they provide toward total output. At the same time, those at the lower end don't drive economic growth since they tend to spend on the most basic of necessities, occasionally making an aspirational purchase of a luxury or high-end discretionary purchase. There isn't much that a person in poverty can contribute to bolstering the economy—a family of four earning $21,000 a year is simply trying to make ends meet, not buy a Harry Winston necklace.

The Bloomberg Orange Book is an excellent approach to identify where and which income class is doing well and which is faring poorly; company executives frequently comment about visits by affluent purchasers or the lower-income sector. When the middle class shows signs of stagnancy, that's when the economy

**EXHIBIT 7.9** Fab Five—Jewelry and Watches

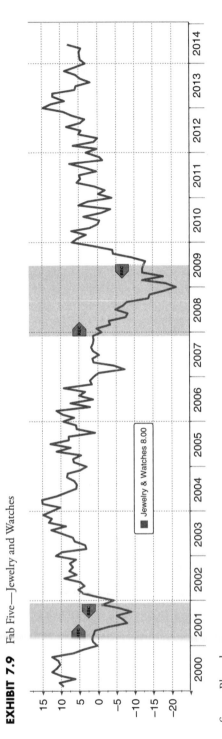

*Source:* Bloomberg

is headed for difficult times. That is the ultimate driver of spending in the United States.

Cosmetics have always played a role in the appreciation of the underlying tone of the economy (Exhibit 7.10). It used to be said that when times were tough, a woman would reduce the purchases of many other items, but never deny herself the luxury of a lipstick. This little extravagance went a long way in providing "retail therapy." For this reason, increased sales of lipsticks were often seen as a predictor of a bad economic climate.

During World War II, extravagances were virtually nonexistent. The war effort used all of the nylon for parachutes, and in order to simulate the appearance of a stocking, women would actually sketch a seam along the back of their leg with an eye pencil. It isn't clear than anybody ever followed eye pencil sales to determine the state of economic affairs; but it certainly suggests that consumers do make adjustments to their beauty aid and fashion-related purchases amid different economic conditions. The level of spending on cosmetics and perfumes had identified recessions in the recent past.

Today, cosmetics and perfumes are seen mostly as a necessity—the 75 million or so inhabitants of the boomer generation isn't getting any younger and possesses a seemingly neverending search of vanity. Sales trends of this category do a fine job at estimating economic downturns.

The last of the Fab Five is my all-time favorite quirky economic barometer, the ultimate Desert Island Indicator, women's dress sales (Exhibit 7.11). Yup, that's right; you tell me how sales of women's dresses are trending, and I'll tell you how the general pace of consumer spending is.

Don't get this confused with the *Hemline Index*, which claims that the length of a women's hemline is representative of market conditions. Higher hem lengths, like those in the 1960s, and the days of miniskirts resulted in stronger financial market performances. The Roaring 1920s was a great time for stocks, and flapper dresses were extremely short (particularly for the times), until of course the Great Crash in 1929. Hem lengths plunged, as did the stock market. Obviously there is no economics behind this "indicator."

Dress sales are different. The economics behind this is that women are traditionally the CFOs of the household. They pay the bills and are responsible for maintaining the operations of the home. They are far more cognizant of economic conditions than their male counterparts, driving kids to school (knowing gasoline prices), and placing food on the table (food costs).

When times get challenging, prices rise, and the climate turns a little darker, what does the CFO do? Make cuts.

Where does Mom make cuts? The kids' dance classes? Soccer, baseball, or piano lessons? No, none of these. She will reduce expenditures of a self-purchase before reducing expenditures on her family—that's why we love Mom. And there is no greater self-purchase for a woman than a dress.

**EXHIBIT 7.10** Fab Five—Cosmetics and Perfumes

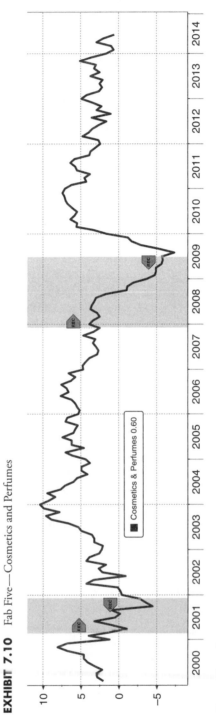

■ Cosmetics & Perfumes 0.60

*Source:* Bloomberg

**EXHIBIT 7.11** Fab Five—Women's and Girls' Clothing

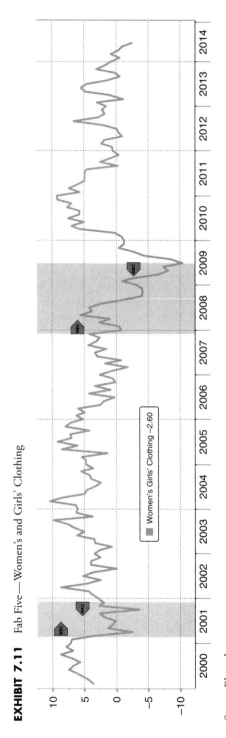

*Source:* Bloomberg

Since the closest component in the expenditures data is women's and girls' clothing, you need to consult the Bloomberg Orange Book to get the detail regarding dress sales. Department stores like Macy's, JCPenney, Nordstrom, or specialty apparel retailers like Ann Taylor, Express, New York & Co, bebe Stores, and so on often provide detail on dress sales.

Ultimately, women determine a good portion of expenditures—searches on the Internet cite studies that suggest they are responsible for upwards of 80 percent of all buying decisions—so it only makes sense to watch their spending habits.

## Government Transfer Payments

In response to the recent financial crisis and profound contraction in economic growth, fiscal policy makers bolstered incomes by expanding government spending on programs like unemployment benefit insurance and the Supplemental Nutrition Assistance Program (food stamps). In addition, reduced taxes helped stabilize softening incomes. These deficit-mounting factors propped up the level of real disposable incomes.

Today, America's economic dependency on the government is more than twice as high as it was over four decades ago. Transfer payments as a percentage of disposable personal incomes are lingering around 20 percent compared to 9 percent in 1970 (Exhibit 7.12). Clearly, this is uncomfortable territory. Whether you agree or disagree with this level of assistance, adding to it or reducing it will ultimately carry major economic consequences—either choice is not very favorable.

Our fiscal policy makers will need to address this since we cannot kick the can down the road forever. Think about what would happen to incomes, spending, and subsequently aggregate demand if and when the government adopts a more restrictive stance in order to cut the deficit and roll up those measures. Or what happens if we continue to extend programs and spending? Another legitimate concern is, could the economy—in a fragile state—withstand a sharp reduction in the level of real disposable personal incomes?

As Tom Petty would say, "There ain't no easy way out." But the warning signs will assuredly surface first in the monthly personal incomes and outlays report.

## The "Savings" Rate

The BEA includes personal savings and the personal savings rate in the Personal Income and Outlays Report. Personal savings is defined as the difference between consumers' disposable incomes—the money they have available to spend—and what they actually spend, their personal outlays. This estimation is based on the economic principle that there are only two things that a person can do with

**EXHIBIT 7.12**  Transfer Payments as a Percent of Disposable Income

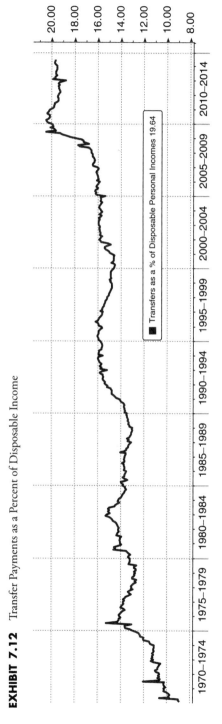

*Source:* Bloomberg

177

income, spend it or save it. In essence, this is an easily appreciated condition. This figure expressed as a percentage of disposable income is the personal savings rate. The May 2014 computation of the personal savings rate, for example, was:

| Disposable personal income | $12,877.2 billion |
| Less personal outlays | $12,256.9 billion |
| Personal savings | $620.3 billion |

Expressed as % of disposable personal income: $620.3 \div \$12,877.2 \times 100$

Equals personal savings rate: Approximately 4.8%

This figure suggests that consumers save about 4.8 percent of their disposable personal income.

There's something inherently misleading about this estimate. Think about your family's savings. What are the two largest holdings that they (or any household, for that matter) might have that make up their savings? A home and stock and bond market investments. While many might not feel as if the purchase of a home is a savings, economists look at homes as if they are. When the BEA estimates GDP, where does residential construction fall? Investment. And the other form of investment, stocks and bonds, is also not included in this calculation.

Such a savings rate lacking these two popular forms of "savings" makes this estimate one of the worst measures that are used on the Street today (Exhibit 7.13). Take this measure with a grain of salt.

## Consumer Spending Inflation Measures

The Personal Income and Outlays Report contains price components for the major personal consumption expenditures (durables, nondurables, and services) as well as some of the more closely watched categories such as personal consumption expenditures excluding food and energy, and just food or energy and goods and services (Exhibit 7.14).

These price deflators are the same indexes used in estimating the quarterly deflators in the GDP report. The only difference is that these are monthly versions.

The BEA also publishes an entire set of detailed price data on its website in the underlying detail section, entitled price index for personal consumption expenditures by type of product (Table 2.2.4U), which includes such categories as household cleaning products, magazines, dental services, Internet access, or televisions.

Investors should get into the habit of knowing the underlying price trends for several major spending categories such as health care, medicine, apparel, food,

**EXHIBIT 7.13** Personal Saving as Percentage of Disposable Personal Income

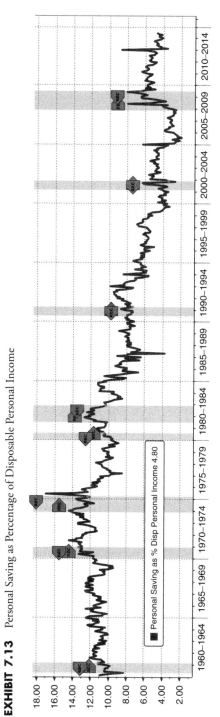

*Source:* Bloomberg

179

**EXHIBIT 7.14**  Personal Consumption Expenditure Deflator, Core (Y/Y%)

*Source:* Bloomberg

housing, tuition, and transportation. Obviously, the higher the prices of these goods, in many cases necessities, the less money there will be available for spending on other things. The other price measures will be discussed in Chapter 10.

## Test Yourself

Answer the following multiple-choice questions:

1. The largest portion of income in the United States is:

   a. wages and salaries.
   b. personal interest and dividend income.
   c. transfer payments.
   d. supplements to wages and salaries.
   e. rental income of persons.

2. Why is the savings rate one of the worst economic indicators?

   a. It only includes values of homes.
   b. It only includes stock and bonds portfolios.
   c. It doesn't include home values or stock portfolios.
   d. It includes only holdings at bank accounts.
   e. a and b only.

3. Why is dining out an excellent economic indicator?

   a. Everyone has to eat, and it is a necessity.
   b. When grocery prices are too expensive, consumers dine out.
   c. It is a measure of discretionary purchases.
   d. Both a and b.
   e. None of the above.

4. The largest component of consumer spending is:

   a. durables.
   b. nondurables.
   c. perfumes and cosmetics.
   d. services.
   e. none of the above.

5. Economists frequently look at real disposable personal income because:

   a. it is income available to spend on disposed goods and services.
   b. it is income available to spend after adjustments for taxes and inflation.
   c. it is income available from the U.S. government.
   d. it is income available to spend after contributions to charities.
   e. a and b only.

## Answers

1. a
2. c
3. c
4. d
5. b

# CHAPTER 8

# Housing and Construction

Housing and construction activity is an economic powerhouse; not because of the direct contribution it has to the U.S. economy but due to the varied and many indirect activities that spur greater spending and hiring. To fully appreciate this power, consider the depth of the 2007–2009 economic downturn, which was exacerbated by a credit collapse, the associated subprime mortgage crisis, and the subsequent housing depression. Many factors influence the pace and level of housing construction spending, and credit conditions are certainly atop that list. When availability of credit evaporates as it had, severe consequences ensue. This chapter will showcase many of the issues associated with that period and how the various components of the housing and construction market responded.

The realization of the American Dream of home ownership is one of the primary drivers of the economy. Residential construction and structures spending is contained in the investment component of the aggregate expenditure equation of gross domestic product (GDP) (see Chapter 3). The construction of new privately owned residential structures, particularly single-family homes, is very informative about consumer sentiment and the health of the economy. After all, a purchase of this magnitude requires the utmost confidence in one's personal financial situation, including employment security and earnings prospects. It also implies favorable conditions in the broader economy. Beyond available income and interest rates, primary influences on housing activity include the general state of economic affairs and demographics. When these factors are aligned correctly, a buoyant housing market can boost total economic activity; when they're not, a slumping market can drag the overall economy into deep recession.

As identified in Exhibit 8.1, essentially every recession since 1950 has some associated decline in residential investment as a percentage of GDP. When economic conditions sour, the housing market is one of the first sectors to

184

**EXHIBIT 8.1** Residential Investment as a Percentage of GDP

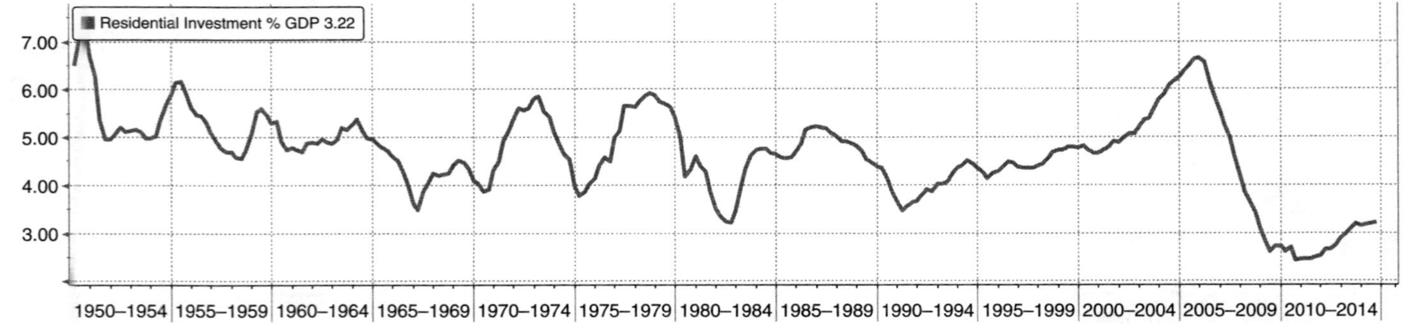

*Source:* Bloomberg

experience a pullback. This wasn't the case during the 2001 recession since it was mild in nature and not a consumer-led contraction, but one that was associated with a buildup of unnecessary and unwanted telecommunication and related equipment. At the time employment was soft, but incomes weren't devastated as during traditional recessions. Interest rates also weren't alarmingly problematic either—particularly in an historical context.

It may seem strange how a component that usually accounts for four-to-five percent of aggregate demand can be so monumental in influencing the overall economic climate. (In more recent times, that percentage has plunged to about 3 percent of total GDP and has remained at that level for over five years, and counting.) Once you consider the associated tremendous multiplier effect of related spending, it's easy to see how the economy simply lumbered along in the wake of the financial crisis of 2008.

Once a home is bought, it must be furnished and decorated; it must be heated and cooled, which results in greater energy demand. Cable, Internet, and sometimes phone installation is often required. All of this means new jobs for utility and construction workers, retail salespeople, and manufacturers; increased tax revenues for local and state municipalities; and greater spending on goods and other related services. Of course, these jobs and revenues fail to materialize if unfavorable conditions, such as rising interest rates, high inflation, low incomes, poor labor market conditions, or general uncertainty stifle demand for new homes.

There are countless indicators that can be employed in the determination of the housing and construction market strength, as well as the outlook. In this chapter, we focus largely on the releases from several different sources including the Census Bureau, the Mortgage Bankers Association, the National Association of Home Builders, the National Association of Realtors, S&P/Case-Shiller, and the American Institute of Architects. These are the most popular of all housing indicators on the Street today. All of these data are available on the Bloomberg terminal and may be conveniently found by typing ECST <GO>.

## Overall Construction Spending

The Construction Spending report is a monthly release of the Commerce Department's U.S. Census Bureau depicting the detail of activity and is segmented by public and private spending. During August 2014, construction spending totaled $960.96 billion, of which $685.0 billion (or 71.3 percent) was in the private sector, and $275.9 billion (or 28.7 percent), was public-sector spending. These two categories are also detailed by residential and nonresidential activity and then detailed again by the type of building or construction activity conducted, including (among others): lodging, residential, office, religious, highway and street, amusement, and health care.

Economists look to this report to see whether there are any trends or developments in the various measures. Exhibit 8.2 identifies the year-over-year pace in spending on public and private construction and how the weakness in total activity plummeted sharply in 2006 and throughout the 2007–2009 economic slump. Since this period coincided with a credit crisis, many banks were reluctant to lend—having just been burned by granting loans to those that could never realistically afford to repay them—and so many would-be borrowers wouldn't dare apply for loans amid such horrible economic conditions, the pace of activity sank.

As the meltdown in the credit market abated, total construction spending climbed in large part by private spending. Businesses took advantage of the zero interest rate environment created by the Federal Reserve and adopted new construction plans.

Interestingly, public spending lagged in the years following the end of the downturn and didn't convincingly return to a positive pace until late 2014. This was due to the inability of policy makers to enact any meaningful legislation to help the dilapidated highway system, fix run-down airports, update railway systems, address poor electrical grids, and upgrade general inadequate infrastructure in the United States. As of today, the United States continues to depend heavily on the public works projects of the Great Depression (Hoover Dam, LaGuardia Airport, the Lincoln Tunnel, highways, and countless bridges). Clearly, this was not a major consideration for the recovery following the Great Recession of 2007–2009.

## Housing Market Index

The National Association of Home Builders releases the Housing Market Index (HMI), as well as a couple of very interesting subcomponents including single-family sales, single-family sales expectations, and prospective buyer traffic (Exhibit 8.3).

These indicators are constructed by asking businesses about conditions—are they better, worse, or the same? The results are compiled and estimated like any other diffusion index whereby any reading above 50 is associated with expansionary conditions and those readings below 50 are contractionary. The HMI correctly identifies the weakness during the housing crisis that commenced in 2004 and ran through 2013.

Because of this accuracy, economists like to incorporate these measures into their econometric models when forecasting housing activity.

According to the HMI, traffic of prospective buyers of new homes has continued to linger around some of the lowest nonrecession levels in history. This may be a function of the inability for first-time buyers to access the credit market, a lackluster pace of real income growth, or less-than-desirable jobs climate.

**EXHIBIT 8.2** Construction Spending (Y/Y%)

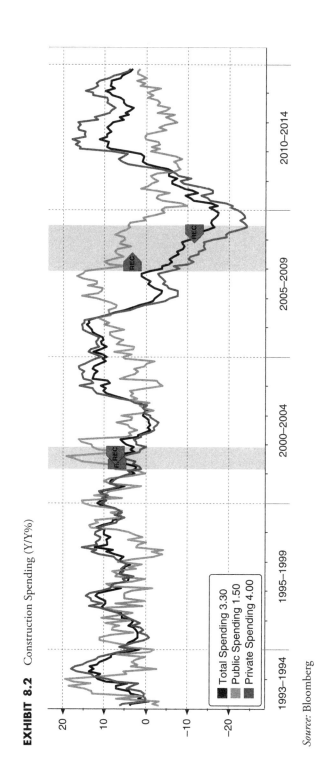

*Source:* Bloomberg

187

188

**EXHIBIT 8.3** Housing Market Index

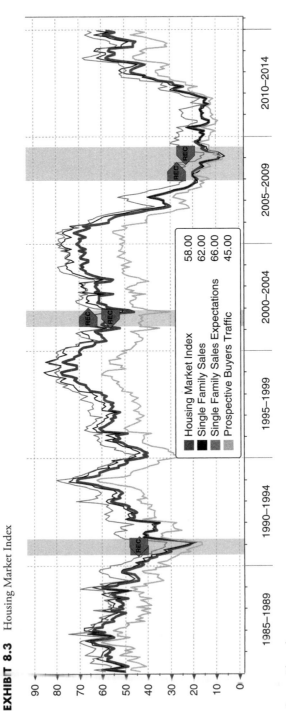

*Source:* Bloomberg

## Housing Affordability Index

In order to purchase a home, several necessary conditions must be met; a primary issue is whether the housing market is affordable. The National Association of Realtors has created an index that determines whether a typical family (one with a median family income estimated by the U.S Bureau of the Census) could qualify for a mortgage on a typical (national median-priced existing family) home (Exhibit 8.4).

Since it takes a mortgage to purchase a home—unless, of course, you are extremely wealthy and can purchase one with cash—the Housing Affordability Index is linked a great deal to mortgage rates.

The NAR adopts an effective mortgage rate when calculating this index.

This quarterly indicator has largely lingered in a range of 100 to 140 for the first 20 years of its history, suggesting that conditions were favorable. The NAR says that an index reading of 120 is to be interpreted as a family earning the median income, possessing 120 percent of the required income needed to qualify for a conventional loan, which would cover 80 percent of the median-priced single-family home. The assumption is that 20 percent of the home price would need to be a down payment.

Notice that during recessions, housing affordability pretty much always advances. This is due to generally lower interest rates. Traditionally, the Federal Reserve lowers its benchmark target rate during economic downturns in order to entice borrowers to the loan market and make purchases of interest-rate-sensitive items like homes. When the Fed adopted a zero-interest rate environment stance in 2008—remaining until late 2014—the HMI was well above 160.

Conversely, in the early-to-mid-1980s, interest rates were extremely high, and mortgage rates were no exception. At several points during 1982, the average 30-year fixed-rate mortgage was over 17.5 percent. This resulted in very low affordability readings.

## Housing Construction Activity

The top housing market attention-getter is the level of housing starts, which is the headline statistic of the New Residential Construction report, cojointly assembled by the U.S. Census Bureau and the U.S. Department of Housing and Urban Development. This release possesses data regarding various stages of housing construction beginning with permits, then starts, homes under construction, and those completed (Exhibit 8.5).

By breaking down the numbers according to stages in the construction process, the tables on building permits, housing starts, under construction, and completions allow economists, investors, and other market participants to pinpoint

**EXHIBIT 8.4** Housing Affordability Index

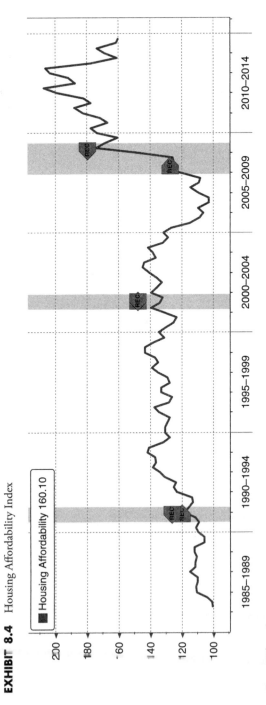

■ Housing Affordability 160.10

*Source:* Bloomberg

**EXHIBIT 8.5** Housing Starts, Permit Applications

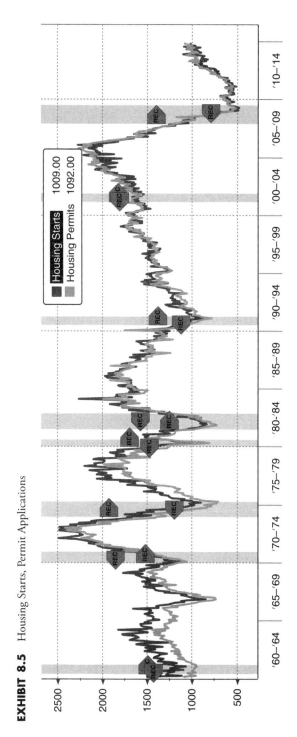

*Source:* Bloomberg

where the strengths and weaknesses lie. For example, should permits, starts, and construction all pick up but completions remain flat, homebuilders may be running up against troubling economic conditions such as an increase in the unemployment rate that could hinder would-be home buyers from purchasing new homes. Also, a rising-interest-rate environment could create difficulties for those buyers attempting to obtain financing at reasonable terms.

Many of the factors that can affect construction activity vary considerably from region to region across the United States. Luckily, the New Residential Construction report has detail for starts, permits, under construction, and completions by regional (Northeast, South, Midwest, and West.)

Midwestern agricultural communities, for instance, will typically suffer disturbances in employment and income growth at different times and under different economic conditions from those in areas with more manufacturing industries, such as the Rust Belt and the West Coast with its concentration of technology companies. Weather conditions also vary regionally, with hurricanes in the Southeast, cold winters in the Northeast and Midwest, and flooding and drought in the South and Southwest. Furthermore, although monetary policy, which determines interest rates, is national, other policy matters, such as tax incentives, differ from state to state. Not surprisingly, then, there is a great disparity between the housing statistics for the different regions represented in the report.

It's simply reasonable to look to the level of new starts to determine the housing and construction climate. Formally, the Census Bureau defines a "start" when excavation begins for the footings or foundation of the building. Clearly, if investors weren't serious about erecting a housing unit, they certainly wouldn't go through the costly endeavor of excavation. This understanding makes starts a reliable gauge.

Permit applications are a wonderful barometer and are used in the Conference Board Leading Economic Index (LEI). They understandably "lead" the level of starts, since a housing unit cannot be constructed without legal documentation. While this is an excellent indicator of future activity, there is a slight issue—applying for and receiving approval for construction doesn't always result in construction. Any number of issues could arise to halt construction, including inclement weather, a sudden turn in economic conditions, an inability to finance the construction process, or simply a general decision to cancel the project.

Exhibit 8.6 identifies the incredible divergence that the housing and construction market experienced in the aftermath of the 2007–2009 Great Recession and associated housing crisis. The jobs situation during this period was devastating—as is usually the case during economic upheavals of this magnitude—and this time around, would-be home buyers weren't granted loans. Incomes for those that were fortunate to get hired weren't that attractive, so the purchase of a home wasn't a viable option for even those who did land a position. But people have to live somewhere.

**EXHIBIT 8.6** Housing Starts—1, 5+ Units

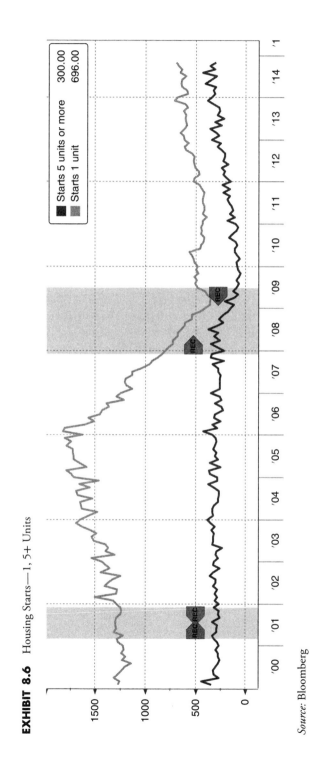

*Source:* Bloomberg

193

## Single-Family Homes and Apartment Construction

Many recent graduates of this period were forced to move back into their parents' homes (since dubbed *boomerang children*). Others grabbed a bunch of friends and leased an apartment together. This caused an abrupt change in the composition of the housing market.

Rather than erect single-family, one-unit homes, businesses appreciated this trend in depressed incomes and ramped up construction of multi-units. While both took a while to post any type of increase, the pace of construction for five-plus units climbed rather briskly, returning to levels prior to the economic downturn. Those for one-unit homes remained stagnant for years and have yet to fully recover to those 2005 levels.

## Applications for Mortgages

Every Wednesday, the Mortgage Bankers Association (MBA) releases its survey of mortgage application activity. The headline index is referred to as the Market Index and comprises two individual components: mortgage refinancings and mortgage purchases (Exhibit 8.7). Both are extremely important in the determination of housing activity, one more so than the other.

Refinancings tell us about the level of underlying mortgage rates and the willingness for homeowners to reduce their monthly mortgage expenses.

Obviously, lower rates send refinancings higher, while an environment of rising interest rates results in a slower pace of activity. Refis reduce the monthly interest expense and place additional funds in the hands of consumers, which may be used for consumption or savings. The MBA Refinance Index does not, however, tell us about the housing market or the likelihood of greater (or weaker) construction or sales activity.

The MBA Purchase Index tells us about the likely pace of residential construction or home sales, since it measures mortgage applications for purchases of single-family homes.

Over time, the MBA Purchase Index provided tremendous insight about the conditions of the housing market that many other indexes had not. The housing bubble popped sometime around 2004–2005, and essentially all measures reveal the existence of the crisis, with precipitous declines prior to, and through, the 2007–2009 economic slump. However, several other indicators (construction spending, existing home sales, even starts and permits) demonstrated some degree of strength. The MBA Purchase Index never emitted such a signal. Instead, it flashed a sideways or flatlined trend for several years. Ultimately, this proved to be the proper path of the housing market.

**EXHIBIT 8.7** MBA Purchase Index

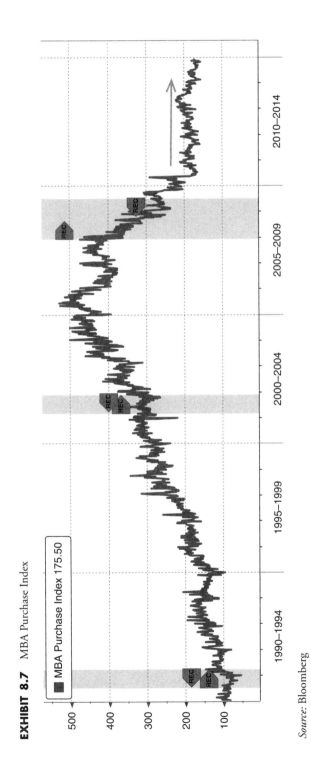

*Source:* Bloomberg

## Architect's "Work on the Books"

The American Institute of Architects has an informative and insightful diffusion index derived from *work on the books*, which is commonly referred to as the Architect Billings Index (ABI).

According to the AIA, this survey is a leading indicator and captures spending on nonresidential construction about 11 months in advance of actual changes in activity. Exhibit 8.8 identifies this close association.

An index reading above 50 denotes an increase in activity that was greater than the previous month, while sub-50 postings imply a deceleration in work. This is an excellent indicator to use for all sorts of construction trends.

## Home Sales

Existing home sales is an ideal measure of the housing market, primarily because of its size—it dwarfs the number of new home sales (Exhibit 8.9). It is estimated and released by the National Association of Realtors (NAR). During the heyday of the housing bubble, sales of existing home sales topped 7.0 million units. Although this level was clearly unsustainable, that number plunged to a cyclical low of about 3.5 million units. This pace was also an extreme level, since lenders were bitten by mass defaults, and widespread fraud was weaved in the industry, causing a reluctance to lend. Would-be borrowers found themselves with no jobs, limited—if any—incomes, and few assets, which are a necessity to qualify for a mortgage and home purchase. The long-term trend probably lies somewhere in between those two extremes at around 5 to 6 million units. Existing home sales are currently running about 10 times the 400,000 to 500,000 unit sales pace of new home sales.

Retail analysts and some industry economists prefer to look at trends in this series since the sale of an existing home has such a large impact on consumption expenditures of remodeling, renovation, decorating, and lawn and garden activity. It is true that many items and services will be needed in a new home purchase; however, an existing home will more likely need plumbing or electrical upgrades, roofing or siding material, or carpeting and paint. New homes, by definition, have the latest appliances and fixtures. Again, the mere size of the existing home market has a considerable impact on consumer expenditures of related goods and services.

The NAR distributes its Pending Home Sales report, which is a measure of existing single-family homes, condos, and co-op sales based on the number of signed contracts. This tends to lead the pace of actual existing home sales by about one to two months, since contracts are signed prior to sale.

New home sales—calculated and reported by the Commerce Department's Census Bureau—are a powerful provider of economic activity because

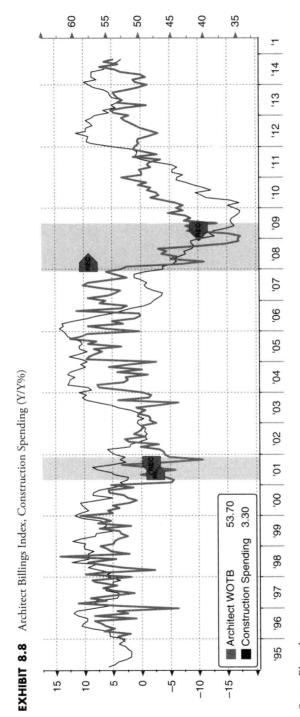

**EXHIBIT 8.8** Architect Billings Index, Construction Spending (Y/Y%)

*Source:* Bloomberg

197

**EXHIBIT 8.9** Existing Home Sales

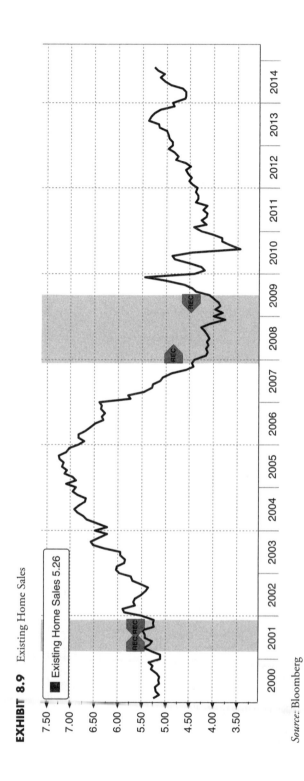

*Source:* Bloomberg

they employ construction and specialty trade workers, requires materials, and necessitates expenditures of particular goods and associated with the construction of a new home. Existing home purchases don't employ the number of workers associated with a new home. Similarly, there are a number of components of a new home that simply are not as prevalent in an existing home.

The National Association of Home Builders (NAHB) routinely estimates the prices of construction components of a single-family home. In a 2011 survey, some of the more expensive components included framing, trusses, and excavation; foundation and backfill; plumbing; electrical wiring; cabinets and countertops; asphalt driveway; shingles; siding; and dry wall. Cumulatively, these account for over 50 percent of the total construction cost. Then, think of the other components, and it's easy to see how a new home contributes so greatly to the pace of overall economic activity.

Exhibit 8.10 identifies the deep trench that new home sales had fallen into after the housing bubble burst. This is considerably more dramatic than that of the existing home market. Years after the slump, the pace of new home sales remains far below that of previous economic recessions. This explains the difficulty the economy has had recovering from the 2007–2009 downturn.

## Home Supply

Like every good or service in an economy, demand isn't the only determinant of housing and residential construction activity. Builders are always conscious of the existing stockpile of homes on the market. When those levels are low, generally in the four- to six-month range, then housing activity tends to flourish, construction advances, and builder confidence rises, resulting in greater housing and related activity to replenish the somewhat depleted inventory.

When new or existing home supply increases to somewhat superfluous levels—arguably, seven or more months—conditions soon become soft as builders reduce new construction until the number of months' supply is reduced (Exhibit 8.11).

There are many obvious influences to home supply: higher interest rates may deter homebuilding, the lack of access to capital—like during the credit crisis of 2008—may sideline many projects, and weather may impede the building process, resulting in a slower pace of sales and greater supply. Conversely, strong economic conditions may convince builders to increase commitments to new projects.

Notice how the months' supply soared during the housing bubble that burst in 2004–2005 and continued to escalate into and throughout the Great Recession of 2007–2009. Clearly, economic conditions were so troubling that home buying wasn't atop the list of desirable purchases—especially in the immediate aftermath of the housing bubble—so supply surged to alarmingly high levels.

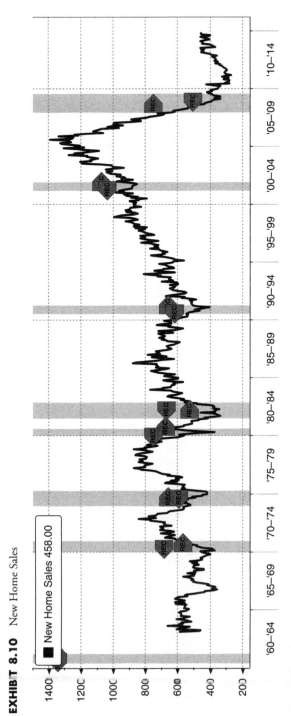

**EXHIBIT 8.10** New Home Sales

*Source* Bloomberg

200

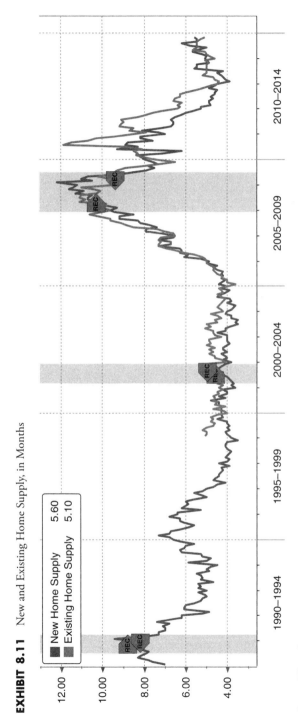

**EXHIBIT 8.11** New and Existing Home Supply, in Months

*Source:* Bloomberg

During one recent economic recession, in 2001, there wasn't a notable movement in the level of months' supply. This may best be credited to the lack of a deterioration in the demand for homes—economic conditions were outrageously bleak—since this recession was not a consumer-led downturn, and one that was predominantly the result of excessive capital spending by businesses.

## Home Prices

When supply and demand change, so too will the price level. Therefore, economists like to keep an eye on home prices. While new and existing home sales releases possess data regarding the median level of home prices, the most popular and respected measure is the relatively new S&P/Case-Shiller Home Price Index. Two broad measures, one of 20 cities and a 10-city composite, measure the values of residential properties in U.S. metropolitan areas. The headline is the 20-city composite.

Location, location, location. That's the rule of real estate, and as such, it is also something to consider when analyzing the housing and construction sector of the economy. And the price level is also contingent on region. If economic conditions are strong in one portion of the country and there are many high-paying positions, and a great pace of hiring, then there's a good chance that home prices will appreciate accordingly. If, however, the area is impoverished, with limited promise to gainfully raise a family, then those values will be depressed.

Exhibit 8.12 depicts the 20 regional indexes and their performances since 2000. Interestingly, a great deal may be gleaned from this chart.

All 20 regions start at 100 in 2000 and appreciate in value—there's no magic in that analysis. By 2004, some areas are accelerating in value, while others struggle. Again, this is consistent with the underlying current of economic activity. The entire nation doesn't experience a similar growth path. So property values will fluctuate as well. In 2004, there are some areas that are experiencing small bubbles—better known as frothy.

But then in 2005, 2006, and some of 2007, some of those little bubbles moved from silly territory into stupid territory. We all remember where they were—Nevada, Miami, Las Vegas, San Diego. When the housing bubble bursts, prices in each regional plunge and enter a long period of stagnation from 2009 through 2012. And then all of the regions experience an increase in their home price levels through 2014.

In hindsight, we know there was an apparent issue developing with respect to home prices, initially in only a handful of areas, which ultimately led to a bubble of epic proportions. This engendered significant consequences on every portion of the economy, demographics, incomes, employment, interest rates, trade, and output. Similarly, there were numerous policy consequences that impacted the domestic and global economies. While the euphoria of home buying in Miami

**EXHIBIT 8.12** S&P/Case-Shiller Home Price Index

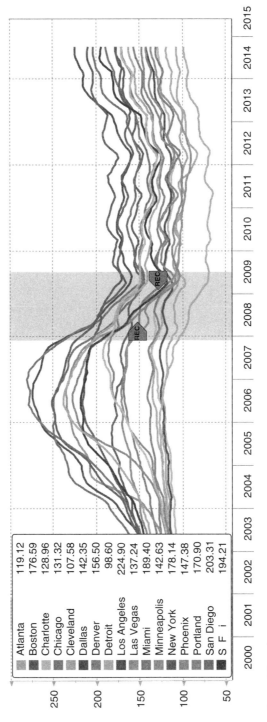

| Atlanta | 119.12 |
| Boston | 176.59 |
| Charlotte | 128.96 |
| Chicago | 131.32 |
| Cleveland | 107.58 |
| Dallas | 142.35 |
| Denver | 156.50 |
| Detroit | 98.60 |
| Los Angeles | 224.90 |
| Las Vegas | 137.24 |
| Miami | 189.40 |
| Minneapolis | 142.63 |
| New York | 178.14 |
| Phoenix | 147.38 |
| Portland | 170.90 |
| San Diego | 203.31 |
| S F i | 194.21 |

*Source:* Bloomberg

may seem like a little, inconsequential event, if unaddressed and permitted to spread, it may have serious influence on a broader, macroeconomic realm.

Some of the other items to keep an eye on when analyzing the housing and construction markets include: anecdotal evidence from the homebuilders themselves. Many of the nation's largest builders—including KB Home, PulteGroup, Toll Brothers Inc., Lennar Corp., the Ryland Group Inc., Hovnanian Enterprises Inc., and Beazer Homes—talk about the issues they are facing in their quarterly earnings statements, which are included in the Bloomberg Orange Book of CEO Comments, all available on the Bloomberg terminal.

It's also a good idea to keep an eye on the loan and default data on the Federal Reserve's website, which can provide early signals of troubles in the industry. It certainly would have helped in projecting the housing slump in 2008. Reluctance by loan officers to extend housing credit may signal that banks are having problems collecting on extended loans. Specifically, interested readers should watch the household detail in the Federal Reserve's Senior Loan Officer Opinion Survey on Bank Lending Practices. These data are also available on the Bloomberg terminal on the FOMC <GO> page.

## Test Yourself

Answer the following multiple-choice questions:

1. Residential construction makes up about how much of GDP?
   a. about 5 percent.
   b. about 10 percent.
   c. about 20 percent.
   d. about 25 percent.
   e. about 40 percent.

2. The largest portion of construction spending is:
   a. public expenditures.
   b. private expenditures.
   c. lodging.
   d. all of the above.
   e. a and b only.

3. The order of housing construction in the Census Bureau's New Construction report is:
   a. orders, processing, digging.
   b. orders, hiring, capital spending, digging, completed.
   c. a and b only.
   d. permit, start, under construction, completed.
   e. none of the above.

4. Why might existing home sales be a better gauge of housing market conditions than new home sales?

    a. There are a lot more of them.
    b. They are bigger and require more materials.
    c. They are used to construct the housing component in the GDP report.
    d. All of the above.
    e. b and c only.

5. Why might economists prefer to observe trends in the MBA's Purchase Application Index over the Refinancing Index?

    a. Refinancings account for only 4 percent of all mortgage applications.
    b. Purchases identify the intent to actually own a home.
    c. Refinancings are only given to the top income earners.
    d. All of the above.
    e. None of the above.

## Answers

1. a
2. b
3. d
4. a
5. b

# CHAPTER 9

# Manufacturing

The size of the manufacturing sector in the United States pales in comparison to what it had been back in the 1950s. According to the folks at the Federal Reserve of St. Louis, the percentage of manufacturing value added by industry as a percentage of gross domestic product during the second quarter of 2014 was about 13 percent. This seems about correct, since the associated level of private manufacturing employment was roughly 10 percent (12.217 million manufacturing employed out of a total private employment level of 118.112 million workers).

The diminished dependency on production doesn't make manufacturing data less important as an economic indicator; it only means that the U.S. economy has a different composition than it once did. Factory output is a critical base, and it helps identify the overall pace of aggregate demand as well as trends in the performance. Watching orders and shipments of aircraft will tell a great deal about the strength of the airline industry, both foreign and domestic. Pricing components in several of the manufacturing surveys like the Institute of Supply Management's Purchasing Managers Index will help identify pipeline inflation and subsequently the pace of demand for manufactured goods.

## Industrial Production and Capacity Utilization

The Industrial Production and Capacity Utilization report, estimated and released by the Board of Governors of the Federal Reserve, is one of the oldest measures of economic activity in the United States. Its 1919 origin predates the GDP data and was used as the benchmark of business cycles for decades before the national income and product accounts (NIPAs) were developed in the 1940s. Despite having a lessened dependency on manufacturing, the growth rate in industrial production is closely correlated with real GDP and is a component of the Conference Board's index of coincident indicators.

The National Bureau of Economic Research uses the index to discern turning points in the business cycle. As the chart in Exhibit 9.1 shows, each of the NBER-designated recessions has coincided with a precipitous drop in the 12-month growth rate of industrial production. The converse, however, is not necessarily true: the manufacturing sector can be in recession while the broader economy continues to prosper.

The total Industrial Production Index is constructed from 312 components or individual series such as copper, instruments, computers, and lumber. The report presents these components according to two different classification schemes: by industry, representing the supplier perspective; and by market, representing the demand perspective.

The industry schema is based on the North American Industry Classification System (NAICS). The three primary industry groups are manufacturing, mining, and utilities. Manufacturing is subdivided into durable and nondurable goods.

In the classification by market groups, the total index is divided into two major groups: final products/nonindustrial supplies, and materials. Final products/nonindustrial supplies is itself divided into consumer goods (further subdivided into durable and nondurable), business equipment, defense and space equipment, construction supplies, and business supplies.

One attractive quality of the industrial production index is that it is available on a monthly basis, so this is extremely beneficial for the forecaster attempting to decipher the trend in the overall economic picture before the quarterly GDP report is released.

The industrial production indexes measure the quantity of output (i.e., in terms of production units like tons, cubic feet, or kilowatt hours), not the dollar volume. The Federal Reserve obtains the production data used to construct these indexes both directly and indirectly, mostly from manufacturing trade and industry associations.

Since the consumer plays such a considerable role in the U.S. economy, economists look to the production of consumer goods to determine any potential signs of strength or weakness. Production of consumer-related goods includes durables (automotive products, home electronics, appliances, furniture and carpeting) as well as nondurables (foods and tobacco, and clothing.)

During expansions, the 12-month pace of production tends to fluctuate in a relatively narrow band of 1 to 4 percent (Exhibit 9.2). When the rate dips below zero, the overall economy generally finds itself in recession.

Something to consider when analyzing this series: U.S. manufacturers produce goods for domestic consumption, as well as for export. So, large gains could arise as foreign demand increases. This could send a false signal that the source of the strength is domestic, particularly households. In a related influence, when the U.S. dollar weakens, U.S.-produced goods are more attractive relative to those countries with appreciating currencies, so changes in production activity may also be a function of currency-related factors. While this would be a clear sign

**EXHIBIT 9.1** Industrial Production versus GDP (Y/Y%)

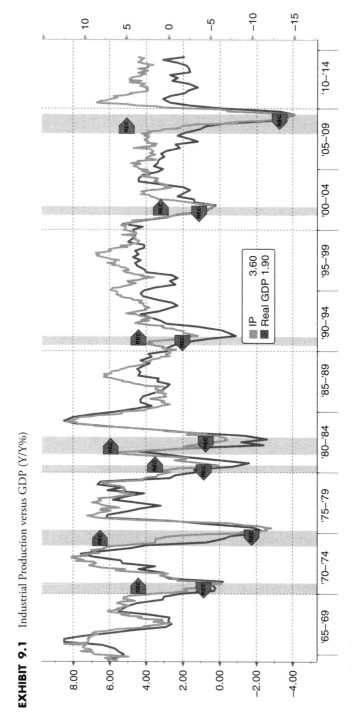

*Source:* Bloomberg

209

**EXHIBIT 9.2** Industrial Production of Consumer Goods

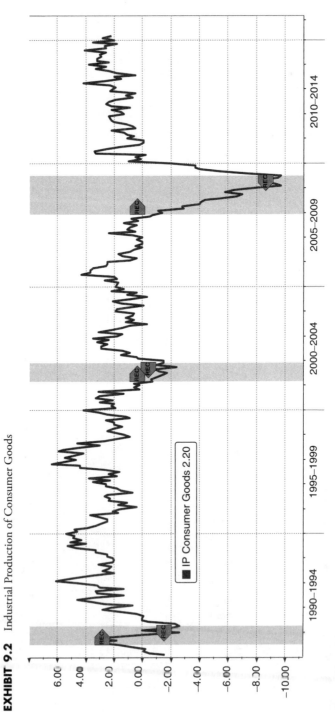

*Source:* Bloomberg

of improving U.S. economic climate (output and most likely employment) it shouldn't necessarily be interpreted as a definitive sign of domestic consumer strength.

## Production and Employment

An interesting relationship can be identified by observing the trends in industrial production and the level of manufacturing jobs in the country. During the three expansionary periods of industrial production in Exhibit 9.3, 1996–2000, 2001–2007, and 2009–2015 the level of manufacturing employment moved sideways, with little-to-no upward trend. Conversely, whenever industrial production contracted during recessions of 2001 and 2007–2009, manufacturing employment appropriately fell. This suggests that the government's expansionary fiscal and easy monetary responses had no influence on job creation in the manufacturing sector.

There may be many reasons for this trend, but none more explanatory than the increase in productivity. American manufacturing has managed to make more with less. That includes less of all inputs: land, capital, and labor. Automation on the assembly line and factory floor with enhancements like robotics in assemblies, stamping, and welding has helped streamline the manufacturing process.

The increase in globalization has led to a diminished need for U.S. domestic manufacturing employment. The United States simply cannot compete with abundant labor forces of highly populated, low-wage countries with little-to-no oversight or protection of workers.

## Capacity Utilization

Capacity utilization is a measure of how close the nation's manufacturing sector is to running at full capacity. Formally, it is the ratio of the industrial production index to an index of full capacity.

Economists, particularly central bankers, look at the total capacity utilization rate to discern trends in production, general economic activity, manufacturing conditions, and inflation. In addition, the rates for particular industries can pinpoint areas of overcapacitization (production that pushes capacity to its limit) that could become manufacturing bottlenecks, constraining production farther down the line and possibly pushing up prices. Such information is useful not only to economists but also to company managers trying to forecast costs and plan production schedules.

Low levels of capacity utilization—79 percent or below—indicate that the economy is headed to, or already in, recession. In fact, as Exhibit 9.4 illustrates, each of the last seven economic recessions was characterized by utilization rates in that range. This relationship is logical: Subpar economic conditions simply don't warrant strong production.

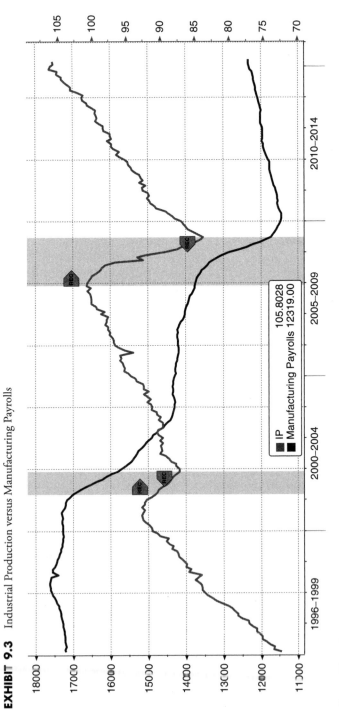

**EXHIBIT 9.3** Industrial Production versus Manufacturing Payrolls

*Source:* Bloomberg

**EXHIBIT 9.4**  Capacity Utilization, Fed Funds Rate

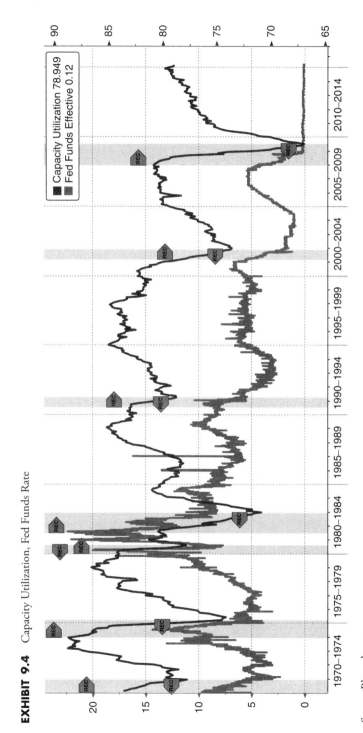

*Source:* Bloomberg

213

When demand and commerce are booming, on the other hand, factories tend to ramp up and produce at rates closer to their capacity. The downside to this is that the higher production rates tend to stoke inflation.

Exhibit 9.4 also shows that from 1970 through 2003, whenever the capacity utilization rate rose into the high 80s, the federal funds rate rose as well.

Similarly, when the capacity utilization rate fell sharply as in the 1990–1991, 2001, and 2007–2009 recessions, the Federal Reserve reacted by reducing its borrowing target. The conclusion: Although the relationship has loosened in recent years, the Federal Reserve clearly believes that capacity utilization is still a powerful inflation marker and watches the reported rate carefully.

## Utility Production

Economists have long looked at the trends of utility production to determine the underlying strength of the economy. Traditionally, electric and natural gas production reveals a great deal about the pace of activity in an economy—reduced demand for utilities would be a sign of weakness, whereas increased activity implies some degree of strengthening. Most of the time, this indicator is highly desirable.

One issue with this analysis is that the year-over-year trends tend to be very noisy and volatile. There are several influences for these abrupt changes, with the foremost being the weather. During sweltering summer months, electricity demand surges as Americans increase usage of air conditioners and fans. Business establishments need to cool offices, malls, stores, and restaurants, resulting in elevated periods of demand. Conversely, during the winter months, the need for heat also boosts demand and subsequently production. The major issue is that the periods of extreme shifts in demand fall in different weeks and months, which distorts the 12-month changes. Temperatures in July of one year may be considerably different from the following July.

More recently, in 2014–2015, utility production fell rather precipitously because of the onslaught of alternative energy resources that came about because of fossil-fuel discoveries in the United States. An abundance of supply, combined with a lessened demand due to the prolonged and sluggish recovery from the 2007–2009 downturn, sent production sharply lower. Also, more energy-efficient infrastructure of late has lessened the amount of energy in demand.

Nevertheless, by observing the six-month moving average of the year-over-year rate of growth provides a smoother, less erratic trend, which may be quite telling of overall macroeconomic trends (Exhibit 9.5).

The Federal Reserve doesn't always receive data on a basis that allows a complete estimate of all the detail in the industrial production and capacity utilization report. When the actual data are not available, the Federal Reserve may estimate industrial production based on some of the data contained in

**EXHIBIT 9.5** Industrial Production—Utilities (Y/Y%) 6-Month MA

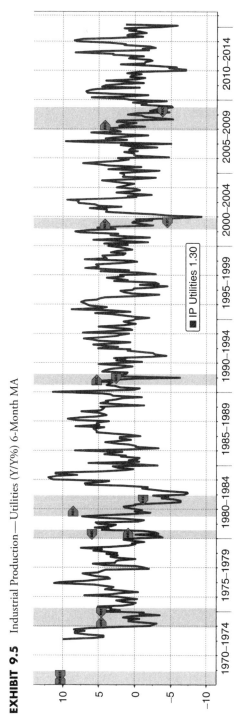

*Source:* Bloomberg

215

the monthly Employment Situation report. Wall Street economists use the same statistics in a simple back-of-the-envelope calculation to obtain a crude estimate for the industrial production index up to two weeks before it is released. Here's what the computation would look like using the data in the Bureau of Labor Statistics' December 2014 Employment Situation report, released on January 9, 2015.

The report stated that in November 2014, 12.222 million people were employed in manufacturing, working an average of 41.1 hours a week, whereas in December, 12.239 million people worked 41.0 hours a week on average. The first step in the computation is to calculate the total number of manpower hours (mh) worked in each month:

November: 12.222 million workers $\times$ 41.1 hours = 502.324 mh

December: 12.239 million workers $\times$ 41.0 hours = 501.799 mh

The next step is to determine how many more or fewer manpower hours were worked in December:

$$501.799 - 502.324 = -0.5252$$

The last step is to derive the month-over-month percentage change:

$$(0.5252 \div 502.3242) \times 100 = -0.1 \text{ percent.}$$

So the predicted change in the Fed's December Industrial Production Index, based on the number of manufacturing workers and the hours they worked, is −0.1 percent. The actual Industrial Production Index reading in the report released in January was indeed −0.1 percent. The result of the calculation is not always that accurate. But the method is certainly simple, and it is helpful in determining the direction, if not always the magnitude, of change in the index—an extremely important statistic.

## Institute for Supply Management Indexes

The Purchasing Managers Index (PMI) is the headline index of the ISM Report on Business and is estimated by the Institute for Supply Management (ISM). Each month the ISM Report on Business describes and discusses the current readings of 10 seasonally adjusted diffusion indexes constructed by the ISM from the responses to a survey of approximately 300 purchasing managers across the United States.

The ISM polls participants about their opinions on prices paid for materials used in the production process, production levels, new orders, order backlogs, the speed of supplier deliveries, inventories, customer inventories, employment, new export orders, and imports.

The headline PMI is a weighted composite of the following five indexes: new orders, production, employment, supplier deliveries, and inventories.

Movements in the ISM's PMI closely parallel those of the swings in real GDP, and have been known to predict recessions months before the National Bureau of Economic Research (NBER) declares them. This may not be so surprising: What better way is there to find out about manufacturing activity and associated spending than from those businesspeople who are responsible for making the purchasing decisions for the nation's manufacturers?

The financial markets—in particular, the fixed-income market—react greatly to the monthly postings of the ISM's Purchasing Managers Index. The PMI has frequently been identified as the biggest market mover in the monthly reporting cycle of indicators.

As already noted, the 10 diffusion indexes contained in the Report on Business reflect the survey responses of purchasing managers from the United States. In addition to direct responses, which are used in the calculation of the diffusion indexes, the ISM asks for remarks after each question regarding the reasons for higher or lower commodity prices, or greater or less employment. The ISM also asks its participants to report specific commodities that they purchase that are in short supply. These invaluable remarks are used in the text prepared for the monthly report and are greatly analyzed by Wall Street analysts.

The ISM separates the responses to each question into positive, neutral, and negative groups and calculates the percentage of the whole that each represents. It then plugs the appropriate percentages for each question into the following formula:

Percentage of positive responses + ½ (Percentage of neutral responses)

The result is a diffusion index. Suppose the question regarding the level of imports received 350 responses, of which 20 are negative, or "lower than a month ago"; 275 neutral, or "same as a month ago"; and 55 positive, or "higher than a month ago." Plugging those numbers into the formula would give a value for the ISM imports index as follows:

$$\text{Imports index} = [(55 \div 350) \times 100] + \tfrac{1}{2} [(275 \div 350) \times 100]$$

$$= 15.7 + \tfrac{1}{2} (78.57)$$

$$= 15.7 + 39.28$$

$$= 55.0$$

Indexes calculated in this manner have values between 0 and 100. Values above 50 are interpreted as indicative of expansion; those under 50, contraction.

Thus, the expansion-contraction cutoff level is 50, not 0. Historically, most of the individual ISM indexes have tended to fluctuate between 35 and 70, depending on the current phase of the business cycle and the individual index.

For example, during severe contractions like in 2007–2009, the headline PMI plunged to 33.1, while during the recession of 2001, the trough was 40.8.

Price activity is generally prone to whipsawing, and the associated price gauge in the ISM survey possesses a similar extreme range, fluctuating between 30 and 90, whereas another indicator less volatile like the export index has maintained a range of about 40 to 70.

## The Headline Purchasing Managers Index

Five of these indexes, as noted above, are equally weighted—20 percent each— and summed to create the headline PMI. The February 2015 PMI, for instance, was calculated as follows:

$$\text{PMI (February 2015)} = \text{New orders } (0.20 \times 52.5) + \text{Production } (0.20 \times 53.7)$$
$$+ \text{Employment } (0.20 \times 51.4)$$
$$+ \text{Supplier deliveries } (0.20 \times 54.3)$$
$$+ \text{Inventories } (0.20 \times 52.5)$$
$$= 10.50 + 10.74 + 10.28 + 10.86 + 10.50$$
$$= 52.88, \text{ or } 52.9$$

The PMI is not solely an indicator of manufacturing activity. Exhibit 9.6 shows that monthly movements in the index closely mirror the year-over-year percentage change in real GDP. This makes the PMI extremely valuable as a predictor of total macroeconomic conditions. The strong correlation with changes in real GDP make the ISM report a considerably important barometer.

Although a level of 50 is considered the cutoff between expansion and contraction for manufacturing conditions, when it comes to movements in the broader macroeconomy, different levels are associated with expansion and contraction. For example, the February 2015 Report on Business said that a reading of about 43.1 percent in the PMI is indicative of an expansion in the overall economy. Economists tend to watch the level of the headline index once it slips below 50 since successive sub-50 readings could be identifying a trend toward that 43.1 level and identify a possible turning point in the overall business cycle.

The Purchasing Managers Index by itself depicts the general state of the manufacturing sector and of the larger economy. It does so in very broad strokes, however. For a more detailed view, economists and traders look at the subindexes,

**EXHIBIT 9.6** ISM PMI and Real GDP (Y/Y%)

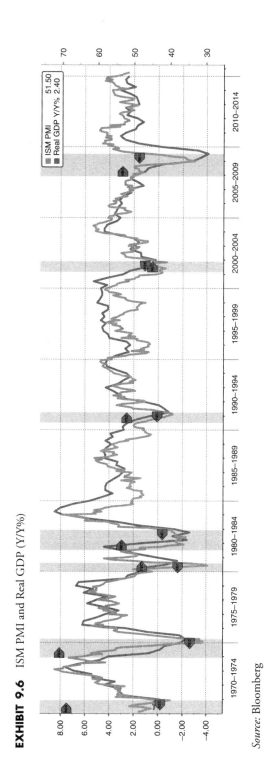

*Source:* Bloomberg

219

each possessing varying degrees of predictive power with respect to the particular aspect of manufacturing condition and activity that it portrays.

The ISM Employment Index, which is compiled from the answers to how the current level of employment compares with last month's, has a solid relationship with the trend rate of growth in manufacturing payrolls in the Bureau of Labor Statistics' monthly employment report. Economists frequently look to the ISM report for insight to the payrolls release when estimating the monthly change.

Since manufacturers are responsible for such a great portion of U.S. exports, the ISM exports index is often looked at for insight into trade activity.

Exhibit 9.7 shows the relationship between the overall ISM PMI, the ISM Export Index and the 12-month trend in U.S. exports. All three measures are closely correlated. Perhaps unsurprisingly, the ISM export index possesses a slightly tighter relationship with exports than the headline ISM index.

With only a few exceptions, sub-50 readings in the export index are associated with contractions in the pace of U.S. exports. The same cannot be said about the below-50 readings in the ISM PMI.

This is often one of the first measures that economists use when modeling export activity and demand for U.S. manufactures. Another critical determinant of export demand is the value of the currency. The impact of significant fluctuations in the value of the dollar will often surface in the ISM Export Index before they arrive in the actual level of exports. This is largely due to the ISM being a sentiment index, not an actual measure of production.

## "Tweaking" Some of the ISM Measures

Economists are always in search of quirky indicators that signal potential strength or weakness in the macroeconomy, and ISM provides the ability to create a number of those measures.

One of the more creative practices performed by Wall Streeters is to take the difference between the ISM's New Orders Index and the Inventories Index. The resulting statistic, depicted in Exhibit 9.8, has displayed a relatively strong correlation with the year-over-year percentage change in real GDP as well as changes in the business cycle.

There are a number of reasons that this gauge is so desirable. For starters, gross domestic product is reported on a quarterly basis and is prone to rather lengthy delays; some economists find this "new orders minus inventories" index a timely (available monthly as opposed to quarterly) and accurate depiction of the economic growth rate.

The economics behind this measure is that *new orders* is a proxy for future demand, basically what businesses expect they are going to need to facilitate production. The inventories index is what businesses already have stockpiled. So, by taking the difference between what manufacturers currently have and their expected need is essentially creating a measure for demand, which is what GDP is.

**EXHIBIT 9.7** ISM PMI, ISM Exports, U.S. Exports (Y/Y%)

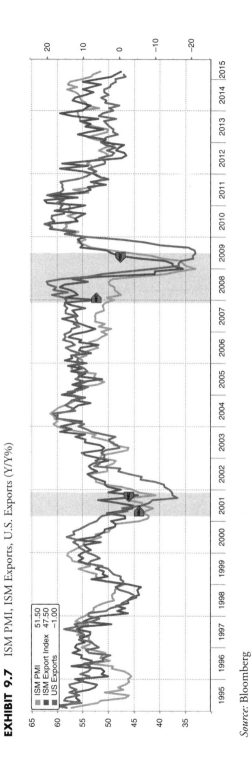

*Source:* Bloomberg

**EXHIBIT 9.8** New Orders Index-Inventories Index, Real GDP (Y/Y%)

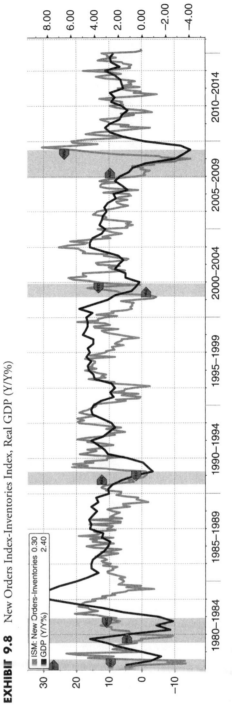

*Source* Bloomberg

Like the many diffusion indexes examined in this chapter, the "new orders minus inventories" index doesn't project a specific magnitude for real economic growth, or GDP, but it is quite telling about the likelihood of economic contraction or expansion. During some phases of the business cycle when the identification of recession isn't exactly clear, this index can help clarify expectations months before the GDP report is released.

Economists look out for low or negative readings in the "new orders minus inventories" index. Anytime there is no difference between the inventories and new orders indexes, that is, when the "new orders minus inventories" index is zero, the economic growth rate tends to contract. Historically, negative readings have been associated with economic recessions. Readings in the "new orders minus inventories" index of 10 or higher historically have equated to real economic growth rates in excess of 3.5 percent—a rate generally considered to be strong.

Are these specific levels definitive predictors of recession or growth? Of course not. The chart clearly identifies several subzero postings, while the growth rate in real GDP remained in expansionary territory. This is nothing more than a crude guide to projecting economic activity on a monthly basis (because GDP is not readily available). However, as this indicator has, on occasion, possessed something of a leading quality, some economists look for trends in the index to forecast GDP growth.

Economists have also tinkered with the difference between the new orders index and the price index as a predictor of changes in total return of the S&P 500 Index. The explanation here is that the price index is a representation of costs, while new orders are a revenues proxy. Again, there are times that this measure works exceptionally well, and those when it breaks down. Nevertheless, it is an interesting gauge and deserves a place on all economists' dashboards.

## Price Trends in the Manufacturing Sector

Investors and economists look to the ISM report for insight into the underlying price trends in the economy. The ISM's Price Index provides a solid relationship with the year-over-year growth rate in wholesale prices (also referred to as the Producer Price Index (PPI)) (Exhibit 9.9). This makes sense because manufacturers produce goods from various inputs and purchasing managers make buying decisions of materials and commodities used in the production process.

The index receives a considerable amount of attention from the Street, especially the credit markets, because inflation rates influence the value of fixed-income securities. And because the Federal Reserve is so concerned with the possibility of rising inflation (as well as deflation), it is atop the Fed's economic-indicator watch list as well.

Since the PPI is a measure of inflation at the wholesale level, it may be considered a somewhat leading indicator for price changes on the retail level. Sometimes businesses pass along higher costs of goods to the final user.

224

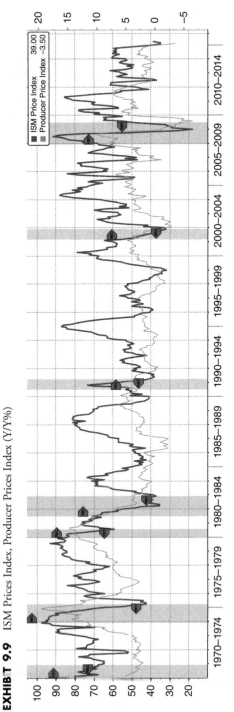

**EXHIBIT 9.9** ISM Prices Index, Producer Prices Index (Y/Y%)

*Source:* Bloomberg

If price pass-alongs are widespread and sustained, the general price level could increase, which, by definition, signals inflation. In addition to reducing the value of fixed-income securities, inflation impedes the pace of consumer spending because workers have to earn more (i.e., by working longer) just to afford the same amount of goods and services they used to get at lower prices.

The PPI is thus a useful indicator of the potential for inflation, in both the manufacturing sector and the broader economy. According to the February 2015 Report on Business, a PPI above 52.1 for a sustained period of time is generally consistent with an increase in the BLS's index of manufacturing prices, which is one of the measures of price inflation on the wholesale level.

Often times, the individual commodity prices, like crude oil, possess solid correlations with the ISM Prices Index.

As with all sections of the ISM's Report on Business, the anecdotal commentary and remarks following each subindex contribute greatly to this report's value.

Included in each monthly report is a list of "commodities up in price," "down in price," and "commodities in short supply." This detail is extremely helpful in the determination of overall trends in macroeconomic activity. When economically sensitive commodity prices such as copper, aluminum, steel, and fuel oil are advancing, it's a pretty good sign of economic vitality. Conversely, deteriorating prices of these critical commodities could be an indication that economic growth is moderating, since the need for inputs in the manufacturing process has receded, resulting in lower prices.

Not all commodities emit this signal. For example, one early-2015 release reported an increase in butter prices. This is clearly not a gauge of overall economic demand. It may be an early indication that food producers, restaurants, and some home purchases might soon be on the rise, but it isn't likely going to identify runaway inflation in the general price level.

Another price-related measure in the ISM report that deserves mention is the supplier, or vendor, deliveries index. This is essentially a measure of time, specifically how long it takes suppliers to deliver parts and materials that are integral to the production process. When the index exceeds 50, it means that delivery has slowed, indicating that greater demand is making it more difficult for suppliers (vendors) to get crucial materials to manufacturers. Sub-50 postings, conversely, indicate faster deliveries.

## Manufacturers' Shipments, Inventories, and Orders

The Manufacturers' Shipments, Inventories, and Orders report from the U.S. Census Bureau is one of the more meaningful sets of factory or production indicators. It is a two-part publication that includes the advance report on durable goods, and then about a week later, the revised and more comprehensive Manufacturers' Shipments, Inventories, and Orders report—commonly referred to on the Street as *factory orders*—hits the newswires. The latter release includes information on the nondurable goods sector.

## Durable Goods Orders

The advance report on durable goods contains four categories of data: shipments, new orders, unfilled orders, and inventories. Shipments comprise products actually sold by establishments. The dollar figures reported are the net sales values of domestically manufactured goods shipped to distributors during the month of record. (For larger goods with lengthy fabrication schedules, such as aircraft and tanks, the reported figures are estimates of the value of work performed during the survey period.)

Some of the larger categories of shipments include capital goods (products, such as machinery, that are used to make other products), machinery, transportation equipment, computers and electronic products, and fabricated metal products. For the most part, the Street focuses on the trends in new orders.

Manufacturing orders constitute a leading economic indicator, because they reflect decisions about optimal inventory levels given the demand businesses anticipate based on their economic forecasts. In this regard, new orders for durable goods have proved to be particularly accurate predictors, since demand for such products is especially contingent on the expectations of overall economic health.

Because of this predictive nature, the Conference Board has incorporated two of the components from the report into its index of leading economic indicators: manufacturers' new orders for nondefense capital goods and manufacturers' new orders for consumer goods and materials. Over time, they can accurately identify turning points in the economy.

Although there is a true forward-looking tendency in the orders components, there is a drawback to these data: They are extremely noisy. Month-to-month fluctuations are often quite extreme, and as depicted in Exhibit 9.10, rarely identify any meaningful trend when observed on this basis. In fact, durable goods orders are the most volatile of all top-tier economic barometers.

Durable goods are those with an intended lifespan of three or more years. They include communications equipment, primary metals, motor vehicles, appliances, and defense aircraft. These products tend to be quite pricey and are not usually purchased on a regular basis. As a result, data connected to their manufacture fluctuate significantly from month to month and are difficult to predict. This is particularly true with regard to defense-related goods, such as ships and aircraft, whose valuation is exceptionally complex.

**EXHIBIT 9.10** Durable Goods Orders (M/M%)

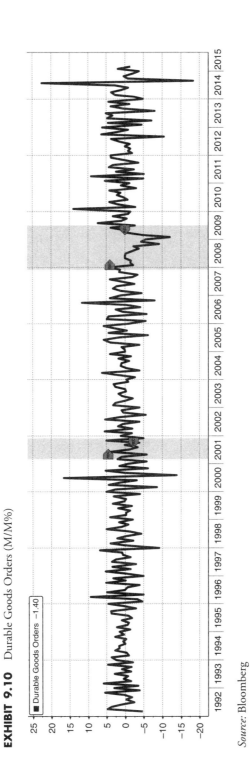

*Source:* Bloomberg

New orders are product orders received during the record month, including both those to be filled during the month and those for goods to be delivered sometime in the future. It is important to bear in mind that orders can at times be canceled. This ability to be canceled adds to the volatility.

Looking at the pace of durable goods orders (and shipments) on a year-over-year basis reveals the less-erratic trend that can better identify changes in the business cycle. Also note that the pace of orders is considerably more volatile than actual shipments, as depicted in Exhibit 9.11. Orders can, and do, get canceled; actual shipments do not, so they are less volatile than the orders data.

## Core Orders and Shipments

To reduce the volatility even more, economists look at trends without the transportation component—big items are not ordered on a routine basis. In fact, it is an even better idea to watch the level of orders and shipments of nondefense capital goods spending excluding aircraft (NDCGXA)—also referred to as "core" orders or shipments. The BEA uses the reports' figures for shipments of NDCGXA in determining the nonresidential equipment spending component of the GDP report. As Exhibit 9.12 shows, the 12-month pace of NDCGXA shipments is highly correlated with the year-over-year trend in nonresidential equipment spending.

Because of this relationship, shipments of nondefense capital goods, excluding aircraft, often serve as a proxy for the level of total capital goods investment in the economy. This is very useful; because investment in capital drives economic activity, economists want to spot trends in this component as early as possible. But capital-investment figures are available only on a quarterly basis, in the GDP report, and three months is a very long time to wait. NDCGXA shipments are among the few monthly surrogates for this important indicator—and the only one that is given in dollar-denominated values, rather than as a representative index, like the industrial production or the Institute for Supply Management's new orders diffusion indexes.

The total level of shipments is composed of nondurables and durables (Exhibit 9.13). The more comprehensive factory orders report contains revisions to the advance report on durable goods, as well as the first presentation of nondurable goods data and greater detail on all of these data by stage of fabrication.

Since we've covered durables, we need to define a nondurable good. Essentially, a nondurable is considered to be anything you leave outdoors in the elements, and after three years it disappears. That's not the technical definition, but it certainly works to explain the difference between nondurable goods. Included

**EXHIBIT 9.11** Durable Goods Orders and Shipments (Y/Y%)

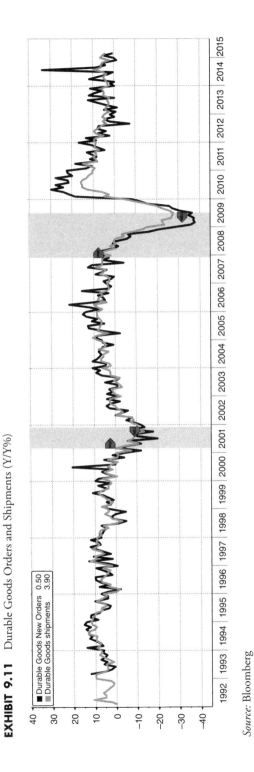

*Source:* Bloomberg

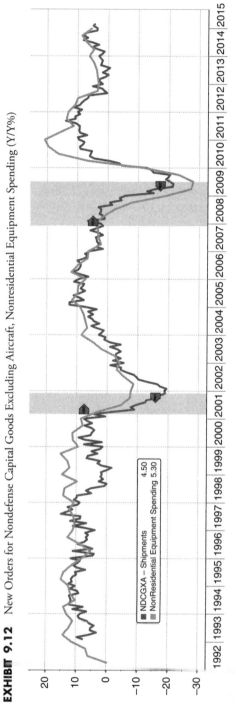

**EXHIBIT 9.12** New Orders for Nondefense Capital Goods Excluding Aircraft, Nonresidential Equipment Spending (Y/Y%)

*Source:* Bloomberg

**EXHIBIT 9.13** Total, Nondurable, and Durable Shipments

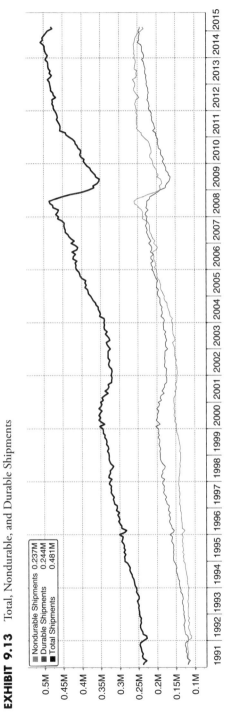

*Source:* Bloomberg

231

in this category are food and beverages, tobacco products, textiles, apparel, paper and allied products, chemicals and allied products, and petroleum and coal products.

Nondurables don't enjoy the headline status of their cousins, durables. Durable goods such as turbines, engines, household appliances, and machinery are sexier and easier to visualize as factory-produced goods than are nondurables such as pesticides, tobacco, and paints. That doesn't mean nondurables aren't an integral part of the economy, however. Nondurable goods account for about half of total manufacturing industry shipments. In March 2015, for example, nondurables made up 49 percent of total shipments, compared with 51 percent for durables. Over time these percentages change, but rarely deviate too much from each other.

There's one last entry that deserves some mention: Inventories are essentially the value of produced goods held at the end of the month that haven't been sold or shipped. The Street rarely, if ever, focuses on the level of inventories. As a standalone indicator, it doesn't really tell the analyst much.

However, when inventories are considered with respect to the level of sales or shipments, they can become among the most useful numbers in the MTIS report (Exhibit 9.14). Basically, the inventory-to-sales ratio (I-S ratio) indicates how many months it will take, at the current sales pace, until inventories are entirely liquidated—that is, until nothing is left to be sold. An inventories-to-sales ratio of 1.40, for example, means that at the current sales rate, businesses have 1.40 months of inventories left on their shelves. From 1990 through early 2015, the average ratio of total business inventory to sales was 1.38.

## The Inventory-Shipments Ratio

Because different types of goods have varied shelf lives, production schedules, and sales rates, the inventories-to-sales ratios for different industries normally move within separate ranges. This is clearly illustrated in Exhibit 9.15, which graphs the ratios for the manufacturing, retail, and wholesale sectors. The chart shows that for the most part, from 1992 through 2015, retailers had the highest ratios of the three groups, followed by manufacturers and then wholesale merchants.

Economists look for pronounced movements in the ratio that are sustained over several months. When the inventories-to-sales ratio rises over time, it means that sales are not strong enough to reduce inventories or that goods are being accumulated at too fast a pace. The bottom line is that sales are slower than companies had anticipated. This is a bad sign for the economy. Conversely, when the ratio of inventories to sales falls over several months, it means that sales are growing faster than inventories and that manufacturers may soon have to boost production. This, of course, is good for overall economic activity.

**EXHIBIT 9.14** Total Factory Orders, Industrial Production, Total Factory Shipments (Y/Y%)

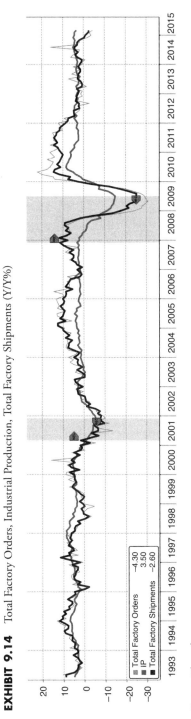

| Total Factory Orders | −4.30 |
| IP | 3.50 |
| Total Factory Shipments | −2.60 |

*Source:* Bloomberg

**EXHIBIT 9.15** Inventory-to-Shipments Ratios: Manufacturing, Wholesale, Retail

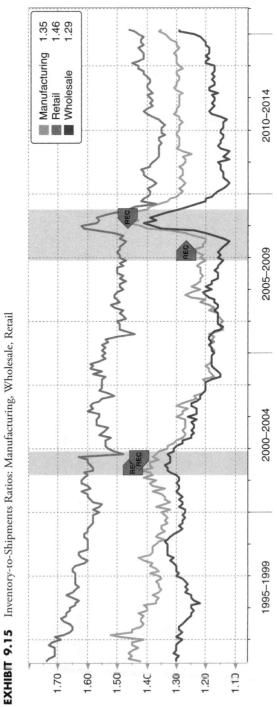

| | |
|---|---|
| Manufacturing | 1.35 |
| Retail | 1.46 |
| Wholesale | 1.29 |

*Source:* Bloomberg

## Test Yourself

Answer the following multiple-choice questions:

1. One back-of-the envelope way to guesstimate the month-to-month change in industrial production index is to:

   a. calculate the month-to-month percent change in man-hours worked.

   b. calculate the month-to-month percent change in weekly manufacturing earnings.

   c. calculate the month-to-month percent change in manufacturing payrolls.

   d. calculate the month-to-month percent change in manufacturing overtime.

   e. c and d only.

2. Why is industrial production a valuable economic indicator?

   a. It has an extremely long history.

   b. It closely parallels overall economic output in the nation.

   c. It is available in a timely, monthly fashion.

   d. All of the above.

   e. None of the above.

3. The Institute for Supply Management's Purchasing Managers Index measures:

   a. the actual number of manufactured goods produced in the U.S. economy.

   b. the actual value of manufactured goods produced in the U.S. economy.

   c. the value of all the manufactured goods produced for export in the U.S. economy.

   d. an estimated sentiment of manufacturing activity in the U.S. economy.

   e. None of the above.

4. Why is new orders for durable goods a desirable economic indicator?

   a. It is rarely volatile.

   b. It accurately predicts nondurables, which include food, and is the largest economic good.

   c. It is a forward-looking statistic, which often identifies turning points in the economy.

   d. None of the above.

   e. a and b only.

5. The inventory-to-sales ratio identifies:

   a. the pace of inventories given the underlying pace of sales.

   b. the forecast for new orders of durable goods.

   c. the size of the sales balance over a one-year period.

   d. all of the above.

   e. none of the above.

## Answers

1. a
2. d
3. d
4. c
5. a

# CHAPTER 10

# Prices and Inflation

Inflation exists when the price of an item or service increases. Over the course of the business cycle, it is common for price measures to exhibit particular patterns, which will tell an investor a great deal about the underlying tone and current of the economy. For the most part, a certain level of inflation in the economy is normal, even desired. Accelerating inflation, however, can cause severe problems, sometimes triggering a recession. A declining price level is also a caustic condition and may result in undesirable economic consequences.

The inflation rate can tell us a great deal about economic activity. When the economy is strengthening and people are employed with solid incomes, companies experience increased demand for their products and so can charge higher prices for them. As a result, revenues increase, lifting profits and permitting companies to boost capital investment and create new jobs. At a particular level, however, higher prices squeeze consumers, who may have to choose where to allocate limited funds: the more they have to pay for one good or service, the less they have for others. In addition, if those price gains are not associated with similar increases in wages and salaries, then consumers might have to cut back on the purchases of even more goods.

The price measures aren't generally considered leading indicators. Changes in the general price level aren't as predictive of business cycle turning points as are many of the indicators discussed in previous chapters. They do tell a great deal about the supply and demand of individual commodities or industries, however. Price indexes, even those excluding energy and food, can be affected by any number of influences. Legislation and taxes, for example, can push up prices on items like liquor and tobacco quite dramatically from one month to the next. That said, it is wise to observe trends over a period of time like three months or a year.

Prices can possess three trends: inflation, a sustained increase in prices; disinflation, a slowing of the rate of increase; and deflation, a sustained decrease in the price level.

**EXHIBIT 10.1**   Consumer Price Index (CPI), Core CPI (Y/Y%)

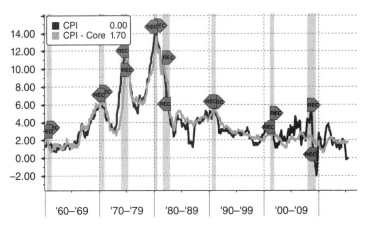

*Source:* Bloomberg

Consider Exhibit 10.1 of two consumer price measures. With the exception of a brief period in 2009 and a slight dip in 2015, the line graphing year-over-year changes in consumer prices remains above zero for the entire chart. That means the inflation rate was positive for the whole period. In other words, 1970 through 2008 and then from 2010 to 2014 saw rising prices for consumer goods. The increases have not been uniform, however.

The price–growth line falls sharply from 1972 to 1974, 1975 to 1977, 1980 to mid-1983, 1991 to 1992, and then again from 2010 to 2014. Those drops indicate slower rates of price growth—that is, disinflation—in consumer goods.

Deflation, a contracting price level, occurred in 2009 when the 12-month trend contracted (below zero). Deflation is consistent with the deep decline in economic growth. The only truly economically compromising bout of consumer price deflation that occurred in modern day United States was during the Great Depression, when a prolonged collapse in prices occurred for several years.

Some price measures, particularly the volatile indicators like commodities, energy, and industrial goods, are prone to extreme changes and therefore may experience temporary bouts of deflation on a more routine basis.

Deflation is as damaging to economic health as high inflation. When prices are falling, consumers postpone purchases in anticipation of even lower prices in the future. This is sometimes referred to as a deflationary mind-set. It also occurs when people are given steep discounts or coupons during weak economic periods. Without the engine of consumer expenditures (the largest component of GDP), economic growth slows and may even contract if the situation continues. Deflation also hurts corporate profits due to the inability to raise prices, thereby causing companies to cut production and reduce staff.

In recent years, economists have fretted about the possibility of deflation in the United States. Growing globalization has sent production facilities to low-wage nations such as China and India, which send incredibly low-priced footwear, toys, textiles, telecommunication devices, and foods back to the United States. Prices of nonimported services, such as tuition, medical care, and electricity, however, continue to rise. So, although certain industries have experienced deflation, the economy as a whole has not. In a true deflationary spiral, all prices decline at all levels, wholesale and retail.

## The Consumer Price Index

The Consumer Price Index (CPI) is the most popular measure of inflation on the retail level. It represents prices on the demand side of the economy. To gather the data used to construct the index, field economists from the BLS visit supermarkets, department stores, gasoline stations, hospitals, and other establishments in 87 urban areas all around the nation, recording prices of food, fuel, beverages, apparel, health care, and other goods and services.

The Consumer Price Index tracks the change in price, at the consumer level, of a weighted basket of 211 goods and services categories in 38 geographic areas for a total of 8,018 item-areas combinations. The composition of this basket reflects households' typical monthly purchases, as revealed in the Consumer Expenditure Survey, which the Census Bureau conducts for the Bureau of Labor Statistics. The weight given each item is determined by its percentage of total household expenditures.

The Consumer Price Index has two basic versions: the CPI-U, which reflects the buying habits of all urban consumers, and the older CPI-W, which relates only to urban households that include a wage earner or clerical worker. The two versions employ data from the same survey and are constructed using the same methodology. They differ only in the weight given certain basket components.

Wall Street and the media focus on the CPI-U, because it represents roughly 87 percent of the noninstitutionalized population, compared with the CPI-W's lowly 32 percent. National and local governments, businesses, and organizations employ the CPI-U in forming and implementing policies. Economists use it to adjust nominal-dollar-based indicators, such as retail sales, for inflation. All of the discussions of the Consumer Price Index in this book refer to the CPI-U.

The index's basket of goods and services does not, of course, capture every individual's or every group's consumption pattern. The elderly, for instance, probably spend more of their monthly allowances on health care, medicine, and food, whereas the younger generation spends more on tuition, apparel, and entertainment. The categories and their weights, however, present a fairly accurate picture of Americans' *average* monthly spending habits.

The month-to-month changes can be quite volatile, and little insight can be inferred from any single monthly posting. For this reason, the Street focuses on the 12-month rate of change as depicted in Exhibit 10.1. This way, a temporary spike in the CPI due to something like a weather-related incident that may have sent food or energy prices higher, can be interpreted with more clarity.

Along these lines, economists often look at trends excluding the noisy food and energy components, commonly referred to as the *core* rate of inflation. These two components have a tendency to whipsaw rather wildly and have at times distorted the interpretation of the true trend of inflation.

Contrary to some arguments, economists are not dismissing the trends in food and energy prices altogether—they simply look at an alternative perspective with less volatile influence. Food prices are prone to changes due to extreme weather conditions like frost, drought, floods, or storms. This can disrupt planting cycles, damage crops, and impede transportation of these products. Similarly, energy prices are susceptible to geopolitical strife. It seems as if every energy-producing country is located in a hotbed, which alters supply and distribution. There are also countless weather-related conditions that effect demand.

Removing these components and their erratic movements makes it easier to discern longer-term inflationary trends. Economists at the Federal Reserve Bank of Cleveland have gone one step further in reducing consumer price index "noise," lopping off those components with the biggest gains or declines in a given month; the so-called median index—also referred to as the Cleveland Fed index—is a more trusted version of the CPI.

This approach provides a much-welcomed representation. As Exhibit 10.2 shows, the headline CPI is considerably more volatile and prone to sending several false trends over time. The Cleveland Fed's version of the CPI is obviously a clearer and more believable representation of price trends.

**EXHIBIT 10.2** Cleveland Fed Median CPI, and the Consumer Price Index (Y/Y%)

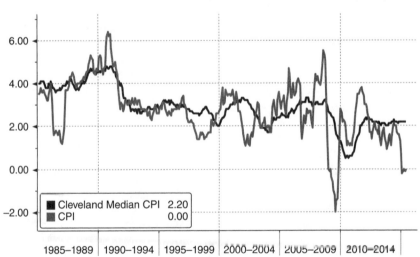

*Source:* Bloomberg

## The Producer Price Index

The Producer Price Index tracks price trends from the seller, or supply-side, perspective. Every month, the BLS collects some 100,000 prices for thousands of goods at various stages of production, from voluntary surveys completed by some 25,000 reporters. Using these prices, the BLS compiles more than 3,700 commodity price indexes and 800 or so for services, which are organized according to several different classification systems.

The Producer Price Index, also referred to as the wholesale price index, tracks changes in the selling prices of goods and services that are received by the producers of those items (Exhibit 10.3).

The Producer Price Index incorporates data about prices usually before the retail level is determined. It covers items that are not in the Consumer Price Index, such as raw materials, commodities, and industrial goods. Economists looking at the Producer Price Index data can generally see how far in the production process inflation pressures have traveled and how close they are to emerging in the retail or consumer sector. They can also get a feel for whether any rise in business costs is driven by demand or by supply.

Because of these characteristics, and because of its earlier release date, the Producer Price Index is used by some analysts to predict Consumer Price Index readings. This can be misleading, however. The two indexes are very different, both in the way they are constructed and in the items they include. The Producer Price Index, for instance, doesn't contain any information on prices on many of the services in the retail level, the largest part of the U.S. economy. On the other

**EXHIBIT 10.3**   Producer Price Index Final Demand, Core PPI (Y/Y%)

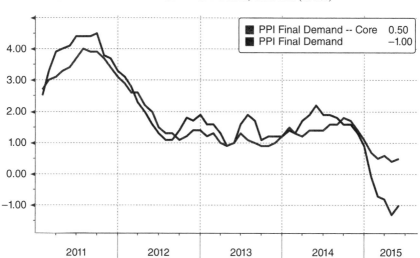

*Source:* Bloomberg

hand, it does incorporate information about the prices of raw materials, industrial goods, and crude products, which are extremely sensitive to weather conditions. This makes the PPI one of the most erratic of all indicators. As a result, monthly readings of the PPI are extremely volatile and can be quite different from those of the CPI, although the two indexes do show a high degree of correlation over the longer term.

The BLS changed its aggregation system from the stage-of-processing (SOP) to the Final Demand-Intermediate Demand (FD-ID) in early 2014. This new system has a limited data history dating back to 2009 or 2010, while the SOP had price indexes dating back to the 1970s or even earlier. The FD-ID system includes government purchases and exports, whereas the SOP system did not. In addition, the new FD-ID possesses prices on services and construction.

The FD-ID is quite an attractive approach detailing final demand for goods, services, and construction. Intermediate demand is broken down by processed and unprocessed goods, services, and construction. There are seemingly countless detailed tables by four different stages of production flow.

Fed-watchers have found some components of the producer price report to be an excellent indication of the near-term direction of Fed policy changes.

By looking at the core (excluding food and energy) intermediate PPI, analysts can identify inflationary pressures that may be building along the pipeline (Exhibit 10.4). Since 1975, when pressures begin to climb, the Fed reacts by increasing borrowing costs. Conversely, when the strains of pipeline inflation recede, the central bank withdraws restrictive rates and lowers its target rate.

**EXHIBIT 10.4**   Producer Price Intermediate, Excluding Food and Energy, Fed Funds Rate (%)

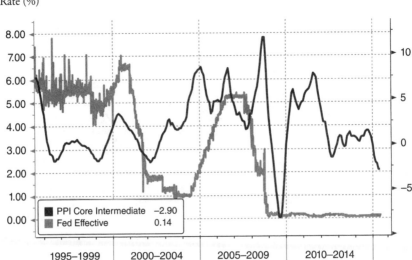

*Source:* Bloomberg

Admittedly, this relationship broke down somewhat in the early months of 2010, with prices trending higher than desired levels. However, the Fed understands that the economy was prone to other issues and was susceptible to market-related shocks, as it had not entirely recovered from the profound weakness experienced during the collapse in economic activity in 2007–2009. Therefore, interest rates were kept at or near 0 percent for more than economic reasons—namely, to restore confidence and help strengthen the financial system.

Traditionally, to cool the economy down and dampen inflationary pressures, the Fed raises its target for the federal funds rate (the rate banks charge each other for overnight loans used to meet reserve requirement). Longer-maturity interest rates usually follow suit. High rates discourage consumers from buying assets—particularly for the most interest-rate sensitive sectors of the economy like houses and motor vehicles, whose purchases are financed with loans. Companies may also put off construction and other projects that would necessitate forays into the debt markets. If rates rise to truly restrictive levels, they might be forced to eliminate workers.

## Commodity and Raw Material Prices

Economists frequently look to daily commodity price movements to get a possible feel for upcoming changes in the monthly release of producer and consumer price indexes. There is a lot to be said about commodity price changes. If raw materials are advancing, then there's a good chance that they will be passed along to the next stage of production. Ultimately, these increases could wind up on the retail level, which would impact the CPI and garner attention by the investment community as well as with policy makers.

Price movements at the crude or basic materials level can lead to price hikes farther down the production pipeline. This is known as cost-push inflation—an industry experiencing rising costs for materials, capital, labor, or land passes the increase on to another sector of the economy by charging higher prices for its own goods or services. When copper prices rise, for instance, homebuilders and buyers feel the pinch.

Similarly, natural gas and aluminum price movements have many knock-on effects. Natural gas not only heats millions of homes in the winter but also is the second-largest resource, behind coal, used in electricity production. One of the most energy-dependent operations is aluminum manufacturing. Higher prices for natural gas can thus push up the price of aluminum. That, in turn, boosts the prices of goods such as cars, which use aluminum or aluminum derivatives in fenders, motors, axles, bodies, wheels, and other components.

It is not enough to discern movements in commodity and raw-materials prices; you must also identify the causes of those movements. Price increases that are due to heightened demand (so-called demand-pull inflation) are more likely to be long term and passed on to end users than those caused by supply-related factors such as strikes, bad weather, factory explosions, and other production disruptions.

Broad-based composite commodities indexes are attempts to aggregate economically relevant materials into a single, and often tradable, index. With a composite of the most meaningful commodities in the economy, investors are given an alternative asset class. In recent years, the arrival of exchange-traded funds (ETFs) has made investing in individual commodities or commodities baskets as simple as investing in an individual stock. These too are wonderful economic indicators, but they do not have a very long history.

The concept of commodities as economic indicators may be the simplest, most elementary economic concept. It makes sense that as the economy accelerates, so will the demand for commodities and related materials. This increase in demand generally results in price appreciation, itself a useful economic indicator. Conversely, as economic activity cools, so too will the demand for most materials, lowering their respective prices. In addition to being a distinct and important asset class, commodities and their respective prices reveal a great deal about underlying economic conditions and provide insight into the outlook for inflation.

Over 100 years ago, when the economy was much more dependent on natural resources, the link between economic performance and commodities prices was considerably stronger. Back then, macroeconomic performance was directly measured by tallying the amounts of metal, glass, textiles, chemicals, food, paper, and rubber being produced. Today, services industries dominate the economic landscape. Yet they, too, are dependent on commodities, if less directly.

Trends in several commodity indexes, including the individual commodity series such as gold, crude oil, lead, lumber, cotton, gasoline, and copper, are an excellent barometer of the business cycle. As long as materials are needed in the creation of goods and the provision of services, commodities will have a reserved spot on Wall Street economists' dashboards. The fact that commodities indicators are determined by trading in the financial markets adds to their allure.

Because commodity prices are determined by supply and demand, any unforeseen interruptions to either of those economic determinants can greatly influence the overall price picture. It is important to observe the individual commodities markets because noneconomic developments may be driving supply and demand in some of them, causing fluctuations in prices. For example, commodities prices can be greatly influenced by climate, so it is always a good idea to know the weather conditions, which will help differentiate short-term temporary movements from longer-term structural changes. Newly enacted laws or regulations regarding environmental controls taxes or can influence the supply and demand of particular crops.

Because the United States has morphed into a services-dominated economy, the once-strong correlation between commodities prices and U.S. economic growth has relaxed a bit. Americans have greatly reduced their domestic manufacturing presence, sending workers and facilities offshore to nations that are more efficient at producing hard goods and products. The United States, with its highly educated workforce, excels in innovation—designing, creating, and developing new types of goods and services—whereas nations with supplies of cheaper labor concentrate on manufacturing processes. For that reason, commodity activity is more closely linked to world economic growth than growth in the United States alone.

Exhibit 10.5 shows the solid relationship a serious commodity-dependent nation like China shares with a broad-based commodity index like the Bloomberg Commodity Index.

The Bloomberg Commodity Index contains 22 commodities weighted two-thirds by trading volume and one-third by world production. It is a diverse index where no single commodity (e.g., corn or copper) may make up more than 15 percent of the index, and no group of commodities (e.g., industrial metals, grains, soy meal) can constitute more than 33 percent of the index. No commodity is permitted to make up less than 2 percent of the index.

It takes a great deal of energy to produce the largest amount of economic output in the world. So it isn't very surprising that the prices of crude oil are closely aligned with trends in U.S. GDP. Of all the individual commodities that have been analyzed over the years, crude oil and its derivatives—gasoline, home heating oil, and jet fuel—have received the most attention. The promise of ethanol as a fuel source has added a new dimension to the analysis, with ethanol influencing the prices of other commodities and consumer prices generally.

**EXHIBIT 10.5**   Bloomberg Commodity Index, China GDP (Y/Y%)

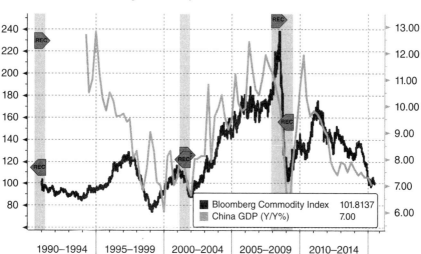

*Source:* Bloomberg

The U.S. Department of Energy's (DOE's) Energy Information Administration (EIA) releases the weekly crude-oil, gasoline, and natural-gas inventory numbers, as well as publishes countless data regarding prices, inventories, and demand, on everything related to energy petroleum, natural gas, electricity, coal, nuclear, and renewable and alternative fuels. All of these, and so much more, are available on the Bloomberg terminal.

Oil, of course, is the basis of other fuels like gasoline, diesel fuel, residual fuel (tankers), and jet fuel. It is also the source for many plastics and other petrochemicals.

The rising popularity of ethanol as a fuel source has added a new dimension to the analysis of influencing the price of energy. Furthermore, nothing has upended the energy market more than the recent hydraulic fracturing and horizontal drilling technologies in U.S. shale formations like the Bakken, Eagle Ford, and Barnett. Drilling in these areas helped boost supply to such lofty levels that the price of crude oil fell over 50 percent, and hurt many other global producers including Russia, Canada, and several OPEC nations.

As Exhibit 10.6 shows, there is indeed a positive relationship between crude oil prices and the four-quarter growth rate of GDP. Notice how spikes in 1990, 2000, 2007, and 2011 were soon followed by a moderation in economic activity. Four of these five periods were actual recessions.

Other than the obvious—that exorbitant energy prices can send the economy into recession and cripple consumer spending—why do investors find it so important to keep abreast of developments in the crude-oil market? Well, the Federal Reserve Board finds the trends in West Texas Intermediate crude oil quite

**EXHIBIT 10.6**   Crude Oil Prices, Nominal GDP (Y/Y%)

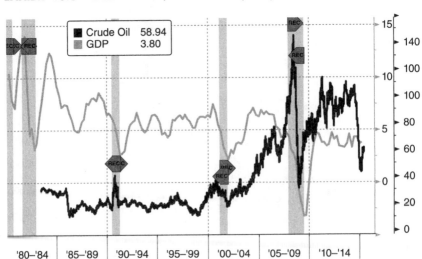

*Source:* Bloomberg

interesting. Although we seriously doubt that the Fed conducts monetary policy solely with respect to the price of crude oil, we do believe it is on the Fed's radar screen. Anything that is powerful enough to cause a widespread inflation threat throughout the economy is an attention-getter for the central bank. And if the Fed watches it, Wall Street watches it.

Since the comeuppance of the U.S. shale drilling, supply hasn't been an issue. The other side of the equation, demand, might keep prices many years. Many of the engines that we use today (automobiles, trucks, jets, buses, etc.) are considerably more efficient than yesteryear. Many vehicles have adopted some sort of hybrid between gas and electricity. Electricity is now a legitimate and accepted fuel source, whereas it was an unthinkable means only a decade ago. In addition, plants and factories are running in a more resourceful manner.

The *Journal of Commerce* is one of the oldest trade publications in use today, dating back to 1827. It has reported on the nation's shipping, trade, and commerce, including daily prices of commodities like wheat, rubber, wool, sugar, and linseed oil. It was only natural that this distinguished newspaper (currently only in electronic format) would eventually develop a measure of commodities prices. The *Journal of Commerce*'s industrial price index was created in the mid-1980s and later updated in the late 1990s by the New York–based Economic Cycle Research Institute (ECRI). Its composition was most recently readjusted in early 2006.

Of all the composite commodity indexes, the *Journal of Commerce*–Economic Cycle Research Institute (JOC-ECRI) Industrial Price Index is the most respected on the Street. Although the index's components and their respective weights are proprietary secrets, the index differs from the other top composite indexes because it doesn't rely entirely on exchange-traded components but includes other industrial materials as well, such as burlap and tallow. And since the JOC-ECRI Industrial Price Index actually has predictive power—an impressively accurate history of forecasting turns in the inflation cycle—it has become a much-relied-on reference for Wall Street investors. If you have to follow only one commodity index, make sure it's this one.

There is a very solid correlation between prices of industrial commodities as measured by the JOC-ECRI Industrial Price Index and the year-over-year change in the industrial production index (Exhibit 10.7).

The JOC-ECRI Industrial Price Index is everything an economist would want in an indicator. Rather than getting bogged down in an attempt to have a tradable group of commodities, the JOC-ECRI tracks materials that drive industry. Only commodities that fuel commerce are included in this 18-industrial material index. Just looking at the components, you get the feeling of the production process at work: machines and turbines pumping, massive heavy-construction trucks unearthing mineral deposits, hot-rolled steel moving out of mills, and lumberyards filling with the scents of plywood and red oak. An economist can almost smell the economy cranking out goods.

**EXHIBIT 10.7**  JOC-ECRI, IP (Y/Y%)

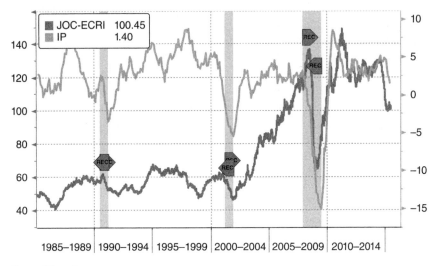

*Source:* Bloomberg

The JOC-ECRI index is preferred to other commodity price measures because it contains non-exchange-traded commodities. The other measures like the Reuters/Jefferies CRB index and the S&P GSCI use futures prices and therefore include a speculative component. Many times, investors—particularly hedge funds—will buy a commodity future in anticipation of a change in the movement of a particular commodity. This has been known to inject a great deal of added volatility into commodities markets and mask the true underlying trend in commodities prices. Furthermore, farmers often hedge against poor crop yields by purchasing commodities futures. Because some of the components in the JOC-ECRI are not futures, there isn't a concern about these speculative influences.

Of all the industrial commodities, one in particular is so solid at identifying turns in the business cycle it is said that it has earned a PhD. Frequently referred to as "Dr. Copper" or "red gold," it is one of the most widely used commodities; it is used in home construction (plumbing, piping, fittings, tubing, wiring, roofing, and flashing), electronics, and industrial, automotive, and marine applications. Like the composite commodities indexes, it shows a very strong relationship with overall economic activity. It is also one of the best indicators of global economic conditions.

As identified in Exhibit 10.8 the trend in copper prices are closely correlated with that of World GDP, particularly in 2005 and 2006. There are a number of events that coincide with this run-up in copper prices.

From 2000 to 2006, the United States experienced one of the largest increases in homebuilding in its history. The demand for copper, integral in

**EXHIBIT 10.8** Copper and World GDP (Y/Y%)

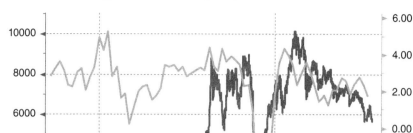

*Source:* Bloomberg

home construction, doubled as demand for related materials surged. This was, in fact, the initial stages of the housing bubble that ultimately burst in 2006–2007. Prices whipsawed for a few years as other nations—especially the emerging markets—experienced their own phases of strengthening. Ultimately, in late-2008, prices and world GDP plunged as the global economy succumbed to the simultaneous credit crisis, economic recession, and U.S. housing slump.

As fiscal infrastructure projects were announced around the world—less so in the United States—prices of copper and global economic output recovered. China's remarkable buildup was responsible for much of the increase in demand for copper and many industrial materials.

For centuries, gold has been recognized as one of the greatest forms of wealth. The desire to possess it has resulted in countless wars and conflicts. In addition to its use in jewelry making—its greatest use—it possesses a few industrial abilities. Since it is soft, heavy, and malleable—three qualities that are desired by manufacturers—it is used in some industries including electronics, dentistry, fashion, furniture, and art.

Investors have long used commodities, particularly precious metals like gold, as a hedge against inflation. Because the price of gold moves in concert with the general price level, traders, portfolio managers, and hedge fund managers purchase gold to protect their assets in a rising-price environment. Inflation erodes the value of fixed-income securities and hurts the valuation of other investments like stocks. Gold has also served as a safe haven against uncertain times or periods of intense geopolitical strife.

The gold-inflation relationship isn't exactly the strongest of all commodity-economy indicators. One of the problems with using gold as a measure of inflation expectations is that you cannot separate "inflation expectations" from the value of gold's "safe-haven" status. Notice in Exhibit 10.9 how prices as measured by the GDP deflator have moved in tandem—for the most part—with the price of gold from 1975 to 2007.

But in 2007, the two indicators diverge; the price of gold started to escalate as the United States and other nations experienced a deep slide in economic output, which is traditionally associated with a muted inflationary climate. Rather than slumping, gold's safe-harbor status kicked in when investors around the world feared a prolonged and deep economic depression, a collapse in the financial markets, the default of several sovereign governments, and the possible end of the European Union. This, in turn, sparked the possibility of a speculative bubble in gold as it approached $1,800 an ounce.

Since 2011, gold prices have remained elevated, but receded to less daunting levels.

Economists don't view gold as an intelligent investment since it doesn't do anything—again, most of it is used in the construction of jewelry. Silver, for instance, differs from gold in its industrial applications which largely include electronics and circuitry because it is the best thermal and electrical conductor. There are also coin, medal, and silverware uses.

According to the Street.com, investing legend Warren Buffett has criticized gold as an investment vehicle claiming, it "gets dug out of the ground in Africa, or

**EXHIBIT 10.9** Gold GDP Deflator (Y/Y%)

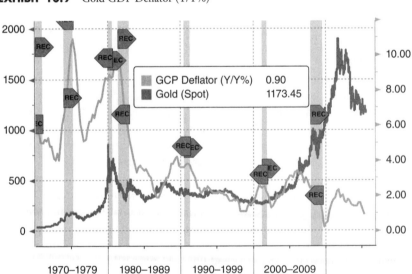

*Source:* Bloomberg

someplace. Then we melt it down, dig another hole, bury it again and pay people to stand around guarding it. It has no utility. Anyone watching from Mars would be scratching their head."

We've seen how following the price of metals, oil, commodities, and so on is a desired practice when attempting to decipher the tone of underlying economic strength. Similarly, watching the trends in prices of the means of transporting those materials is also quite a revealing economic indicator.

The Baltic Dry Index (BDI) is a daily composite index of shipping rates of dry bulk materials like cement, fertilizers, coal, iron ore, steel, forest products, and foodstuffs.

The BDI is a composite of the time charter averages (TCavg) of routes made by four vessel types: Capesize, Panamax, Supramax, and Handysize. Until mid-2009, the calculation was based on an equally weighted average of the BCI, BPI, BHSI, and the BSI indexes, where

BCI = Baltic Capesize Index 2014 (180,000 deadweight tons),

BPI = Baltic Panamax Index (74,000 dwt),

BHSI = Baltic Handysize Index (28,000 dwt), and

BSI = Baltic Supramax Index (52,454 dwt).

According to the Baltic Exchange, the BDI is currently calculated using the following formula:

$$((\text{Capesize 2014 TCavg} + \text{PanamaxTCavg} + \text{SupramaxTCavg} + \text{HandysizeTCavg})/4) \times 0.110345333$$

where TCavg = Time charter average.

As global demand increases for inputs, prices to ship traditionally advance. When economic conditions deteriorate, there is a pullback in the prices charged to ship materials.

This indicator is attractive for a number of reasons. It is a measure of prices at an early stage of processing. That is, prior to being cut into planks of lumber or forged into steel, these crude materials represent anticipated demand for finished products. Also, this is a measure of actual economic transactions. The materials have been purchased, and are being shipped. This is very different than an *order*, which might be canceled or a sentiment indicator that doesn't represent actual exchange or trade. The BDI is a measure of commerce. Finally, the BDI is a daily figure, and since it possesses some predictive qualities, it is a desirable leading indicator. Like all indicators, however, the BDI does have its flaws. Countless factors affect the pricing of any commodity, and that's no different for the prices of shipping them.

**EXHIBIT 10.10**   The Baltic Dry Index

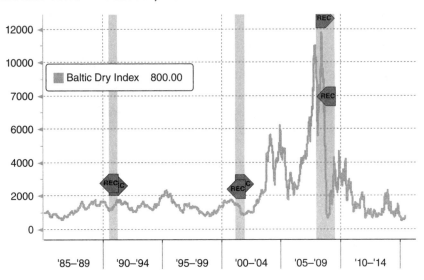

*Source:* Bloomberg

In late 2008, China announced an unprecedented $586 billion stimulus package, which was largely composed of countless large-scale infrastructure projects. The associated run-up for the massive demand for commodities and raw materials could be seen in the BDI (in Exhibit 10.10). The sharp increase was also driven by higher fuel prices, which are an added cost to chartering a cargo vessel.

Another influence is the supply of ships. When the commodity-demand boom developed in the wake of the Chinese stimulus there were shortages of ships. Ports were heavily congested and prices were pressured higher. Shipbuilders took notice and added to the supply, and some price pressures abated.

More recently, world trade had slowed, a greater supply of vessels are in the market, and fuel prices have tumbled. These three drivers have sent the BDI to some of its lowest readings in over three decades.

## Import Prices

The top three price reports released by the U.S. government's Labor Department are the CPI, the PPI, and the Import and Export price indexes. This troika are usually released within five trading session of each other.

Most books on indicators lump the import and export price report in the conversations regarding trade. While that is understandable, it might make sense to present it with the inflation and prices stats since import inflation (and deflation) can and does have a notable effect on the price level of domestic goods.

During the first quarter of 2015, Americans imported $2.09 trillion of goods and services from abroad and sent $2.6 trillion of exports to the rest of the world. Consumption of this magnitude has considerable sway on the general economic performance, and the associated price movements have a similar influence on the general price level.

For the most part, the export price portion of the release is ignored. When attempting to decipher the level of inflation in the U.S. economy, the changes in the prices to those purchasing our exports tells us little. This isn't to say that export prices aren't an important barometer; we use them for several purposes like adjusting nominal exports for inflation. It's just that import inflation identifies possible pressures from an important source of economic activity.

Total import prices is the headline indicator of this 16-page release. And since the U.S. imports a sizable amount of crude oil—admittedly less in recent years—and energy can be quite volatile, economists look to a "core" value of nonfuel import prices. The Bureau of Labor Statistics also showcases a fuel import price series.

Some of the more popular industrial import price categories are depicted in Exhibit 10.11, which are charted along with the value of the U.S. dollar (inverted scale) to show the strong correlation with input price trends.

The value of the currency can, and does, possess a considerable impact on inflation. It is often said that a strong dollar is in the best interest of the United States. For the most part, that phrase is correct. As the dollar appreciates in value against another currency (or basket of currencies) the value of goods and services declines for Americans. Conversely, when the dollar weakens against other currencies, goods and services from those nations are more expensive to Americans consuming them. So it's easy to see how a stronger dollar and the associated lower prices are, as Martha Stewart would say, a good thing.

But when the dollar appreciates sharply against a broad basket of currencies, the economy may invite import deflation, which could be a debilitating condition. In late 2014–2015, the value of the U.S. dollar experienced a rather precipitous increase, which sent several import prices into deflationary territory. For U.S. consumers purchasing imports of foreign automobiles, industrial supplies, capital goods, and nonautomotive consumer goods, this was very much welcomed. For those businesses in the United States that compete with foreign producers of those goods, conditions would be difficult since—on a relative basis—U.S. exported goods are seen as more expensive.

## Labor Market Price Activity

*Productivity and Costs* is a quarterly report with monthly revisions, where the headline index, labor productivity, is defined as the total amount of real output in the economy produced per labor hour worked. It is, in essence, a measure of efficiency.

**EXHIBIT 10.11** Import Prices—Various Measures

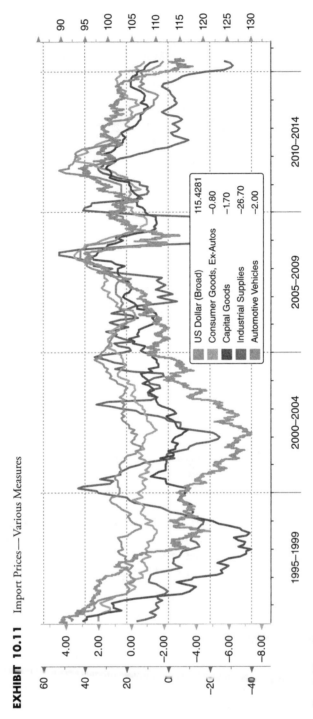

| | |
| --- | --- |
| US Dollar (Broad) | 115.4281 |
| Consumer Goods, Ex-Autos | −0.80 |
| Capital Goods | −1.70 |
| Industrial Supplies | −26.70 |
| Automotive Vehicles | −2.00 |

1995–1999    2000–2004    2005–2009    2010–2014

*Source:* Bloomberg

The higher the level of productivity (efficiency), the lower costs will be. Savings on labor costs can be passed along to shareholders (dividends) or invested in greater productivity-enhancing technologies, equipment, and capital spending, which elevates the level of aggregate demand in the economy. Also, this traditionally engenders greater job creation.

The estimates (and subsequent revisions) are not market-moving indicators. In fact, economists play down the productivity portion of the release primarily since the estimates of hours worked are probably not very accurate, particularly in the services sector of which the U.S. economy is dominant.

The soaring popularity of working from home and the ability to do so many job-related tasks outside a traditional office obscures the calculation of actual hours worked. There are so many fields—finance, advertising, fashion, information technology, publishing—where work can now be performed outside a traditional office. This tends to escape detection. Countless vacations are interrupted by a client request, emergency meeting, or potential new business opportunity.

The most respected and closely watched component of the Productivity and Costs report deal with the price of labor. Since this chapter deals with inflation, we include this measure because it assesses the price of labor. Unit labor costs may be defined as the cost of labor needed to produce one unit of output.

Since labor costs generally account for 70 percent of a company's expenses, the trends in this indicator tell us—among other things—about inflationary pressures, corporate profit margins, and subsequently the direction of stock prices. The general health of the economy can be explained by the growth rates in unit labor costs.

To estimate the level of unit labor costs, economists divide the average rate of compensation per hour by the index of real industry output.

Exhibit 10.12 presents the unit labor costs for several business sectors. For the most part, unit labor costs have been well behaved, with the exception of durable manufacturing and manufacturing, which were low (subzero) for most of the 1990s, and then spiked during the economic collapse in 2007–2009. Both industries returned to negative trends from 2010–2015.

The best explanation may be due to escalating technological advances on the factory floor, which resulted in a diminished need for workers. Labor costs were compressed because employees were replaced by robots, machines, and other productivity-enhancing software, computers, and technology.

Another respected measure of labor costs is the quarterly Employment Cost Index (ECI). This release tells us the total compensation, benefits, and wages and salary costs to civilian, private, and state and local government businesses. There are several subcomponents, including costs of goods- and services-providing industries and several insightful categories, including bargaining status (union or nonunion) and a regional prospective. As noted, wages and salaries make up about 70 percent of the total amount of compensation costs, while benefits account for the remaining 30 percent.

**EXHIBIT 10.12** Unit Labor Costs—Various Measures

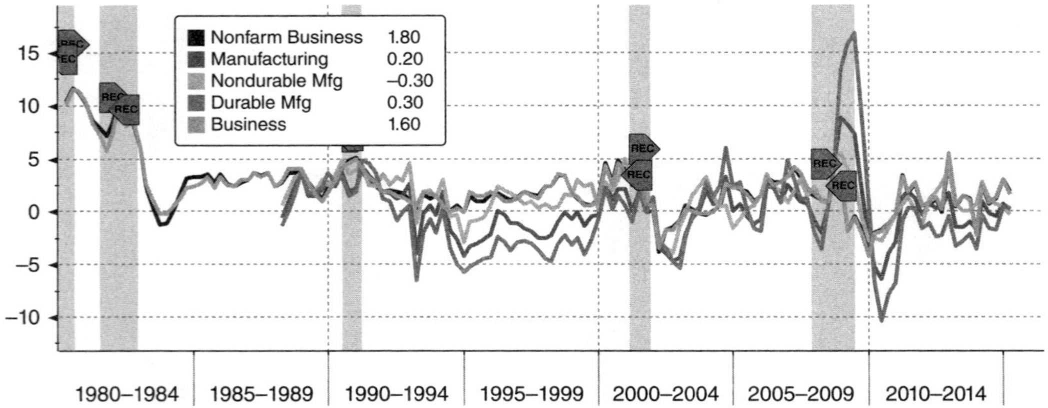
Nonfarm Business 1.80
Manufacturing 0.20
Nondurable Mfg –0.30
Durable Mfg 0.30
Business 1.60
REC
15
10
5
0
–5
–10
1980–1984
1985–1989
1990–1994
1995–1999
2000–2004
2005–2009
2010–2014

*Source:* Bloomberg

The costs of labor are a critical measure. While commodity inflation accounts for roughly 15 to 20 percent of the costs for the economy, those of wages and salaries are upwards of 70 percent. So when attempting to decipher the potential price pressures in the economy, it is best to observe those influencing the wage channel rather than the commodity or materials sector.

The Street tends to focus on the ECI and the major components wages and salaries, compensation costs, and benefits of civilian workers. Those involved in individual industry research, or a microeconomic approach, may look to just the total compensation of construction or manufacturing.

Exhibit 10.13 depicts the current trends in the ECI for total compensation, benefits and wages and salaries. The large increases in benefits in 2001–2003 were predominantly due to escalating health care costs (benefits).

When the economic collapse occurred in 2007–2009, total compensation costs sank—obviously, reduced staffing slashed labor expenses to businesses. The pace of wages as well as total compensation remained stagnant—from 2009–2014 (below 2.0 percent) until finally advancing in 2015. Benefits costs actually surged from 2010–2011 as the recovery advanced, returning to the pre-recession pace of 3.25 percent. This was largely a function of higher health care costs in general. Then, as businesses began to pass along these higher prices to the employee, the costs to companies fell from a better than 3.5 percent pace to a less daunting 2.10 increase.

Historically speaking, the latest trends are far from those that would cripple or upend the economic expansion—despite some increases in 2015 from higher minimum wage legislation and Obamacare. Still, the Federal Reserve is always on the lookout for potential inflationary pressures, and will undoubtedly notice these increases and pay heed in ensuing deliberations.

## Inflation Expectations

In early 1997, the U.S. Treasury Department introduced a new bond called the Treasury inflation-indexed security. Apparently this name was difficult to sell to retail clients, so the terminology was tweaked by salespeople and became Treasury Inflation-Protected Securities, or TIPS. These securities are indexed to the level of inflation, so the investor is protected against a rising price environment.

TIPS, like conventional Treasury notes and bonds, are direct obligations backed by the full faith and credit of the U.S. government and are available in several mid- to long-term maturities. The difference is that the par value (principal amount at issuance) is periodically adjusted for changes in the Consumer Price Index.

Because the primary difference between TIPS and Treasury notes is inflation, or the market's expectation of inflation over the remaining time to maturity of the TIPS, economists can in theory measure inflation expectations by subtracting

**EXHIBIT 10.13** The Employment Cost Index

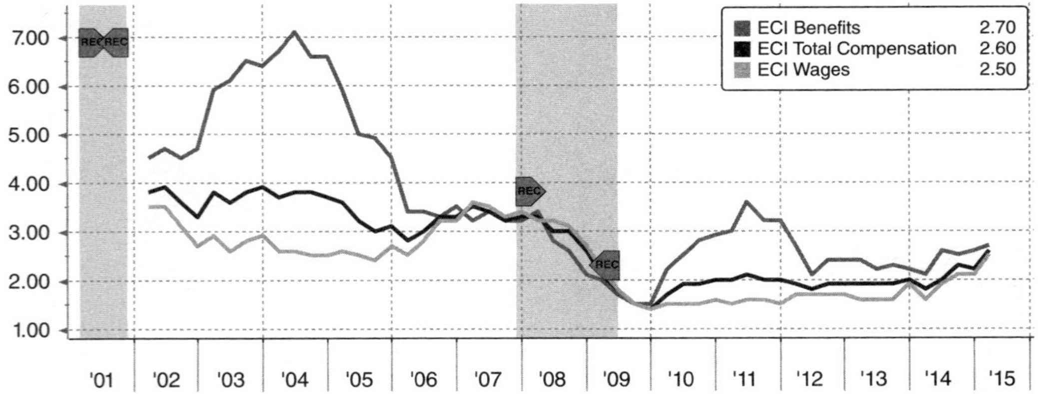

*Source:* Bloomberg

258

**EXHIBIT 10.14** The Breakeven Rates, CPI (Y/Y%)

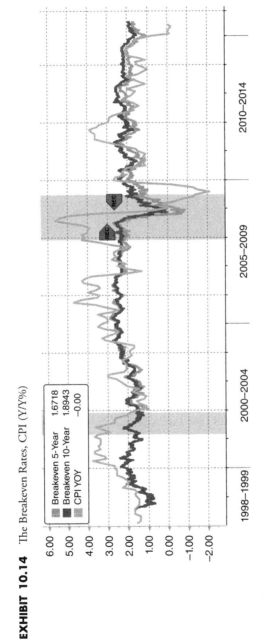

| | |
|---|---|
| Breakeven 5-Year | 1.6718 |
| Breakeven 10-Year | 1.8943 |
| CPI YOY | –0.00 |

*Source:* Bloomberg

the yield of the TIPS from that of a Treasury security with comparable maturity. This spread, also known as the breakeven rate, makes for a reasonably accurate measure of inflation.

The two most common indicators are constructed using the spread between the 5-year Treasury note and the 5-year TIPS (Exhibit 10.14) and the spread between the 10-year Treasury note and the 10-year TIPS.

From this chart of inflation expectations based on the 5-year Treasury–5-year TIPS spread, the most meaningful inference to be drawn is that since 2003, inflation expectations have not exceeded 3.0 percent. There are several possible explanations for this phenomenon, including rapid gains in productivity, globalization—freer exchange of goods, services, ideas, and money—and technological advances. Some people credit the inflation-fighting resolve of the Federal Reserve in the 1980s through the early 2000s for dampening fears of runaway prices. No matter what the actual reason is, we can say that according to the 5-year-TIPS-spread indicator, the fixed-income market in late 2006 did not see any economically compromising inflation in the near-term future.

Like most indicators, the TIPS spread isn't foolproof. The assumption behind the TIPS spread is that outside of inflation expectations, the yields on the two securities (the conventional Treasury note and the TIPS) should be the same. If there are any influences that disrupt this condition, then bias creeps into the equation, distorting the measure. Many will argue—perhaps successfully—that differences in the liquidity of the two securities (the Treasury note and the TIPS) make an exact comparison impossible. In that view, the TIPS spread wouldn't indicate precise inflation expectations. Nevertheless, it is an important indicator, used in some capacity by virtually all of the economics departments on Wall Street today.

Treasury Inflation-Protected Securities, or TIPS, provide protection against inflation. The principal of a TIPS increases with inflation and decreases with deflation, as measured by the Consumer Price Index. When a TIPS matures, you are paid the adjusted principal or original principal, whichever is greater.

## Test Yourself

Answer the following multiple-choice questions:

1. Deflation occurs when:
    a. the rate of the price level advances so fast, it deflates the consumer's ability to spend.
    b. the rate of the price level is contracting.
    c. the rate of the price level is advancing, but by a pace only 1.0 to 2.0 percent.
    d. the rate of the price level is advancing by a pace slower than the Fed's so-called comfort zone.
    e. c and d only.

2. Economists look to the "core" rate of inflation because:

   a. some components are susceptible to extreme volatility.
   b. some components are simply not used in an economy.
   c. some components are only exported.
   d. all of the above.
   e. none of the above.

3. The Producer Price Index (PPI) is extremely volatile because:

   a. it contains many commodity prices, which fluctuate greatly.
   b. it contains energy prices, which tend to whipsaw on a daily basis.
   c. it comprises many crude and raw materials used in the manufacturing process, which are erratic in nature.
   d. all of the above.
   e. none of the above.

4. The price of labor (wages) is important to the overall inflation picture because labor-related costs generally account for:

   a. 30 percent of a firm's total expenses.
   b. 50 percent of a firm's total expenses.
   c. 70 percent of a firm's total expenses.
   d. 70 percent of a firm's net expenses.
   e. none of the above.

5. The breakeven rate is a gauge that measures:

   a. the implied inflation rate from market-traded Treasury securities.
   b. when the consumer price index breaks even with the producer price index.
   c. the import inflation rate 5 to 10 years down the road.
   d. the difference between CPI and PPI.
   e. none of the above.

## Answers

1. b
2. a
3. d
4. c
5. a

# CHAPTER 11

# Confidence and Sentiment

Economists garner a great deal of information simply by asking questions. One of the best ways to take the temperature of the consumer is via surveys and questionnaires. Just as no politician would ever dare to run for office without the information from a few polls to know what constituents want, neither should any economist attempt to understand current economic conditions and the expected outlook without the assistance of a sentiment survey. All of the consumer confidence measures are top-tier indicators and deserve a great deal of attention and study.

When it comes to gauging the economy, consumers are king, accounting for upwards of 70 percent of gross domestic product through their spending on goods like toaster ovens and iPhones, to services like airfare and hockey games. That said, it is always good to know how the king is feeling. When people feel confident about their financial situation and future, they are usually reacting to some positive economic fundamental, such as solid employment growth or rising personal incomes. It is not surprising, then, that measures of consumer attitude have produced an impressive record of predicting business-cycle turning points.

Several surveys of consumer confidence and sentiment exist. Some research institutions and investment firms have proprietary surveys to get the responses directly into their models and transformed into forecasts and strategies as quickly as possible. Although differing in specifics, the various surveys share one crucial characteristic: They ask ordinary people questions that probe their feelings about the current and future state of the economy, inflation, and their spending plans for purchases like vehicles and homes. The survey participants may not know the difference between recession and depression, but their answers provide insights into the likelihood of these situations occurring.

Of all the surveys and measures, the three best known and most respected are the Conference Board's Consumer Confidence Index, the University of Michigan's Index of Consumer Sentiment, and the Bloomberg Consumer Comfort Index.

The Conference Board's Consumer Confidence Index is generally released on the last Tuesday of each month, while the University of Michigan survey usually issues its consumer sentiment index on the second to last Friday of each month, followed by the revised final estimate two weeks later. Both of those releases hitting the tape at 10:00 a.m. ET. The Bloomberg Consumer Comfort Index is released every Thursday at 9:45 a.m. ET, and contains information gathered for the week ended the previous Sunday.

Every Wall Street economics department watches the details of these surveys. They are also frequently cited by policy makers such as Federal Reserve and White House officials and are the objects of countless studies by government agencies seeking to determine if economic policies are working as intended. Politicians are also big users of the information found in the consumer sentiment reports.

The markets generally react most sharply to the confidence measures when the business cycle is close to a turning point. The indexes won't indicate how much the economy may grow or contract. But when the indexes decline sharply, you can bet on tough economic sledding ahead. Conversely, when the indexes spike upward, you can look forward to more prosperous times.

The Conference Board's indexes are based on surveys conducted by Greenwich, Connecticut–based NFO Research Inc. (Exhibit 11.1). NFO polls a panel of about 5,000 households on their assessment of current economic conditions, their expectations for the future, and their plans for major purchases in the next six months.

The Conference Board constructs three diffusion indexes from the responses to five questions: (1) how they rate general business conditions in their area; (2) what conditions they foresee in six months; (3) how they would characterize current job availability in their area; (4) how they think availability will compare in six months; and (5) how they think their family income in six months will compare with their current income. The Consumer Confidence Index is constructed from the responses to all five questions; the Present Situation Index from answers to questions 1 and 3; and the Expectations Index from questions 2, 4, and 5. All three indexes are calculated relative to a base year, whose value is set at 100.

The Conference Board receives preliminary results 18 to 21 days into the record month, so the indexes reflect the conditions of the month's first three weeks. Any late surveys are retained and used in the revision contained in the next month's release.

It is important to know the cut-off date for the survey responses, since any confidence jarring news that is received after the first three weeks of the month will not surface in the released figures. If, for example, there was a stock market skid that hit the last week of the month, some observers might be inclined to

**EXHIBIT 11.1** Conference Board Consumer Confidence, Real GDP (Y/Y%)

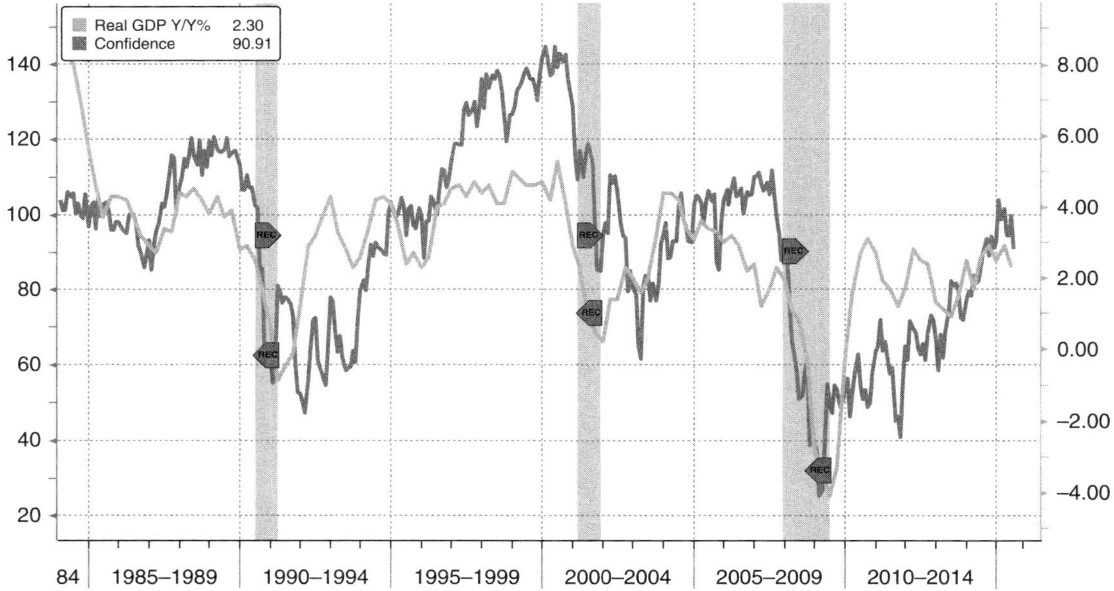

*Source:* Bloomberg

ratchet down their estimates for the confidence measures. But since the event transpired after the survey collection date, it couldn't possibly impact the data. Market observers would have to wait another month before they would find out whether the stock market slump dampened consumer spirits.

For its indexes, the University of Michigan's Survey Research Center polls 500 households in the lower 48 states by telephone, asking participants about their personal finances, general business conditions, and planned purchases (Exhibit 11.2). The entire survey consists of more than two dozen core questions, which serve as the basis for several indexes. The Index of Consumer Sentiment (ICS) is created from the responses to five questions:

1. Are consumers better or worse off financially than a year ago?
2. Will the year to come be better or worse for them financially?
3. How will businesses fare in the next 12 months?
4. During the next five years or so, will the country experience good times or widespread unemployment and depression?
5. Is it a good or bad time to buy major household items?

Responses are classified as positive, neutral, or negative. Two subindexes are formed from different subsets of the five responses: the index of current economic conditions (ICC), from replies to questions 1 and 5, and the index of consumer expectations (ICE), from questions 2, 3, and 4.

These three indexes are all constructed using diffusion methodology: The positive responses are added together and the result divided by the sum of positive and negative responses to yield a relative value. The index values are calculated relative to a base month, whose value is set at 100.

The Bloomberg Consumer Comfort Index is a weekly report, asking roughly 1,000 consumers per month (250 per week aged 18 or older) to evaluate their perspectives on the economy, the buying climate, and personal finances. They are prompted to rate each as poor, not so good, or excellent. This dates back to 1985.

In mid-2014, the Bloomberg Consumer Confidence Index experienced a rebase to a 0–100 scale, which differed from the previous –100 to 100 scale. The index is estimated by taking the average of three subindexes (national economy, good or bad time to buy, and the state of personal finances). This series is considered to be the best weekly measure of consumer attitudes (Exhibit 11.3).

The level of finances is greatly correlated with the 12-month trend growth rate in nonfarm payrolls. People clearly have an appreciation for the tone for the labor market, and its largely reflected in the Bloomberg comfort personal finances index.

Every indicator becomes a more useful tool when you understand the factors that affect it. Such understanding can aid in both interpreting and anticipating the indicator's readings. Measures of consumer attitude, however, differ from other indicators because the sentiment deals not with something tangible—such as the number of cars produced, the level of machine orders, or the value of

**EXHIBIT 11.2**  University of Michigan Sentiment, Index of Coincidental Indicators

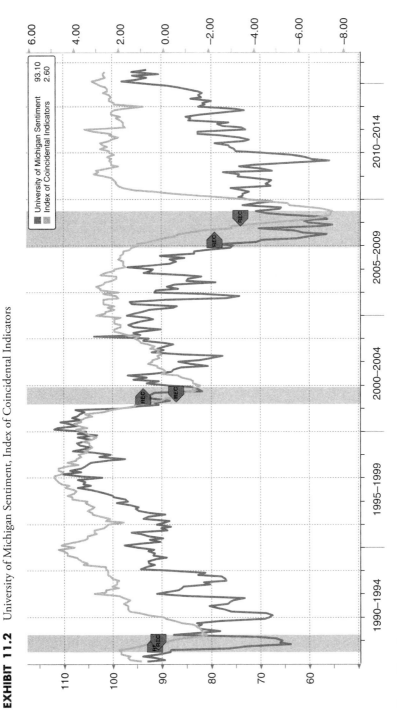

*Source:* Bloomberg

**EXHIBIT 11.3** Bloomberg Comfort, Personal Finances, NFP

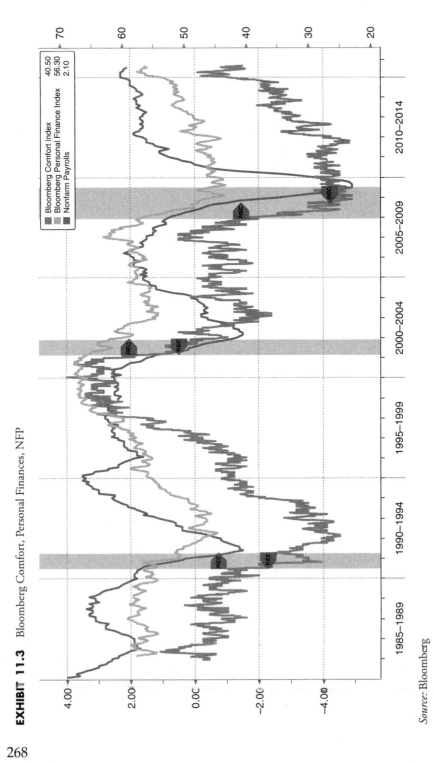

*Source:* Bloomberg

construction put in place—but with psychology. Using consumer sentiment measures effectively thus requires knowing how consumers' emotions are brought into play and whether these emotions are sufficiently strong to change spending habits and thus have an impact on the general economy.

## Tweaking the Confidence Measures

One way economists use the sets of consumer sentiment indexes to predict changes in economic variables is to chart the spread, or difference, between the Conference Board's Expectations and Present Situation Indexes. The reasoning behind this strategy is simple: If the expectations index is less than the present situation index, generating a negative spread, the implication is that people are happier with where they are now than with where they see themselves in the near future. Conversely, a positive spread implies a belief that greater prosperity lies just around the corner, a good sign for spending and the economy. The wider the spread in either direction, the drearier or dreamier future conditions are expected to be relative to the present.

Exhibit 11.4 shows the present–expectations situation spread and the 12-month moving average of the year-over-year trend in real disposable personal income. Notice how the spread generally bottoms out just before a recession begins and peaks just after it ends. In February 2001, the spread widened considerably, putting it into record negative territory.

Apparently, consumers were spot-on with their concerns, because a recession began two months later and lingered for eight months to November 2001. Consumers retrenched as their incomes dwindled and stock markets fizzled. Similarly, in December 2007 consumers felt more confident about the present and less enthusiastic about the future. This turning point signal was the beginning of the 2007–2009 collapse in the economy, the credit crisis, and the housing bubble.

The Conference Board's consumer confidence report contains a few insightful components regarding the employment situation, specifically are jobs plentiful, not so plentiful, or are jobs hard to get? Tracking any of these three barometers individually can be quite telling. However, when you take the difference between the jobs plentiful index and the jobs hard to get index, you have a very powerful tool used in the prediction of the unemployment rate. And since the confidence index is released before the monthly Employment Situation report, this is usually considered a key variable in Wall Street economists' forecasting models.

The economics behind the so-called *labor market differential* is that when jobs that are hard to get are larger than those plentiful, labor market conditions are seen as less desirable since consumers are irked by the difficulty in finding a position. Conversely, when the number associated with plentiful positions exceeds those hard to get, then the jobs climate is seen as improving. Inverting the scale of the labor market differential in Exhibit 11.5, we can see the incredibly strong relationship this metric has with the unemployment rate.

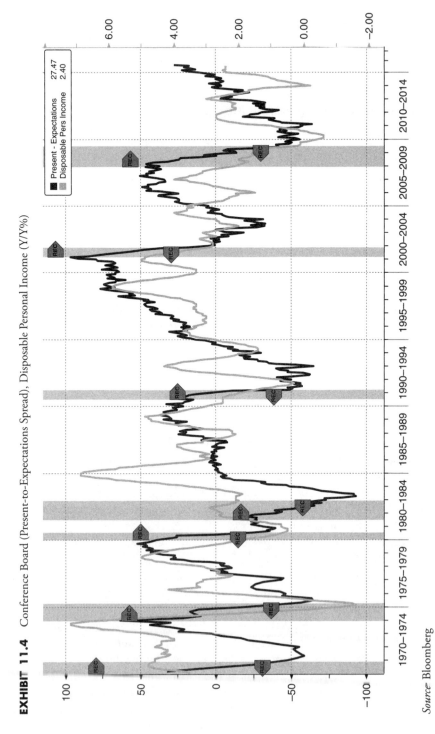

**EXHIBIT 11.4** Conference Board (Present-to-Expectations Spread), Disposable Personal Income (Y/Y%)

*Source* Bloomberg

**EXHIBIT 11.5** Conference Board Jobs Plentiful and Jobs Hard to Get, Unemployment Rate

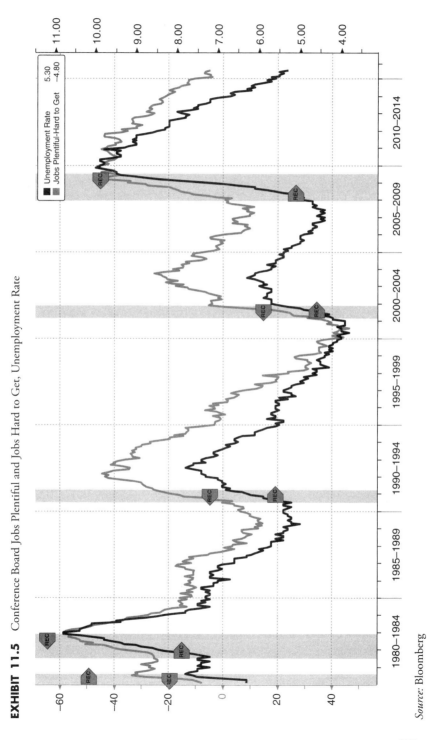

*Source:* Bloomberg

271

There isn't a key level of the labor market differential that identifies recession. For example, the 1982 recession had an associated −23 reading, while the 2001 slump was +20. So rather than watch a specific reading, look at the trend. When the differential registers four or five consecutive monthly declines, it's time to start considering the possibility of recession.

The Bloomberg National Economy Expectations Diffusion Index is based on 500 random-sample telephone interviews conducted during the first two weeks of each month. Consumers are asked whether they think the national economy is staying the same, getting better, getting worse, or if they have no opinion. The responses are then reported as a percentage of total polled respondents. Like most diffusion indexes, the National Economy Status Diffusion Index is estimated by taking the percentage of respondents who responded "getting better" plus one-half of the percentage who claimed the economy is "staying the same." This series possesses an excellent relationship with real consumption expenditures, which makes economic sense. One thing to consider is how meaningful an optimistic perspective has on spending.

Another correlation is that the confidence measures can sometimes miss the mark when it comes to turning points in the economy.

The Bloomberg Comfort Diffusion Index fell sharply in 2004–2005, yet consumers maintained a solid, above 3 percent, rate of spending (Exhibit 11.6). Also in 2011, the Index tumbled in half from 54.0 in January to 27.0 in November. During this time, the 12-month pace of real consumer spending tumbled sharply, from 3.2 percent to 1.2 percent. While many had issued warning signs of a recession at that time, a downturn never ensued. Several other measures are good at estimating turning points, but few are better at capturing trends in consumer spending.

## Confidence by Income Status

Exhibit 11.7 depicts the level of confidence by income cohort. All strata fluctuate pretty sharply on a month-to-month basis. That's to be expected, since conditions change relatively frequently that could alter confidence. Most measures advance during expansions and decline during recessions. The most startling difference is the pace at which each income category reacts to underlying conditions.

For the most part, the higher the income level, the more confident are the assessments of economic conditions—apparently, money can buy you happiness. Equally unsurprising, the least confident are those residing in the lowest of the income spectrum. This isn't to say that either group, or any of those in between, is more important than any other; it simply suggests that the underlying level of confidence varies by incomes.

Those at the higher end of the income spectrum tend to react more to changes in the financial markets and global economic conditions than those at

**EXHIBIT 11.6** Bloomberg National Economy Diffusion Index, Real Consumer Spending (Y/Y%)

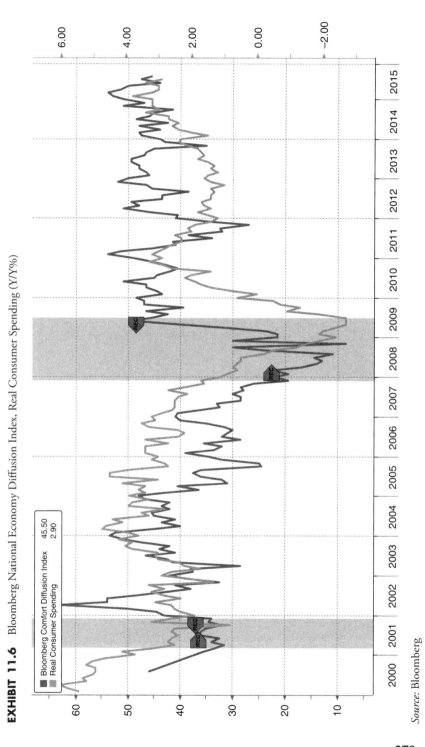

*Source:* Bloomberg

**EXHIBIT 11.7** Conference Board Confidence by Incomes

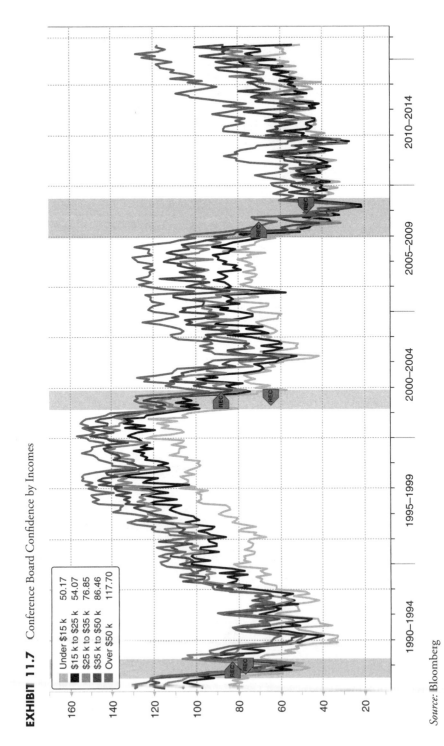

| Under $15 k | 50.17 |
| $15 k to $25 k | 54.07 |
| $25 k to $35 k | 76.85 |
| $35 k to $50 k | 86.46 |
| Over $50 k | 117.70 |

*Source:* Bloomberg

the lowest tier. This is in large part due to having a greater exposure to those types of investments. Those at the lower end are more impacted by prices at the pump. Changes in minimum wage legislation also tend to influence those lower-income earners.

These measures all tend to move in concert, with only the magnitudes changing by varying degrees. Notice the declines that commenced in 2002. Fears on Wall Street were that the economy was about to experience a *double-dip* recession (a second recession quickly following the 2001 downturn). The confidence measure of those earning more than $50,000 fell from 128 in May 2002 to 71.5 in March 2003—a drop of about 56.5 points. At the same time, those earning under $15,000 experienced a 33-point drop from 74.8 to 42.0.

Another interesting trend can be seen during the recovery of the 2007–2009 Great Recession. It took several (roughly six) years for confidence to be restored to prerecession levels. Those in the top two income brackets have sharper gains, while those lower-tier income earners had muted, almost stagnant, movements. Again, this may be credited to the stock market valuations, which skyrocketed to all-time highs after the Federal Reserve adopted a zero-interest rate policy, which fueled the gains.

When we look at the level of confidence by age, we see a tighter relationship between the groupings than those by incomes (Exhibit 11.8). The interesting take from this is that those under the age of 35 are generally more optimistic than those aged 35 to 54 or even those over 55. Those in the oldest category are usually the least optimistic.

These trends may be credited to any host of reasons. Younger people may be more optimistic because they are ambitious and are just beginning their professional journey, fresh off of a graduation, excited about what lies ahead.

Make no mistake about it, when tough times come about, that optimism quickly turns sour and economic conditions deteriorate. The middle age group (35 to 54) are a key cohort, particularly when attempting to decipher overall economic trends. Those in this age bracket are in the sweet spot of their earnings lifecycle. They probably have paid off student loans, maybe own a home, a car or two, and have children. In other words, they're bringing money in, and spending it. They are established, have careers, and presumably possess a steady income. This is the true driver of the U.S. economic spending and subsequently aggregate demand. The younger group is largely just figuring things out; an appropriate career path, desirable place to reside, should I get married?, etc. These years are associated more with struggles than a consistent path of steady spending.

Older workers (55 to 64) are in the twilight of their careers, possibly thinking about their retirements. Although they might no longer have a mortgage or any outstanding loans, there is plenty for them to be worried about: Did I save enough? Will I be healthy? Many are also dealing with elder care for their parents.

Senior citizens (65 and older) are often concerned about living on fixed incomes, which are eroded by increases in the inflation rate. Higher medical cost

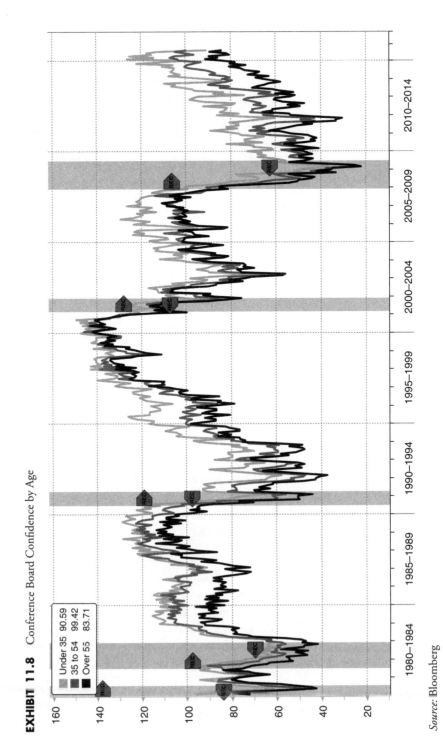

**EXHIBIT 11.8** Conference Board Confidence by Age

| | |
|---|---|
| Under 35 | 90.59 |
| 35 to 54 | 99.42 |
| Over 55 | 83.71 |

*Source:* Bloomberg

inflation is also taking its toll on this group—the largest consumer of medical expenses.

Watching the trends in the Conference Board's 35–54 age group may be the single most important sentiment indicator in this entire chapter. If this group isn't confident, then spending will not flourish and aggregate demand will not advance by any desirable pace. Economists don't look to the lower-earning younger or retiring, older cohorts to spark economic growth. Neither ends of the income spectrum are ever responsible for determining the overall pace of spending or economic activity.

## The Misery Index

Two of the largest influences of consumer attitudes are inflation and unemployment. High levels of either are enough to rattle confidence, but if both increase, conditions could become quite challenging and spell bad times for the consumer sector. Fears of job loss or a rising price level dampen consumer spirits and, if prolonged, result in reduced spending and weaker overall economic activity.

Economists have combined these "twin evils" of consumer price inflation and the unemployment rate and called it the Misery Index.

Exhibit 11.9 identifies the close correlation that the Conference Board's Consumer Confidence measure has with the Misery Index (inverted scale). Here we see a solid increase in attitudes as the economy emerged from the 1973–1975 recession with a surge in the consumer confidence index and a decline in the Misery Index from 20 percent to about 12 percent. Then building up to the double-dip recession of 1980–1982, there was a spike in the Misery Index to 22, which carried an associated slump in attitudes to below 60! This solid relationship continued through the mid-2010s.

One intriguing observation is that there isn't a particular level in the Misery Index that coincides with the Conference Board's consumer confidence index and recession. From the 1970s to 1980s, the economy was in recession once the misery index breeched 19+ percent, and confidence plunged into the 60s. Then, during the 1990–1991 downturn, the Misery Index had an associated Misery Index of 11 percent, while confidence plunged 70 points to the sub-60 level.

Then the economy experienced yet another recession in 2001—mild by historical measure. The Misery Index was quite low, which was largely a function of low inflation (in 2001 the CPI ran about 3.0 percent, and pretty much stayed below that incredibly low level for the next 14 years), so it was the unemployment rate that determined the level of misery. Also, confidence plunged after the end of the recession, mostly because there was a protracted jobless recovery, which weighed on consumer attitudes. Also, there are a number of non-economic-related events that can influence consumer feelings.

**EXHIBIT 11.9** Conference Board Confidence, Misery Index

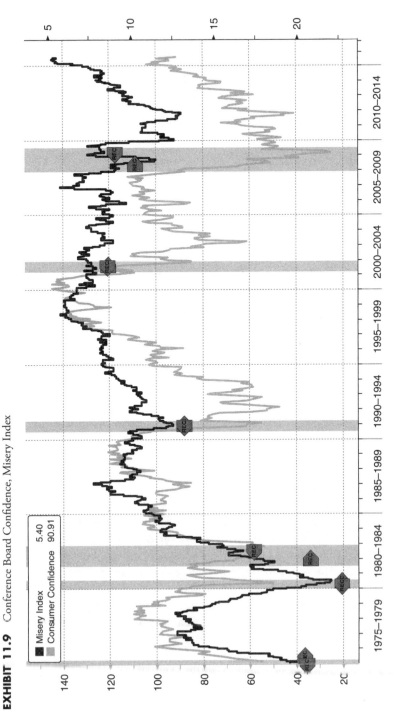

*Source:* Bloomberg

Consumers react to many things besides employment and perceptions of general economic health. War, peace, and politics can all shake or bolster consumer confidence. The emotional ride is particularly turbulent today because of the tremendous growth in news outlets on the Internet and cable, and the instantaneous dissemination of information over these channels. The result is often a false economic signal. Economists, analysts, and traders must learn to differentiate between news that will stimulate or stop spending and information that consumers will simply find uplifting or irritating.

The University of Michigan's Sentiment report has some measures of expected price changes based on two questions asking respondents whether they believe prices will rise, fall, or remain stable in the next 12 months and in 5 to 10 years, and by what percentage they expect them to change. The end product, as Exhibit 11.10 demonstrates, is a highly accurate predictor of near-term inflation. Because inflation influences both consumer spending and the fixed-income market, this is a very useful and highly respected indicator.

Throughout the 35-plus years covered by the graph, growth in the two price expectations indexes were closely aligned with the trend in the consumer price index (CPI). Only in 1979–1981, 1987, and 1990–1991 did the actual inflation rate differ significantly from consumers' expectations. During these periods, the U.S. economy was either in recession (1980–1981 and 1990–1991) or concerned over tumbling oil prices (1986).

In recent years, 2007 to 2015, consumers polled on their inflation rate outlook missed the mark. Inflation as measured by the CPI sank during the crisis in 2008–2009, and pretty much lagged below expectations. The combination of a slow economic recovery that hindered the ability for businesses to raise prices and slumping energy prices pushed the inflation rate to some extremely low levels, which at times bordered or fell into deflation.

Watching the price of gasoline can tell you a great deal about confidence. It is a measure of inflation, and since labor and inflation are the two largest influences of confidence, it should be considered in the assessment of the economy. As Exhibit 11.11 shows, every time the price of regular grade gasoline rises, there is an equal and opposite reaction to consumer attitudes. And when prices at the pump decline, the consumer becomes more optimistic with this price savings. Gasoline prices matter to most Americans, particularly those living outside of major inner cities where public transportation is not readily available.

It is common to hear executives of consumer-related companies like restaurants, hoteliers, food and grocery stores, casinos, and household product producers talk about energy prices and their impact on consumer sentiment and subsequent spending on their goods and services.

Two notable trends in the associated graph are that elevated levels from 2011 to 2014 (ranging between $3.00 and $4.00 per gallon) yielded both weak sentiment and low (mostly below 80) expectations.

**EXHIBIT 11.10** University of Michigan Inflation Expectations, CPI (%)

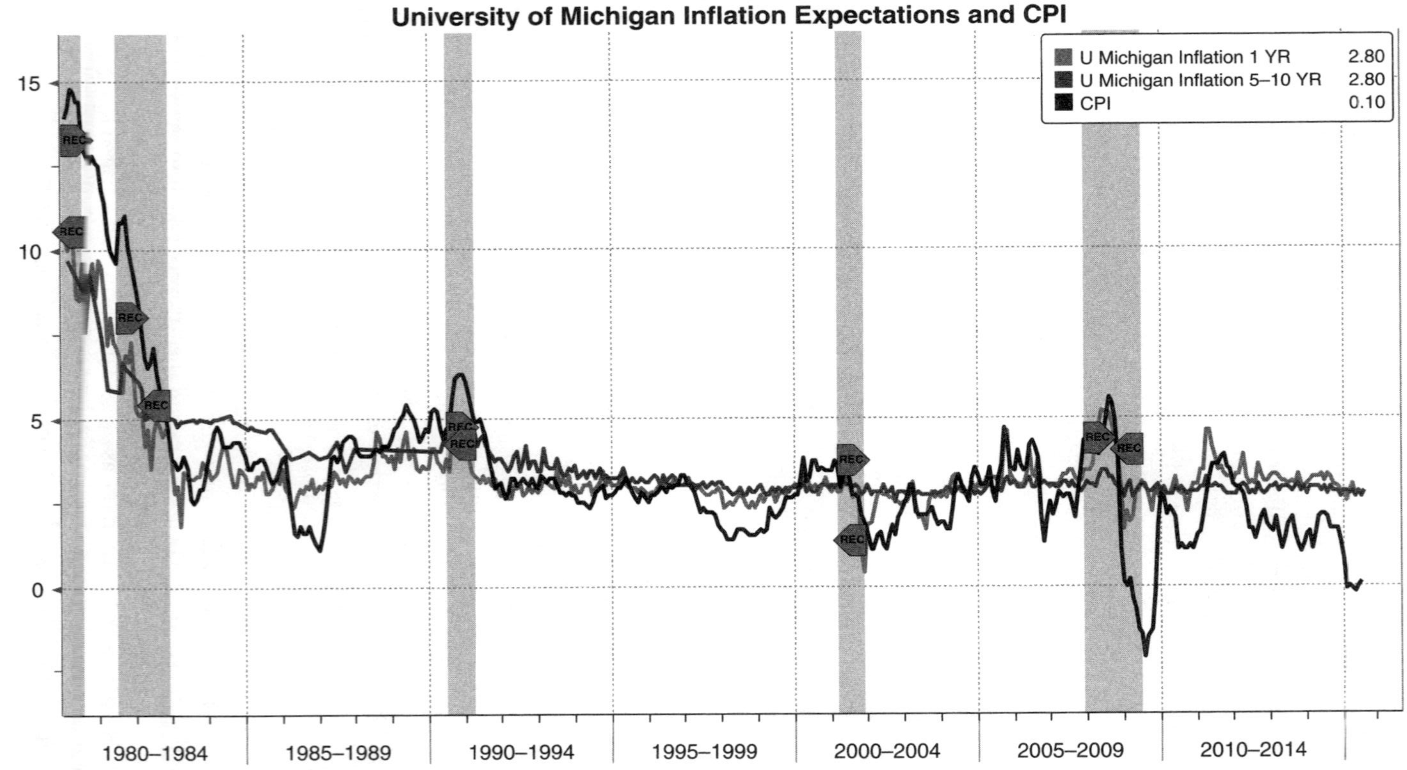

University of Michigan Inflation Expectations and CPI

| U Michigan Inflation 1 YR | 2.80 |
| U Michigan Inflation 5–10 YR | 2.80 |
| CPI | 0.10 |

*Source:* Bloomberg

**EXHIBIT 11.11** University of Michigan Sentiment, Expectations, Gasoline Prices

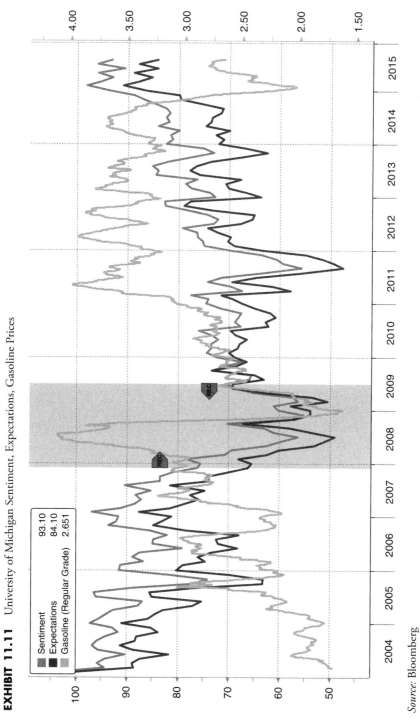

*Source:* Bloomberg

281

But when gasoline prices plunged from $3.68 per gallon in mid-2014 to $2.05 in early 2015, the University of Michigan's sentiment and expectations indexes climbed about 20 points each. Clearly, consumers care about the cost of gasoline and should always be considered in the analysis of household spending.

Whether they know it or not, consumers have an excellent idea of where growth in incomes is headed. When asked about their personal finances compared to a year ago, their responses are strongly correlated with the 12-month growth rate in wages and salaries—the largest component of personal incomes (Exhibit 11.12). Incomes are critical economic indicators and therefore matter when attempting to estimate consumer spending. Simply put, you need money to buy things.

The month-to-month level of personal finances confidence is pretty erratic—it frequently posts changes of 10 points in any given month. Nevertheless, the truly predictive power lies in the direction of the trend. If you wanted to use this barometer in a forecasting model for incomes, wages, salaries, and spending, it might be best to incorporate some sort of moving average.

It looks as if readings of 105 are when the yellow warning flags get hoisted, though this level isn't etched in stone. The economy was in recession in 2001 when the personal finance confidence measure was above 120. One explanation for this may be that that particular downturn was not a consumer-driven slump, but one where businesses overbuilt inventories, particularly in telecommunications equipment.

It's often said that if you needed only one gauge to forecast the tone of consumer attitudes, go with the trend in stock prices. Exhibit 11.13 identifies the solid relationship the Conference Board's consumer confidence measure possesses with the year-over-year change in the S&P 500 index. This is clearly an excellent indicator.

This relationship makes economic sense and is easily understood. The wealthier people feel, the more confident they become, and subsequently, the more they can be expected to spend. Alternatively, the less wealthy consumers feel, the less confident they tend to be, which would result in a slower pace of spending. Economists have attempted to estimate this so-called *wealth effect* and have come up with several different estimates for expected spending increases given various gains in the broader stock market measures.

This is a very easy concept to accept, but terribly difficult to measure. For example, only a portion of Americans have access (direct or indirect) to stocks. So gains in the equity markets may not be evenly felt throughout the spending public.

Also, extrapolating specific gains (or losses) in wealth and equating them to trends in consumer expenditures doesn't jive with a number of real-life situations.

Consider a stock market correction. Lower valued stocks would presumably result in a less optimistic attitude and send people to the sidelines until the stock market recovered. It is doubtful that consumers all around the country are going

**EXHIBIT 11.12** Conference Board Personal Finances, Wages, and Salaries (Y/Y%)

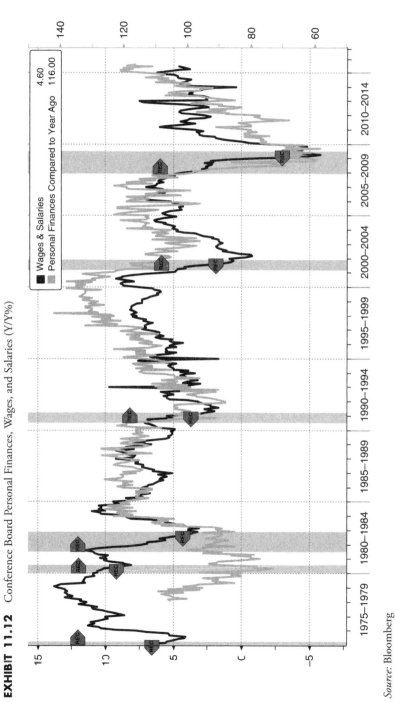

*Source:* Bloomberg

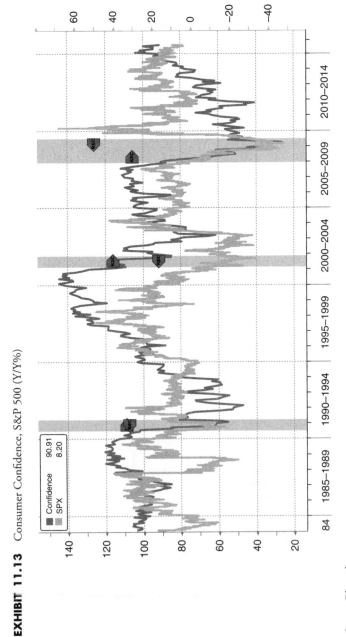

**EXHIBIT 11.13** Consumer Confidence, S&P 500 (Y/Y%)

*Source:* Bloomberg

to pull back on the spending reins. It is doubtful that you'll ever hear a mother pushing a child in a shopping cart in Target telling the kid, "You can't have that toy; don't you know the stock market is down for three consecutive sessions?" Also, will record stock market postings push those with no equity holdings or very low incomes to go out and ring cash registers and make aspiration purchases like Balenciaga handbags or a new set of Callaway golf clubs?

Despite the uncertainty regarding the wealth-effect and economic performance, the stock market is a notable influence on consumer attitudes and should be considered when evaluating the tone of the household sector and spending.

Of all the purchases one makes in their lifetime, a home will be the largest. And if you are considering such a large purchase, you better be confident in the ability to make the payments, which are usually over a 30-year period (360 monthly installments.) Of course, housing is a function of several economic factors—the prevailing interest rate, supply of homes, tax rates, and incomes—but if you feel pessimistic about your job prospects, the interest rate environment, or your ability to hold down a job, you won't make that purchase. Watching the income expectations and home sales is a very telling indicator with respect to the overall sentiment of the macroeconomy.

As Exhibit 11.14 shows, the month-to-month change in the confidence measure of income expectations varies greatly. So rather than have a specific level to determine a possible recession, it's better to observe ranges.

When the top 33 percent has income confidence in the 100–120s, the middle 33 percent is running in the 80–100 range, and the bottom 33 percent in the 70–80 range, existing home sales tend to perform very well. Look at the surge in sales from 1999 to 2005—this was undoubtedly due to many favorable influences like a solid jobs climate and a low-mortgage-rate environment. But one overriding factor was rising incomes and improved expectations of future income growth.

Then, in 2004, the housing bubble burst, resulting in a collapse in sales. At first glance, it looks somewhat odd that the pace of home sales plunge, yet the income confidence measures held up well, particularly the top 33 percent. Existing home sales plunged from better than 7.2 million uso 4.5 million units at the end of the 2007–2009 economic downturn. Meanwhile, the confidence measures fell only modestly by the time the economy began to contract. This divergence may best be explained by the economic fundamentals during 2004 to 2007.

It is true that the housing market began its precipitous decline in 2004, but other conditions, especially income growth, remained solid. And despite the slump, real disposable personal incomes advanced by about 3.1 percent over that time, while spending increased by roughly 3.25 percent.

That's what makes this indicator so meaningful, it is reflective of consumers' perceptions about economic conditions, particularly incomes, which are the ultimate determinant for spending: You can't spend what you don't have—or think you're going to have.

**EXHIBIT 11.14** University of Michigan Sentiment Incomes (Top, Middle, Bottom 33%) Existing Home Sales

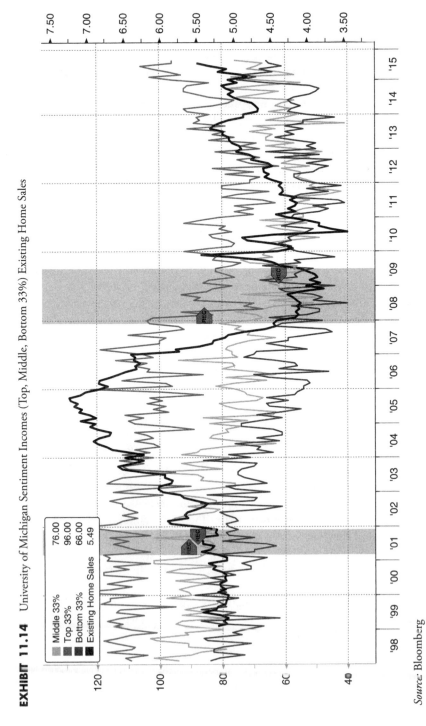

*Source:* Bloomberg

286

**EXHIBIT 11.15** Michigan Confidence Buying Conditions for Large Durables (Top, Middle, Bottom 33%)

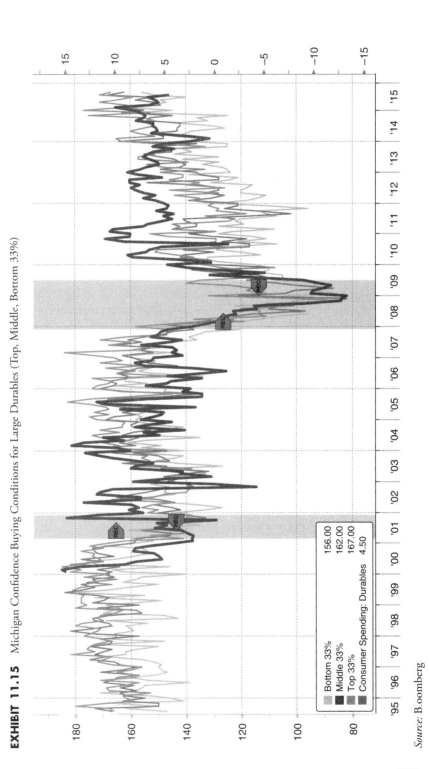

| Bottom 33% | 156.00 |
| Middle 33% | 162.00 |
| Top 33% | 167.00 |
| Consumer Spending: Durables | 4.50 |

*Source:* Bloomberg

In mid-2009, about the time the recession was ending, existing home sales bounced around and gradually returned to a respectable level in mid-2015. The reason for this prolonged sluggish recovery was due to a lofty unemployment rate, poor prospects for recent graduates, which pushed out the first-time home-buying age by about three to seven years, and stagnant wages and incomes.

In the wake of the crisis, banks were overly cautious about lending and had very stern loan standards. So even if you had income, a solid job, and the ability to make a good down payment, you might not qualify for a mortgage.

Again, watching the middle 33 percent is a preferable approach to determining the state of economic conditions; it seems to be the strongest of the cohorts with so many economic variables.

## Confidence and Big-Ticket Items

People generally buy big-ticket durable goods, such as stoves, washing machines, and air conditioners, on credit, which means committing to payments over a period of time. In making such purchases, therefore, consumers need to take stock of their financial future. That entails considering their employment status, potential income growth—even the state of the economy. These are the very considerations covered in the forward-looking questions of the University of Michigan's large durables confidence measure.

In this series, respondents are asked whether they believe it is a good time to purchase furniture, a clothes dryer, a stove, and so on. Exhibit 11.15 shows the Index of Consumer Sentiment for purchases of large durables by three cohorts, top 33 percent, middle 33 percent, and bottom 33 percent.

## Test Yourself

Answer the following multiple-choice questions:

1. The consumer confidence measures are based on the belief that when people feel confident about their situation, they:
   a. possess a greater likelihood to spend.
   b. are reacting to some positive economic fundamental.
   c. think the underlying fundamentals are solid.
   d. none of the above.
   e. all of the above.

2. The confidence measures are very sensitive to which two economic variables?
   a. production and income generation
   b. inflation and unemployment
   c. airfares and taxi usage

    d. inflation and factory orders

    e. durable goods orders and inventories

3. Consumer sentiment is largely linked to expenditures on:

    a. durables.

    b. nondurables.

    c. services.

    d. factory orders.

    e. none of the above.

4. What is a drawback of the confidence measures?

    a. Consumers don't always do as they say.

    b. Consumers may have a negative assessment due to noneconomic events like the weather.

    c. Consumers don't measure any concrete economic variable like employment or output.

    d. None of the above.

    e. All of the above.

5. One of the better confidence measures estimated from the Conference Board's survey used to determine the unemployment rate is:

    a. taking the difference between the jobs plentiful and jobs hard to get index.

    b. taking the difference between the inventories and jobs hard to get index.

    c. taking the difference between jobs in transit and jobs hard to get Index.

    d. all of the above.

    e. none of the above.

## Answers

1. e
2. b
3. a
4. e
5. a

# CHAPTER 12

# The Federal Reserve

When it comes to economic data and statistics, there's no greater nongovernment source outside of the Commerce Department or Labor Department than the Federal Reserve System. Between the information reported by the Board of Governors in Washington, DC, which includes industrial production, consumer credit, loans, the *Beige Book,* and flow of funds, or the individual regional bank contributions of manufacturing, services, or general economic data, this is one of America's greatest economic statistical resources.

Much of the information disseminated by the Federal Reserve System deals with the policy tools used by the Fed to fulfill its dual mandate of full employment and price stability. The primary instrument is the altering of its benchmark overnight borrowing rate known as the federal funds rate, or fed funds rate.

The Federal Open Market Committee meets eight times a year, about every six or seven weeks. The Committee comprises 12 members. The seven governors based in Washington, DC, and the president of the Federal Reserve Bank of New York, are permanent members. The remaining four members are chosen on a rotating basis from the other 11 regional Fed Bank Districts.

Exhibit 12.1 shows the fed funds rate and the rate of inflation in the U.S. economy as measured by the GDP deflator. These two series appear to move in tandem since the Fed raises this rate when inflation pressures mount. An accelerating economy traditionally engenders greater inflation. So when that occurs, or when the Fed believes that the economy is on the verge of overheating, it cools the economy down by raising its interest rate target. Conversely, when the economic conditions are deteriorating, the Fed provides a little stimulus by reducing borrowing costs with a fed funds rate cut.

A recent policy tool adopted by the Fed is quantitative easing (QE). This was conducted to arrest the market meltdown and credit crisis in 2008. Essentially, quantitative easing is an expansion of the Fed's balance sheet via the widescale purchase of financial instruments—in the United States, this included longer-dated maturity bonds as well as mortgage debt. When the Fed purchases securities and

292

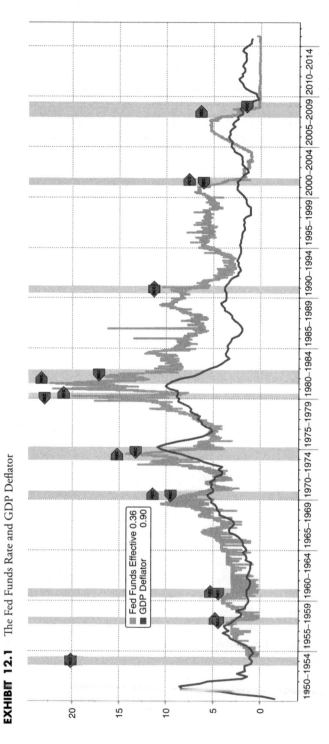

**EXHIBIT 12.1** The Fed Funds Rate and GDP Deflator

*Source:* Bloomberg

places them on its balance sheet, it removes those securities from the market (reducing supply), causing the price of those fixed-income instruments to increase and interest rates to decline.

The Board of Governors of the Federal Reserve System estimates and releases a very insightful report that contains loan activity called "H.8 Selected Assets and Liabilities of Commercial Banks in the United States." The contents of this report—released every Friday at 4:15 p.m. ET—helps identify the appetite businesses and households have to borrow. Obviously, an individual or a business will not seek financing unless they are confident they have a legitimate need for funds and will be able to repay the loan. Also, the pace of borrowing will tell a great deal about whether the prevailing cost of money—the interest rate—is too restrictive or desirable.

Looking at the Fed's H.8 report—as it is referred to on the Street—the assets and liabilities are presented (seasonally adjusted, nonseasonally adjusted, and the percent change) for U.S. commercial banks, domestically chartered commercial banks, small and large commercial banks, and foreign-related institutions in the United States.

While the data contained in this report receive virtually no attention from the business press, and have even less market-moving potential, those attempting to understand trends in the macroeconomy should not ignore this report.

For the most part, the Street observes the total commercial banks data, and looks to only a few of the loans data, particularly, commercial and industrial (C&I) loans, consumer loans, and real estate loans, which are segregated into commercial real estate and residential real estate loans.

Exhibit 12.2 identifies the solid relationship between the year-over-year growth rate in C&I loans and the 12-month pace in nonresidential business investment. Usually, the trends in C&I loans move in tandem with that of nonresidential business investment. The pace, however, isn't always consistent between these two variables, but the direction is largely a reliable indicator.

Not only is a moderating pace of borrowing a sign of economic uncertainty by businesses and households, but a lessened desire for banks and financial institutions to lend, which may be a sign of potentially softer economic climate. Banks aren't about to extend credit to those would-be borrowers that might not be able to repay the loan.

## Consumer Credit

When attempting to determine the pace of consumer spending in the economy, it is best to look at the growth rate of personal incomes, or better yet, the rate of change in real disposable personal incomes—those adjusted for inflation and taxes. The economic reasoning for watching incomes is that consumers—the largest contributor to GDP—tend to spend only what they earn. There is,

294

**EXHIBIT 12.2** Commercial & Industrial Loans and Nonresidential Business Investment

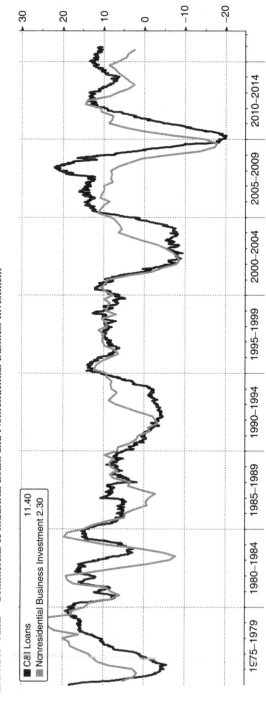

*Source* Bloomberg

however, an additional measure that will help explain the state of consumer affairs and the propensity for consumers to spend, the Federal Reserve's Consumer Credit report.

Each monthly release details the outstanding levels of credit secured by depositing institutions, finance companies, credit unions, federal government, and so on. The Street focuses on the monthly change in the headline amount of total consumer credit and the pace of revolving and nonrevolving credit.

Revolving credit essentially is the level of credit card borrowing. Watching the trends in this series permits the economist to see the desire consumers have to ring the cash registers. If conditions are favorable and consumers feel good in their situations and job prospects are upbeat, then they tend to pull out the charge cards and make purchases knowing that they will have the ability to pay the balance of their purchases over time. So, if you're employed and want to buy an item that may exceed your current budget like a dishwasher, an electronic device, or an air conditioner, you will spend with the understanding that you'll have money in the future. Conversely, a credit card purchase is not likely for an individual who has been furloughed from work or suspects the future environment is not altogether promising.

The other portion of outstanding consumer credit is nonrevolving, which includes loans on motor vehicles, mobile homes, education, boats, trailers, and so on. In more recent times the levels of nonrevolving debt have escalated and grew by a faster pace than revolving. This is, in large part, due to higher prices and demand for student loans. Also, auto loans have picked up amid a historically low interest rate environment. Consumer credit is, of course, very sensitive to the underlying interest rate.

As Exhibit 12.3 shows, during more prosperous times, consumers tend to pick up the pace of borrowing and spending. In more recent times (post 2007–2009 downturn) the pace of revolving credit moved in a "sideways" pattern, advancing by a range of 0 percent and 4.5 percent from 2012 to 2016. Despite the low-interest-rate environment, consumers were still reluctant to use their credit cards since the economic climate remained miserable for so long. Revolving credit growth didn't increase by any desirable pace until 2014, some five years after the NBER declared an end of the recession in July 2009. The pace of nonrevolving credit advanced by double digits, and then trended lower to a high-single digit pace.

Some caution is advised when using the consumer credit data. There are no mortgage-related data contained in this release, even though this is the largest "credit-related" purchase a consumer may make in a lifetime. Also, there is a tendency for revisions to alter the levels due to new sources becoming available, while the loss of other data inputs can be discontinued. Reclassification of data like some of that pertaining to student loans has also been known to inject some volatility in these figures.

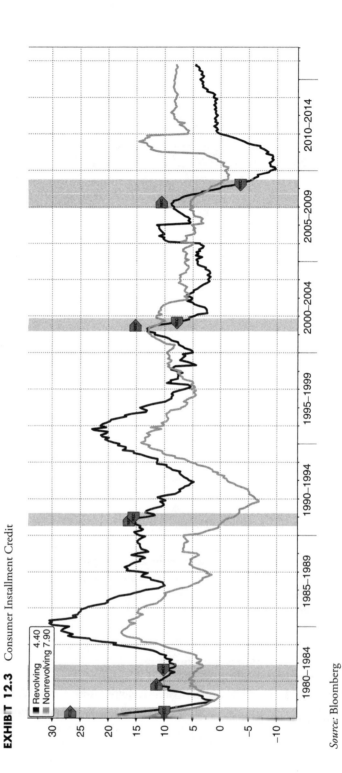

**EXHIBIT 12.3**  Consumer Installment Credit

*Source:* Bloomberg

There are also special memo items that appear in the report on isolated values of motor vehicle loans and student loans. This appears on a somewhat delayed basis.

## The Senior Loan Officer Survey

One of the more interesting set of indicators released by the Board of Governors of the Federal Reserve System is the Senior Loan Officer Opinion Survey on Bank Lending Practices. On the Street, this report is commonly referred to as the SLOOS. The SLOOS asks roughly 70 domestic banks and around 20 branches and agencies of foreign banks about changes in lending standards and terms, as well as the demand for various loan types by households and businesses.

Viewing these quarterly reports (January, April, June, and October) over time signals potential issues or developments in the lending process. Appreciating the demand for residential mortgage loans, consumer loans, and consumer installment loans will tell an economist the appetite that households or businesses have for consumption. If demand for mortgages weakens, then the pace of housing starts, sales, and related construction activity should be set for some degree of moderation. If consumer demand for autos loans was accelerating, then it's a good bet that sales of light vehicles and autos have been solid. These loan categories are also detailed by responses from large banks and "other" banks.

The consumer loan standards and demand are quite telling, especially with respect to the willingness for banks to make consumer installment loans. When this series falls below zero—implying a reluctance to lend to consumers—it's time to start thinking that a consumer-led slowdown may be in the offing. Starting in 2011, the Fed broke the consumer loans data into three separate categories: credit card loans, auto loans, and other consumer loans, which may help identify what area consumers are pulling back in.

When bankers tighten standards, the result—if sustained—is generally one of economic weakness. Notice how in Exhibit 12.4 the sizable increases (above zero) in 1990, 2001, and 2007 all had associated downturns in demand for commercial and industrial loans to large and middle-market firms as well as to small firms. Conversely, when banks ease standards, demand advances engendering greater lending and business activity.

There are many reasons why a bank would want to restrict the ability of a would-be borrower from receiving a loan. The Fed actually asks the banks about the possible reasons for the change it may be making with respect to standards. Among them are: deterioration in the bank's current/expected capital position, a less favorable economic climate, industry-specific problems, a reduced tolerance for risk, and so on.

Perhaps there is a fear that the economy may be taking a turn south, so rather than risk having those consumers or businesses miss payments, or worst care,

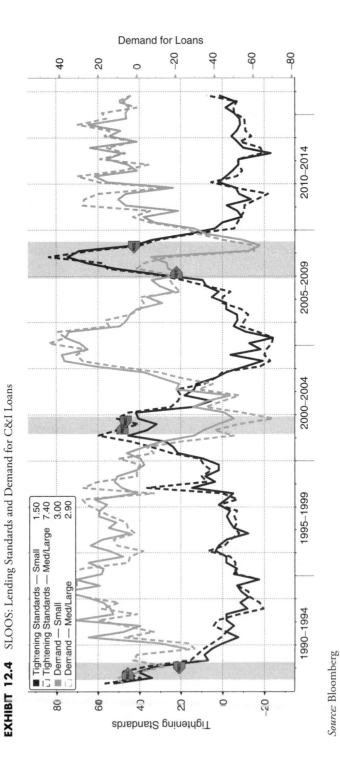

**EXHIBIT 12.4** SLOOS: Lending Standards and Demand for C&I Loans

Legend:
- Tightening Standards — Small    1.50
- Tightening Standards — Med/Large    7.40
- Demand — Small    3.00
- Demand — Med/Large    2.90

*Source* Bloomberg

default, they make it a little more difficult to get loans. The bottom line is, the first time banks ratchet up lending standards, there's a good chance the economy is about to demonstrate a softer performance.

There is excellent detail on the mortgage market in the residential sector, and beginning in 2007 a breakdown of all mortgage loans, prime, nontraditional, and subprime. The commercial real estate sector is also represented with series detail on construction and land development, nonfarm nonresidential, and multifamily real estate loans commencing in 2013.

## The Flow of Funds Report

The Board of Governors of the Federal Reserve System releases a quarterly publication formally titled "Z.1 Financial Accounts of the United States." This comprehensive report contains the flow of funds, balance sheets, and integrated macroeconomic accounts for the United States. This release is not a market-mover, nor are any components forecast by Street economists. The massive 200-plus page report contains data pertaining to the flow of financial assets and liabilities by sector (domestic nonfinancial; households and nonprofit organizations; nonfinancial corporate business; nonfinancial noncorporate business; federal, state, and local governments). There are also scores of tables listed by instruments (e.g., debt securities, loans, corporate equities, mutual fund shares, pension entitlements, etc.). Each report contains data for the six most recent quarters and the previous five annual figures.

Of the thousands of possible data series in the Fed's Financial Accounts, the "headline" is generally considered to be the total net worth of households and nonprofit organizations, which is listed in the balance sheet section of the release.

Exhibit 12.5 depicts the year-over-year change in household net worth, which is composed of nonfinancial assets (real estate, consumer durables, and equipment, etc.) and financial assets (deposits, corporate equities, mutual fund shares, municipal securities, etc.) less liabilities, which are largely loans like home mortgages and consumer credit. During the second quarter of 2015, total household net worth was valued at $85.7 trillion, with single largest holding of real estate ($21.5 trillion), followed by pension entitlements ($21.0 trillion), and corporate equities ($13.5 trillion).

Economists like to observe trends in this series for a number of reasons. Obviously, the higher the net worth, there's a good chance that the economic climate is quite favorable. Conversely, when asset prices like corporate equities or real estate decline, it may be a sign that the economy may not be operating too well. Consumers see this first hand in their monthly brokerage statements or neighborhood home sales activity. This may be best defined as the wealth effect. Asset prices advance and consumers have the perception that they are wealthier, and they tend to spend more.

**EXHIBIT 12.5** Flow of Funds—Household Net Worth

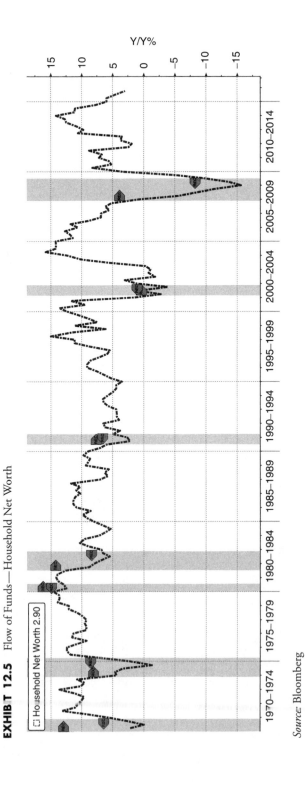

*Source* Bloomberg

## The Philadelphia Fed Economic Measures

The Federal Reserve Bank of Philadelphia is an economic powerhouse, with the greatest assemblage of internally created and publically disseminated economic indicators, surveys, and indexes used by the Wall Street community. In addition to data on state activity, the Federal Reserve's Third District has two of the most acclaimed forecast surveys, The Survey of Professional Forecasters and the Livingston Survey. These reports are summaries of economic projections made by a litany of top-notch economists. Although each and everything the Philadelphia Fed releases should be presented in this chapter, space is limited, so we proceed with two important indicators that are very closely watched.

The Philadelphia Fed's Manufacturing Business Outlook Survey, commonly referred to as the Philly Fed Index, is one of the oldest economic measures released by the regional banks, dating back to May 1968. It shares a solid relationship with many other manufacturing gauges (industrial production, the ISM, and durable goods shipments) and has a similarly strong correlation with broader economic measures.

Exhibit 12.6 identifies the trend that the Philly Fed headline index of business activity has with the year-over-year growth rate in real GDP. This relationship had a much tighter correlation prior to 2000, but that is simply a function of the changing U.S. economy morphing into a services-dominant structure from one where goods and production ruled the roost. Nevertheless, this monthly report deserves a place in the economist's tool bag.

The detail is quite telling with data on average workweek, number of employees, new orders, shipments, and inventories. There are also data for each of these key indicators, and the expected conditions six-months down the road. These are often very desirable leading indicators used in the forecasting process. Economists frequently perform analysis using many of the subcomponents like taking the difference between the New Orders and Inventories indexes, or the difference between the current business index and the six-months forward outlook.

The prices paid and received indexes are quite insightful. During periods of weak economic activity, prices tend to fall so economists watch the price measures for possible softness in economic conditions—in addition to the obvious inflation consequences. Prices paid for materials by businesses and those received for their goods sold are usually felt first for raw materials and commodities and then get passed along at a different stage of production. On many occasions, the Philly Fed Manufacturing Business Outlook Survey will identify potentially higher price pressures in the processed goods market.

In addition to the detail amid the rich history of this top-tier indicator, each report has the responses to "Special Questions" asked by the economists at the Philly Fed. Most deal with various economic topics such as capital spending plans, prices paid and received, and labor market conditions. One late 2015 survey asked about expected change in costs for upcoming 2016. Interestingly, those polled

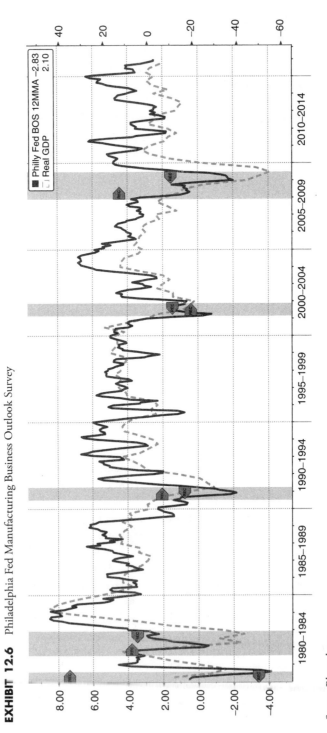

**EXHIBIT 12.6** Philadelphia Fed Manufacturing Business Outlook Survey

*Source.* Bloomberg

said, on average, energy prices would fall 0.7 percent in the new year, while raw materials prices would increase 0.8 percent, wages would rise 2.2 percent, and health benefits were expected to climb 7.5 percent. These responses frequently provide great clues about the broader economic climate.

In March 2011, the Philadelphia Fed introduced a similar version of its Manufacturing Business Outlook Survey for services sector activity called the Nonmanufacturing Business Outlook Survey. Despite its somewhat limited history, it does provide an excellent perspective of services industry activity.

Another excellent indicator from the folks at the Federal Reserve Bank of Philadelphia is the Aruoba-Diebold-Scotti (A-D-S) Business Conditions Index. This series isn't as popular as the market-moving Philly Fed Index; it does not appear on any economic calendars and no economist forecasts the measure. Still, it should be on every investor's dashboard.

In recent years, there has been a growing trend toward an immediate assessment of the overall economic picture. The bulk of the research was born out of the need to appreciate U.S. economic conditions in 2008 and 2009 as the economy was in a free-fall. The Real-Time Data Research Center at the Federal Reserve Bank of Philadelphia, responsible for the maintenance of the A-D-S, was established in August 2008.

Tom Stark of the Philadelphia Fed defined real-time data as "the historical observations before they are subject to revision or the forecasts based on such data." Over time, key economic indicators are often revised and can be quite different from those initially reported values. This calls into questions of accuracy. Using real-time data helps policy makers in the decision-making process, as well as a better understanding of current business conditions.

The A-D-S Business Conditions Index observes economic activity on a daily basis and is updated the moment each of the six variables are released (initial claims, industrial production, payroll employment, manufacturing and trade sales, personal incomes less transfer payments, and real GDP).

The interpretation of the readings in the A-D-S should be considered with respect to an average value of zero. Only when the latest values deviate from zero are there any meaningful signals emitted. Exhibit 12.7 shows the A-D-S since 1960, plotted with the recessions as identified by the National Bureau of Economic Research. With the exception of a few temporary dips in the 1960s and 2004 the economy avoid recession when the index fell below −1.0. There has never been a time when an A-D-S reading of −2.0 didn't result in recession.

## The Chicago Fed's Midwest Economy Index

The Federal Reserve Bank of Chicago provides a great deal of economic insight and data, most dedicated to the manufacturing economy. After all, this Fed District encompasses—along with the Cleveland Fed—half of the nation's Rust Belt, which extends from Michigan through Northern Illinois and Indiana, Ohio

**EXHIBIT 12.7** The Aruoba-Diebold-Scotti Business Conditions Index

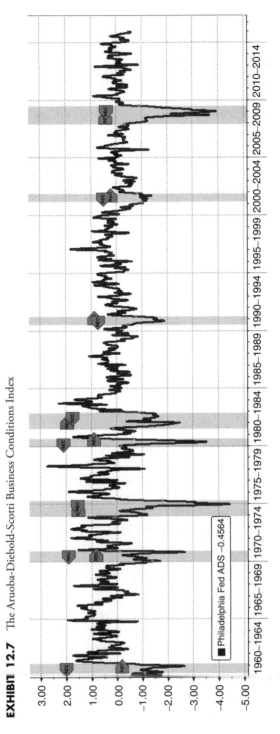

*Source:* Bloomberg

and into Western Pennsylvania. Since this region pretty much holds the keys to the auto industry—pun intended—the information contained in the associated reports can be quite telling.

The Chicago Fed has a couple of insightful economic indicators of overall U.S economic conditions including the National Financial Conditions Index and the Chicago Fed National Activity Index (see Chapter 2, "The Business Cycle"). But from a regional perspective, this critical district provides some exceptionally informative data like Farmland Values, the Michigan Retail Index, and the Chicago Fed Income-Based Indexes.

The most popular report observed by Wall Street economists that is estimated and released from the Chicago Fed is the Midwest Economy Index (MEI). This series is a weighted average of indicators from the region and the five states represented in the Fed's Chicago District (Iowa, Wisconsin, Michigan, Illinois, and Indiana). There are four subcomponents (manufacturing, construction and mining, services, and consumer), and data are reported for all states and the region, in each of the four sectors. In addition, there are two separate measures, the headline MEI and the relative MEI. The MEI utilizes some of the national—and regional—factors influencing conditions, whereas the relative MEI depicts those that are specific to the Midwest economy. That said, the Street tends to observe the headline MEI.

Exhibit 12.8 shows the headline MEI and its consumer and manufacturing conditions components. The proper perspective of these readings is, when the MEI is greater than zero, economic conditions in the Midwest economy are above its historical trend.

Interestingly, we see that over time there are in fact different degrees of above- and below-trend growth in each individual series. The MEI has a tendency to post extreme changes, while those of the consumer and even the manufacturing components are less volatile. During the late-1970s, mid-1980s, mid-1990s, and the 2010s the Midwest region experienced some favorable conditions, with many instances where the expansions approached or exceeded 1.0 percent. During each of those periods, the consumer index rarely deviated from its longer-term historical level. Notice, however, that the only time the consumer ever truly moved from its long-term historical trends was during recessions. This implies that overall activity—and even manufacturing conditions—may be signaling an economic downturn. But only when the consumer experiences a discernable dip does the overall economy experience recession.

## The Cleveland Fed's Inflation Expectations Index

Economists at the Cleveland Fed have developed a number of insightful indicators, including the Cleveland Fed's Median CPI that strips out the most volatile components of inflation in a given month, resulting in a less distorted measure of retail level price inflation. There are the informative Cleveland Fed Financial

**EXHIBIT 12.8**  Federal Reserve Bank of Chicago Midwest Economy Index

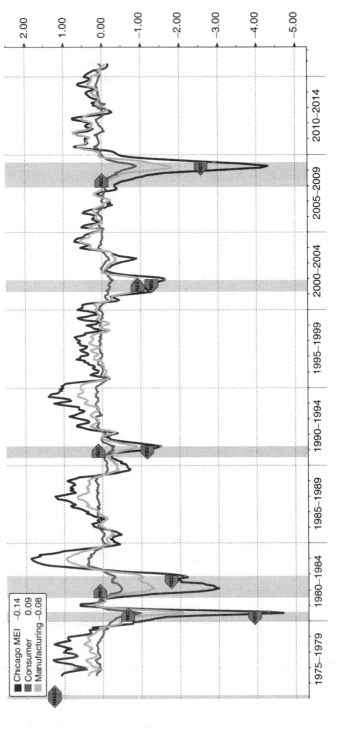

*Source:* Bloomberg

Stress Index, which presents the likelihood of systemic financial distress, and the very recent addition of the Cleveland Fed's nowcasts of inflation, whereby daily updated forecasts are presented for the monthly CPI, CPI-core, the personal consumption expenditure deflator (PCED), and the core-PCED.

One of the unique indicators that the Cleveland Fed disseminates is its Inflation Expectations Index. This series projects the expectations for inflation from 1 through 10 years based on several indicators including the so-called breakeven rate implied from the Treasury Inflation Protected Securities (TIPS) and the underlying Treasury note and survey-based estimates.

Exhibit 12.9 depicts the trend rate of expected inflation from the 1-, 5-, and 10-year perspective. The most obvious trend in this graph is that over the long run, the expected rate of inflation has receded rather precipitously and is currently residing at its lowest levels in decades. From the early 1980s when near double-digit inflation was the norm to the current sub 2.0 percent environment, an incredible transition occurred that changed the economic atmosphere. The rise in the popularity of online shopping had increased competition so much that it had become too expensive to operate—profitably—large big-box stores. Higher costs made it difficult to raise prices, especially against the price-cutting deals offered by online companies that didn't need to heat, secure, or staff bricks-and-mortar stores. Many retailers folded or merged, reducing employment and increasing mall vacancies. This, in turn, reduced the amount of taxes received by local municipalities.

This resulted in a lower inflation expectation environment, which can have a deleterious impact on an economy. Consumers will postpone purchases until they find the retailer offering the lowest price—this may be done online. This process engenders even greater discounting as businesses compete to lower prices even more. Ultimately this results in the lower inflation expectations that we have today.

Exhibit 12.9 shows the core rate of inflation as measured by the Personal Consumption Expenditure Deflator (core-PCED) and the Cleveland Fed's Expectations Index. Interestingly, the economy fairs quite well when inflation expectations are higher than the underlying rate. Consumers are probably encouraged by the existence of a lower priced environment that they believe they are getting a deal. This will permit them to spend more. This condition existed for the most part from 1990 to late-2007, when the economy ultimately succumbed to recession. Note that inflation expectations were also higher than the prevailing inflation rate in 2001, but that was not an economic downturn driven by households, but by the business sector.

## The San Francisco Fed's Tech Pulse Index

The San Francisco Fed's Tech Pulse Index is a lesser known, but important, gauge of economic activity calculated and disseminated by economists at the Federal

**EXHIBIT 12.9** Cleveland Fed Inflation Expectations Index

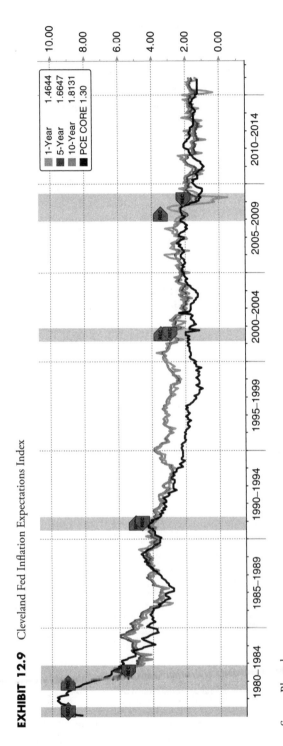

*Source:* Bloomberg

Reserve Bank of San Francisco. This measure is used to track the condition of the tech sector in a coincidental manner and is released on the second Wednesday of every month.

Initially, this series was created by the Federal Reserve Bank of New York, and then ownership was shifted to the Fed's San Francisco District in 2009. Comparisons of the current San Francisco data to the pre-2009 New York Fed estimate are not accurate since the model and sources have changed.

The San Francisco Fed uses several economic indicators in the estimation of this series, including industrial production of computers, communications equipment, and semiconductors, as well as shipments of computers and electronic products, consumer expenditures on computers peripherals, and software. Employment in several tech-related areas like computer systems design, telecommunications, and computer and electronic product manufacturing are also used in the estimation process.

Exhibit 12.10 identifies the index level of the SF Fed Tech Pulse Index as well as the annualized growth rate in the series. Several interesting issues surface when observing these measures. The decline in the Tech Pulse Index was considerably sharper during the historically mild recession in 2001 than during the major economic collapse in 2007–2009. The reason for this contrast in conditions was due to the tech-heavy influence of the 2001 recession. This recession, only eight months in length, was not lead by a pullback in consumer spending, as is traditionally the case, but by a buildup of unnecessary spending on technology and telecommunications equipment prior to the arrival of Y2K and the coincidental bursting of the dot.com bubble.

Notice, too, how the growth rate in the Tech Pulse Index climbed by more than 45 percent after the end of the 1982 recession. This is the beginning of the PC revolution and the comeuppance of the software, desktop, and communication industry. In the 1990s, the Tech Pulse Index continued its ascent, with annualized growth rates frequently approaching 40 percent as the Internet gained popularity.

It is important to understand that not every decline, or lower trend in the growth rate, will result in an overall macroeconomic recession. The U.S. economy is composed of many important industries like services, manufacturing, agriculture, transportation, retail, and trade. Only when a combination of these sectors experience downturns will the economy roll over.

## The New York Fed's Empire State Survey

Of all the regional Fed manufacturing surveys, the New York Fed's Empire State Manufacturing Survey usually provides the first glimpse of factory conditions in any given month. This survey is released around the fifteenth day of the month, and is reflective of conditions for the current month. While there is a shorter

**EXHIBIT 12.10** San Francisco Fed Tech Pulse Index

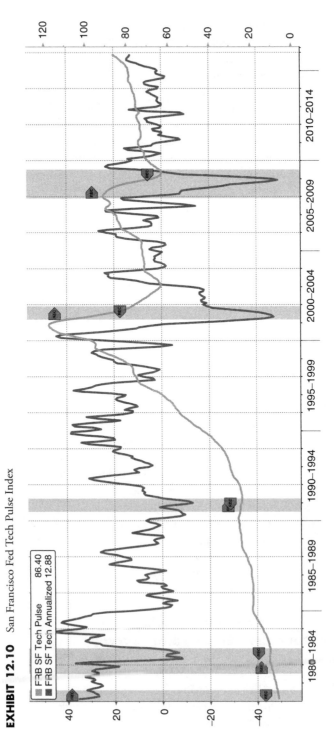

*Source:* Bloomberg

history of the Empire State Manufacturing Survey (commenced in July 2001), it is considered to be as meaningful as its longer-storied cousin, the Federal Reserve Bank of Philadelphia's Manufacturing Business Outlook Survey.

The Empire State Survey, like the many regional Fed manufacturing reports, polls area executives about current conditions as well as those for six months down the road. Positive (above zero) readings indicate expansionary conditions, while negative readings suggest contractionary activity.

While all the components are scrutinized, the most commonly interpreted are the headline General Business Conditions Index, the New Orders Index, Shipments, and the Number of Employees. The Prices Paid and Received indexes are also important, but have diminished in recent years, given a very low inflationary environment. With respect to the six-month forward barometers, the Street favors the headline, the prices, and the technology spending and capital expenditures figures.

As Exhibit 12.11 suggests, there are very volatile readings in this series on a month-to-month basis. Furthermore, there are several times when the current Business Outlook Survey falls below zero, yet no recession occurs in the overall economy. There are a number of reasons for this, the greatest being that the U.S. economy is no longer a manufacturing-dominant economy, so that sector may experience recession while the rest of the economy—largely services-dependent—supports the overall growth rate. In addition, the New York manufacturing economy isn't exactly what it was in the early nineteenth century when the upstate economy was producing large-scale manufactures and when Erie Canal fed the Midwest with imported goods via the Hudson River and west to Lake Erie. Nevertheless, this index is a solid indicator of manufacturing conditions and the first indication of what's going on in the manufacturing sector. It has a solid history revealing the manufacturing conditions of the entire country.

Following the Empire State Manufacturing Survey's release, the New York Fed publishes a Supplemental Survey Report that contains responses to topical questions asked in Empire State Manufacturing Survey and the Business Leaders' Survey of service-sector firms. These responses are often highly enlightening, with interesting insights regarding exchanges rates, expected workforce changes, price trends, and the Affordable Healthcare Act.

## The Richmond Fed Surveys

The Richmond Fed surveys businesses in its district that encompasses essentially the entire Middle Atlantic (Maryland, the District of Columbia, Virginia, West Virginia, and the Carolinas). In addition to its top two reports, the Manufacturing Survey and the Services Sector Survey, the Fed's Fifth District produces reports on agricultural credit conditions in the region and business activity data for the

312

**EXHIBIT 12.11** New York Fed Empire State Manufacturing Survey

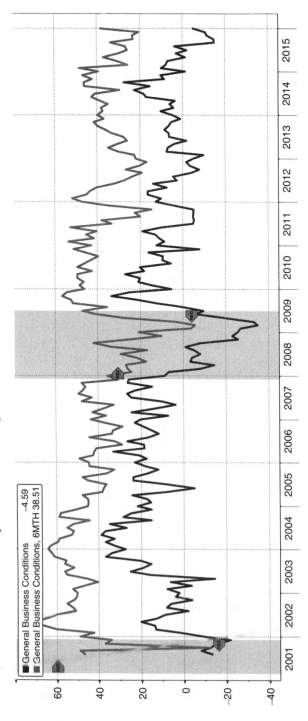

*Source:* Bloomberg

state of Maryland and the Carolinas. These are all quite informative, but hardly observed by the Wall Street community.

Even the Richmond Fed Manufacturing—often considered the headline release—is somewhat ignored by investors since the U.S. economy had morphed into a services-dominant economy. In addition, the presence of so many regional production reports representative of areas that are considerably more meaningful manufacturing areas has made this measure less monitored.

The lesser known report, and even lesser covered by the business press, is the Fifth District Survey of Services Sector Activity, which includes insights into the nonmanufacturing activity in the region, as well as several meaningful barometers regarding retail trends.

Economists like to view the components with respect to the Commerce Department's monthly retail sales report. Among the most watched retail indicators of the survey, the Expected Product Demand, Big-Ticket Sales, and Sales Revenues indexes are atop the list. Trends in retail employment may be witnessed in the Number of Employees and Average Wage components. The price components (current and expected) are insightful when considering retail inflation—some economists employ these measures in their forecasting models for the CPI. The shopper traffic index has had a diminished relevance since so much retail activity has moved from bricks-and-mortar stores to online.

Exhibit 12.12 shows the quarterly average of the Richmond Fed's Retail Sector's expected demand for goods index and the year-over-year pace of retail sales spending excluding autos. This is a very volatile series, and is best viewed with some type of aggregation or moving average. But over time it does demonstrate turning points as well as an underlying trend in retail performance.

## The Dallas Fed Surveys

It's often said that everything is bigger in Dallas, and when it comes to regional economic data and analysis, there may not be a larger set of indicators than those in the Federal Reserve's Eleventh District. The Dallas Fed releases include the Texas Business Cycle Index, the Metro Business Cycle Indexes—which represent nine metropolitan areas in the Lone Star State—and an agricultural survey with information regarding farm, ranch, and the general ag economic conditions in the district.

Three of the most-watched reports released by the Dallas Fed include the Texas Manufacturing Outlook Survey, the Texas Services Sector Outlook Survey, and the Texas Retail Outlook Survey.

While the Texas economy is only the second largest in the country (following California) it would rank in the top 15 national economies in the world. So what happens in Texas economically matters a great deal. And while it is widely believed that the trends in the Lone Star State are dictated solely by the price of crude oil,

**EXHIBIT 12.12** The Richmond Fed Index and Retail Sales

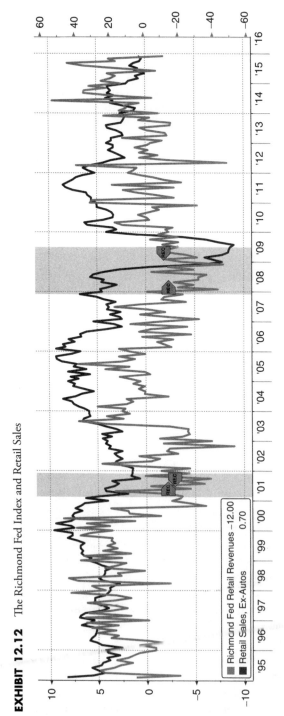

*Source:* Bloomberg

314

investors are better off knowing that there is much more to this region's economy than the operational output of the so-called "nodding donkey" oil pump jacks.

## The Dallas Fed Trimmed Mean Index

But rather than present another manufacturing or regional survey of economic conditions, we look to the most often cited and widely used measure of underlying inflation measures, the Dallas Fed's Trimmed Mean Personal Consumption Expenditure inflation rate index. This measure is adopted and used in essentially all models attempting to decipher the true pace of consumer inflation in the United States. It is a cleaner, less volatile measure of national price trends and is often cited by all districts of the Federal Reserve, as well as the Board of Governors.

The Dallas Fed's Trimmed Mean PCE inflation rate is basically an adjusted version of the Bureau of Economic Analysis's personal consumption expenditure (PCE) deflator price index. The adjustment entails categorizing the monthly changes in each component of the BEA's PCE in an ascending to descending order. Then those components at the extreme ends—24 percent of those at the lower end and 31 percent of those from the higher end—are "trimmed" from the estimate revealing an inflation rate less volatile, smoother, and more realistic representation than the previously conceived core measures of excluding just food and energy.

Exhibit 12.13 shows the Dallas Fed's trimmed mean pace of inflation against the BEA's PCE, which has a tendency to move in a whipsawed fashion.

## The Kansas City Fed Manufacturing Survey

Sometimes clues to the economic outlook can come from the most unexpected places; the Kansas City Fed's Manufacturing Survey is one of those little-known indicators from the Federal Reserve System that has at times revealed shifts in the overall economy earlier than some of the bigger and better-known regional measures with longer histories.

Each month the economists in the Fed's Tenth District gather responses on manufacturing activity from the region's related businesses and release a large set of information regarding current and the six-month forward outlook on production, new orders, shipments, prices, capital expenditures, inventories, and employees.

As Exhibit 12.14 shows, there is a solid relationship between the price of oil and the headline Kansas City Fed Manufacturing Survey. In a somewhat delayed fashion, the Number of Employees Index also possesses a solid relationship with the headline and oil prices. In late 2014, the macroeconomic impact of plunging oil prices was seen first in this series, even before that of the Dallas Fed's Manufacturing Survey—which most would expect to see all the goings on in the energy markets first revealed.

**EXHIBIT 12.13**   Dallas Fed Trimmed Mean Deflator

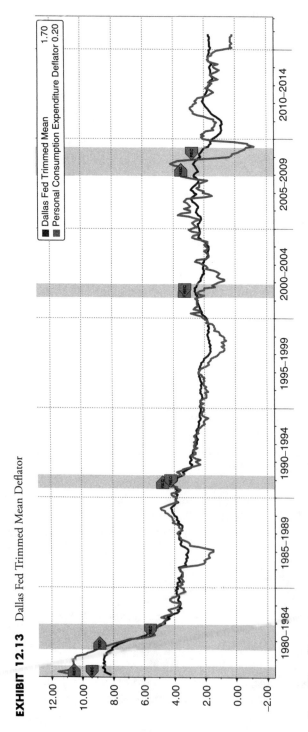

*Source:* Bloomberg

**EXHIBIT 12.14** Kansas City Fed Manufacturing Index, Employees and Crude Oil

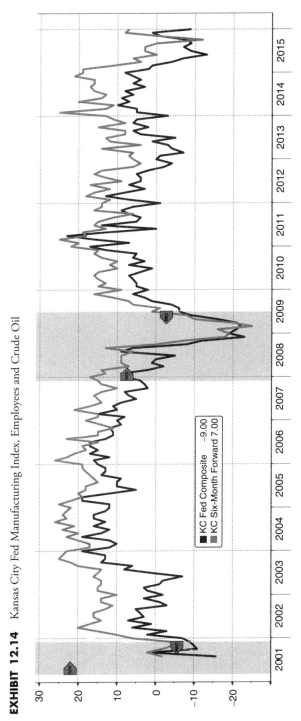

*Source:* Bloomberg

What many may not realize is that the Kansas City District is not just the home of Ford Motor and General Motors assembly plants but also a region that is very much linked to the energy sector. The Fed's Tenth District includes economic activity that stretches as far west as Wyoming, Colorado, and northern New Mexico, to western Missouri, Nebraska, Kansas, and Oklahoma. If you consider the fact that this region is home to some of the largest coal deposits in the country (Wyoming's Powder River Basin) as well as some hefty natural gas producing states like Oklahoma, Wyoming, and Colorado, it becomes easy to see why movements in some of these economic series would be telling a story not able to be told from other regions.

Along with the data contained in this survey, the Kansas City Fed provides extremely important and detailed commentary from its respondents. In the November 2015 report, one contact noted, "The industrial economy as we see it is under attack by low demand, foreign competition and the high cost of government law and regulation. We have reduced headcount and otherwise cut pay of existing employees. Our capital projects are aimed at reducing labor input and increasing efficiencies, rather than growing and creating jobs."[1] Comments like these can tell a much clearer story than some of the data.

## Test Yourself

Answer the following multiple-choice questions:

1. The Federal Reserve has a dual mandate to:
   a. print money by a pace of 5 percent per year.
   b. foster price stability and promote full-employment.
   c. cut interest rates to zero.
   d. help maintain a strong value of the dollar.
   e. none of the above.

2. The Federal Reserve's Consumer Credit report does not include:
   a. credit cards.
   b. mortgages.
   c. auto loans.
   d. student loans.
   e. none of the above.

3. The Federal Reserve's Senior Loan Officer Opinion Survey:
   a. tells economists why the Fed is raising rates.
   b. provides insight regarding the latest monetary policy moves.

---

[1] Federal Reserve Bank of Kansas City Manufacturing Survey, November 21, 2015. Kansas City, Missouri

    c. provides insight regarding new Fed regulations on community reinvestment policies.

    d. provides insight regarding lending standards and demand for loans.

    e. none of the above.

4. The Federal Reserve Bank of Philadelphia's Aruoba-Diebold-Scotti (A-D-S) Business Conditions Index:

    a. projects the trends of underlying economic activity on a real-time basis.

    b. estimates the growth rate of real GDP six months in the future.

    c. projects manufacturing activity three to six months in the future.

    d. all of the above.

    e. b and c only.

5. The Dallas Fed Trimmed Mean PCE inflation rate index:

    a. Trims the CPI from the Personal Consumption Expenditure Deflator (PCED).

    b. Trims wages and salaries from the Personal Consumption Expenditure Deflator (PCED).

    c. Trims the most volatile components from the Personal Consumption Expenditure Deflator (PCED).

    d. All of the above.

## Answers

1. b
2. b
3. d
4. a
5. c

# Sources and Additional Reading

## Chapter 1: The Daily Blotter

Cottle, Sidney, Roger F. Murray, and Frank E. Block. *Graham and Dodd's Security Analysis*. New York: McGraw-Hill, 1988.

Crescenzi, Anthony. *The Strategic Bond Investor*. New York: McGraw-Hill, 2002.

Goldberg, Linda, and Deborah Leonard. "What Moves Sovereign Bond Markets? The Effects of Economic News on U.S. and German Yields." Federal Reserve Bank of New York *Current Issues in Economics and Finance* 9, no. 9 (September 2003).

Hager, George. "Economists Seek Clues in Daily Life." *USA Today* (February 12, 2001).

Yamarone, Richard. "The Business Economist at Work: Argus Research Corporation." *Business Economics* (July 1999): 65–70.

## Chapter 2: The Business Cycle

Anderson, Gerald H., and John J. Erceg. "Forecasting Turning Points with Leading Indicators." Federal Reserve Bank of Cleveland, *Economic Commentary* (October 1, 1989).

Dueker, Michael J. "Strengthening the Case for the Yield Curve as a Predictor of U.S. Recessions." Federal Reserve Bank of St. Louis, *Economic Review* 79, no. 2 (March/April 1997): 41–51.

Estrella, A., and F. S. Mishkin. "The Yield Curve as a Predictor of U.S. Recessions." Federal Reserve Bank of New York, *Current Issues in Economics and Finance* 2, no. 7 (June 1996).

Evans, Charles L., Chin Te Liu, and Genevieve Pham-Kanter. "The 2001 Recession and the Chicago Fed National Activity Index: Identifying Business Cycle Turning Points." Federal Reserve Bank of Chicago, *Economic Perspectives* 26, no. 3 (Third Quarter): 26–43.

Haubrich, Joseph G., and Ann M. Dombrosky. "Predicting Real Growth Using the Yield Curve." Federal Reserve Bank of Cleveland, *Economic Review* 32, no. 1 (First Quarter 1996): 26–35.

Higgins, Patrick. "GDPNow: A Model for GDP 'Nowcasting,'" Federal Reserve Bank of Atlanta Working paper 2014-7 (July 2014).

Kozicki, Sharon. "Predicting Real Growth and Inflation with the Yield Spread." Federal Reserve Bank of Kansas City, *Economic Review* (Fourth Quarter 1997): 39–57.

Moore, Geoffrey H. *Business Cycles, Inflation and Forecasting*, 2nd ed. Cambridge, MA: Ballinger Publishing, 1983.

———. *Leading Indicators for the 1990s*. Homewood, IL: Dow Jones-Irwin, 1990.

National Bureau of Economic Research. *Conference on Business Cycles*. New York: National Bureau of Economic Research, 1951.

————. U.S. Business Cycle Expansions and Contractions. www.nber.orgcycles.html.

Stock, James H., and Mark W. Watson. *Business Cycles, Indicators, and Forecasting*. Chicago: University of Chicago Press, 1993.

The Conference Board. *Business Cycle Indicators*. New York: The Conference Board, several issues.

————. *U.S. Leading Economic Indicators and Related Composite Indexes*. New York: The Conference Board, several issues.

## Chapter 3: Gross Domestic Product (GDP)

Aruoba, S. B., F. X. Diebold, J. Nalewaik, F. Schorfheide, and D. Song. "Improving GDP Measurement: A Measurement-Error Perspective." FRB Philadelphia Working Paper 13-16 (May 2013).

Baumol, William J., and Alan S. Blinder. *Macroeconomics Principles and Policy*, 5th ed. New York: Harcourt Brace Jovanovich, 1991.

Bernanke, Ben S., and Andrew B. Abel. *Macroeconomics*, 3d ed. New York: Addison-Wesley, 1998.

Congressional Budget Office. *The Budget and Economic Outlook: An Update* (July 2000).

————. *CBO's Method for Estimating Potential Output: An Update* (August 2001).

Mankiw, N. Gregory. *Principles of Macroeconomics*. Fort Worth, TX: The Dryden Press, 1998.

Popkin, Joel. "The U.S. National Income and Product Accounts." *Journal of Economic Perspectives* 14, no. 2 (Spring 2000): 214–224.

Prakken, Joel L., and Lisa T. Guirl. "Macro Modeling and Forecasting with Chain-Type Measures of GDP." *National Association of Business Economists News* 113 (September 1995).

Steindel, Charles. "Chain-Weighting: The New Approach to Measuring GDP." Federal Reserve Bank of New York, *Current Issues in Economics and Finance* 1, no. 9 (December 1995).

United States Department of Commerce, Bureau of Economic Analysis. An Introduction to National Economic Accounting, Methodology Papers: U.S. National Income and Product Accounts. Washington, DC (March 1985).

————. *National Income and Product Accounts of the United States, 1929–94*, vols. 1, 2. Washington, DC (April 1998).

————. "GDP: One of the Great Inventions of the 20th Century." *Survey of Current Business* (January 2000): 6–14.

————. Corporate Profits, Profits Before Tax, Profits Tax Liability and Dividends Methodology Paper. Washington, DC (September 2002).

————. Gross Domestic Product Report (various issues).

————. Survey of Current Business (various issues).

————. Website: http://www.bea.doc.gov.

## Chapter 4: The Labor Market and Employment

Baumol, William J., and Alan S. Blinder. *Macroeconomics Principles and Policy*, 5th ed. New York: Harcourt Brace Jovanovich, 1991.

Fleming, Michael J., and Eli M. Remolona. "What Moves the Bond Market?" Federal Reserve Bank of New York Research Paper, no. 9706 (February 1997).

Getz, Patricia M., and Mark G. Ulmer. "Diffusion Indexes: A Barometer of the Economy." *Monthly Labor Review*. Washington, DC: U.S. Department of Labor (April 1990).

U.S. Department of Labor, Bureau of Labor Statistics. "Labor Force Data Derived from the Current Population Survey." *Handbook of Methods* (April 1997).

_____. "Employment, Hours, and Earnings from the Establishment Survey." *Handbook of Methods*. http://www.bls.gov/opub/hom/pdf/homch2.pdf.
_____. "How the Government Measures Unemployment" (July 2001). www.bls.gov/cps/cps_htgm.htm.
_____. The Employment Situation (various issues).

## Chapter 5: Retail Sales

Harris, Ethan S., and Clara Vega. "What Do Chain Store Sales Tell Us about Consumer Spending?" Federal Reserve Bank of New York Research Paper, no. 9614 (June 1996).
Mencke, Claire. "Hot Retail Seems to Cinch Rate Hike Even as Producer Prices Stay Tame." *Investor's Business Daily* (April 14, 2000).
Nakamura, Leonard I. "The Retail Revolution and Food-Price Mismeasurement." Federal Reserve Bank of Philadelphia, *Business Review* (May/June 1998).
U.S. Department of Commerce, Bureau of the Census. *Annual Benchmark Report for Retail Trade and Food Services: January 1992 through March 2002*. Washington, DC (May 2002).
_____. Current Business Reports, Retail e-Commerce Reports, Washington, DC (various issues 1990–2002).
_____. Monthly Retail Services Branch. E-Commerce, Frequently Asked Questions (FAQs). http://www.census.gov/mrts/www/efaq.html.

## Chapter 6: National Federation of Independent Businesses (NFIB) Small Business Economic Trends

Dunkelberg, William C., and Holly Wade, *NFIB Small Business Economic Trends*, NFIB Research Foundation, (various issues).

## Chapter 7: Personal Income and Outlays

Larkins, Daniel. "Note on the Personal Saving Rate." *Survey of Current Business* (February 1999): 8–9.
Mitchell, Wesley C., ed. *Income in the United States: Its Amount and Distribution 1909–1919*. New York: Harcourt, Brace and Company, 1921.
U.S. Department of Commerce, Bureau of Economic Analysis. *Personal Consumption Expenditures, Methodology Paper Series MP-6*. Washington, DC (June 1990).
_____. *National Income and Product Accounts of the United States, 1929–94*, vols. 1, 2. Washington, DC (April 1998).
_____. "Personal Income and Outlays" (various issues, 2016). http://www.bea.gov/national/index.htm#personal.

## Chapter 8: Housing and Construction

Hagenbaugh, Barbara. "More People Refinance to Wring Cash Out of Their Homes." *USA Today*, Money Section (October 28, 2002).
Hancock, Jay. "Amazing Housing Market Bound to Help the Economy." *The Baltimore Sun* (February 27, 2002).
Mortgage Bankers Association, www.mbaa.org.

National Association of Home Builders. "Housing the Key to Economic Recovery" (November 2002). www.nahb.com.

National Association of Realtors, nar.realtor.org.

U.S. Department of Commerce, Bureau of the Census. *Expenditures for Improvements and Repairs of Residential Properties* (Third Quarter 2001).

———. *New Residential Construction* (various issues).

———. New Residential Construction Documentation. https://www.census.gov/construction/c30/c30index.html.

## Chapter 9: Manufacturing

Blinder, Alan S. "Retail Inventory Behavior and Business Fluctuations." *Brookings Papers on Economic Activity* 2 (1981): 443–505.

Board of Governors of the Federal Reserve System. Industrial Production—1986 Edition with a Description of the Methodology. Washington, DC (1986).

———. Federal Reserve Statistical Release, G.17. *Industrial Production and Capacity Utilization* (various issues).

Economic Cycle Research Institute (2016). www.businesscycle.com.

Emery, Kenneth M., and Chih-Ping Chang. "Is There a Stable Relationship Between Capacity Utilization and Inflation?" Federal Reserve Bank of Dallas, *Economic Review* (First Quarter 1997): 14–20.

Gittings, Thomas A. "Capacity Utilization and Inflation." Federal Reserve Bank of Chicago, *Economic Perspectives* 13, no. 3 (May/June 1989): 2–9.

Harberger, Arnold C., ed. *The Demand for Durable Goods.* Chicago: The University of Chicago Press, 1960.

Harris, Ethan S. "Tracking the Economy with the Purchasing Managers' Index." Federal Reserve Bank of New York, *Quarterly Review* (Fall 1991): 61, 69.

Institute for Supply Management. Institute for Supply Management's Manufacturing Report on Business Information Kit (as of September 2002).

———. Institute for Supply Management Manufacturing Report on Business (various issues).

———. Institute for Supply Management Non-Manufacturing Report on Business (various issues).

Klein, Philip A., and Geoffrey H. Moore. "N.A.P.M. Business Survey Data: Their Value as a Leading Indicator." *Journal of Purchasing and Materials Management* (Winter 1988).

Koenig, Evan F. "Capacity Utilization as a Real-Time Predictor of Manufacturing Output." Federal Reserve Bank of Dallas, *Economic Review* (Third Quarter 1996): 16–23.

McConnell, Margaret M., and Gabriel Perez Quiros. "Output Fluctuations in the United States: What Has Changed Since the Early 1980s?" Federal Reserve Bank of New York, *Staff Report* 41 (June 1998).

Rogers, R. Mark. "Forecasting Industrial Production: Purchasing Managers' versus Production-Worker Hours Data." Federal Reserve Bank of Atlanta, *Economic Review* (January/February 1992): 25–36.

U.S. Department of Commerce, Bureau of the Census. Manufacturers' Shipments, Inventories, and Orders: 1947–1963, Revised, Series M3-1. Washington, DC: GPO (October 1963).

———. Advance Report on Durable Goods Manufacturers' Shipments, Inventories, and Orders (various issues).

———. Manufacturers' Shipments, Inventories, and Orders (various issues).

———. Monthly Wholesale Trade: Sales and Inventories (various issues).

———. Manufacturing and Trade Inventories and Sales (various issues).

# Chapter 10: Prices and Inflation

Aluminum Association, Inc. *Industry Overview: From Alumina to Automobiles*, 2003. http://www.aluminum.org.

Bryan, Michael F., and Stephen G. Cecchetti. "The Consumer Price Index as a Measure of Inflation." Federal Reserve Bank of Cleveland, *Economic Review* (December 1993): 15–24.

Bureau of Labor Statistics. "The Consumer Price Index." Chapter 17 in *BLS Handbook of Methods*, April 1997.

———. "The Producer Price Index." Chapter 16 in *BLS Handbook of Methods*, April 1997.

———. "Measurement Issues in the Consumer Price Index" (June 1997). www.bls.gov/cpi/cpigm697.htm.

———. "How Does the Producer Price Index Differ from the Consumer Price Index?" PPI Program Spotlight, No. 98-3 (1998).

Clark, Todd E. "Do Producer Prices Help Predict Consumer Prices?" Federal Reserve Bank of Kansas City Research Working Paper, 97-09 (December 1997).

Copper Development Association. Copper Facts (2003). http://www.copper.org.

Fair, Ray C. *Predicting Presidential Elections and Other Things*. Stanford, CA: Stanford University Press, 2002.

———. "Econometrics and Presidential Elections." *The Journal of Economic Perspectives* (Summer 2003): 89–102.

Hess, Gregory D., and Mark E. Schweitzer. "Does Wage Inflation Cause Price Inflation?" Federal Reserve Bank of Cleveland Policy Discussion Paper, no. 1 (April 2000).

Wu, Tao. "Improving the Way We Measure Consumer Prices." Federal Reserve Bank of San Francisco Economic Letter, no. 2003–24 (August 22, 2003).

# Chapter 11: Confidence and Sentiment

Bram, Jason, and Sydney Ludvigson. "Does Consumer Confidence Forecast Household Expenditure? A Sentiment Index Horse Race." Federal Reserve Bank of New York, *Economic Policy Review* (June 1998): 59–78.

Carroll, Christopher D., Jeffrey C. Fuhrer, and David W. Wilcox. "Does Consumer Sentiment Forecast Household Spending? If So, Why?" *The American Economic Review* 84, no. 5 (December 1994): 1397–1408.

Conference Board. *Consumer Confidence Survey*. New York: Conference Board (various issues).

Curtin, Richard T. "Indicators of Consumer Behavior: The University of Michigan Surveys of Consumers." *Public Opinion Quarterly* 46 (1982): 340–352.

———. "Index Calculations." University of Michigan. Mimeo.

———. "Surveys of Consumers." University of Michigan. Mimeo.

Garner, C. Alan. "Forecasting Consumer Spending: Should Economists Pay Attention to Consumer Confidence Surveys?" Federal Reserve Bank of Kansas City, *Economic Review* (May 1991): 57–71.

Katona, George. *The Powerful Consumer*. New York: McGraw-Hill, 1960.

——— and Eva Mueller. *Consumer Response to Income Increases*. Washington, DC: The Brookings Institution, 1968.

Keynes, John Maynard. *The General Theory of Employment, Interest, and Money*. New York: Harcourt, Brace and Company, 1936.

Mishkin, Frederic S. "Consumer Sentiment and Spending on Durable Goods." *Brookings Papers on Economic Activity* 1 (1978): 217–232.

Tobin, James. "On the Predictive Value of Consumer Intentions and Attitudes." *The Review of Economics and Statistics* 41 (February 1959): 1–11.

University of Michigan. *Surveys of Consumers.* Ann Arbor, MI: University of Michigan Survey Research Center (various issues).

## Chapter 12: The Federal Reserve

Aruoba, S. B., F. X. Diebold, and C. Scotti "Real-Time Measurement of Business Conditions," *Journal of Business and Economic Statistics* 27, no. 4 (October 2009): 417–427.

Board of Governors of the Federal Reserve System. Federal Reserve Statistical Release. H.8 Selected Assets and Liabilities of Commercial Banks in the United States (various issues).

———. Federal Reserve Statistical Release, G.19 Consumer Credit (various issues).

———. Federal Reserve Statistical Release, Senior Loan Officer Opinion Survey on Bank Lending Practices (various issues).

———. Federal Reserve Statistical Release, Z.1 Financial Accounts of the United States (various issues).

Bram, Jason, and Sydney Ludvigson. "Does Consumer Confidence Forecast Household Expenditure? A Sentiment Index Horse Race." Federal Reserve Bank of New York, *Economic Policy Review* (June 1998): 59–78.

Brave, Scott, and Chenfei Lu. "A Snapshot of the Midwest Economy: Past and Present," Federal Reserve Bank of Chicago, Chicago Fed Letter, Number 280 (November 2010).

Deitz, Richard, and Charles Steindel. "The Predictive Abilities of the New York Fed's Empire State Manufacturing Survey." *Current Issues in Economic and Finance* 11, no. 1 (January 2005).

Dolmas, Jim. "A Fitter, Trimmer Core Inflation Measure," Federal Reserve Bank of Dallas, *Southwest Economy* 3 (May/June 2005).

Haubrich, Joseph G., George Pennacchi, and Peter Ritchken. "Inflation Expectations, Real Rates, and Risk Premia: Evidence from Inflation Swaps." Federal Reserve Bank of Cleveland, Working Paper no. 11-07 (2011).

Hobijn, Bart. "The Tech Pulse Index: Recent Trends in Tech-Sector Activity." Federal Reserve Bank of San Francisco Economic Letter (January 14, 2009).

Hobijn, Bart, Kevin J. Stiroh, and Alexis Antoniades. "Taking the Pulse of the Tech Sector: A Coincident Index of High-Tech Activity." *Current Issues in Economics and Finance* 9, no. 10 (2003).

Lessons from the Tenth District," Federal Reserve Bank of Kansas City, *Economic Review* (Third Quarter 2004), 39–70.

Lacey, Robert L. "Gauging Manufacturing Activity: The Federal Reserve Bank of Richmond's Survey of Manufacturers." Federal Reserve Bank of Richmond, *Economic Quarterly* 85, no. 1 (Winter 1999): 79–98.

Price, David A., and Aileen Watson. "The Richmond Fed Manufacturing and Service Sector Surveys: A User's Guide," The Federal Reserve Bank of Richmond Economic Brief, No. 14-03 (March 2014).

Schiller, Timothy, and Michael Trebing., "Taking the Measure of Manufacturing," Federal Reserve Bank of Philadelphia, *Business Review* (Fourth Quarter 2003): 23–37.

# Index

Page references followed by e indicate an exhibit